MEDIATING FAITHS

Religion is living culture. It continues to play a role in shaping political ideologies, institutional practices, communities of interest, ways of life and social identities. *Mediating Faiths* brings together scholars working across a range of fields, including cultural studies, media, sociology, anthropology, cultural theory and religious studies, in order to facilitate greater understanding of recent transformations.

Contributors illustrate how religion continues to be responsive to the very latest social and cultural developments in the environments in which it exists. They raise fundamental questions concerning new media and religious expression, religious youth cultures, the links between spirituality, personal development and consumer culture, and contemporary intersections of religion, identity and politics. Together the chapters demonstrate how belief in the superempirical is negotiated relative to secular concerns in the twenty-first century.

Mediating Faiths

Religion and Socio-Cultural Change
in the Twenty-First Century

Edited by

MICHAEL BAILEY
University of Essex, UK

and

GUY REDDEN
University of Sydney, Australia

ASHGATE

Published by
Ashgate Publishing Limited
Wey Court East
Union Road
Farnham
Surrey, GU9 7PT
England

Ashgate Publishing Company
Suite 420
101 Cherry Street
Burlington
VT 05401-4405
USA

www.ashgate.com

British Library Cataloguing in Publication Data
Mediating faiths:religion and socio-cultural change in the twenty-first century.
   1. Religion–History–21st century. 2. Religion and sociology. 3. Social change–Religious aspects. 4. Mass media in religion.
   I. Bailey, Michael. II. Redden, Guy.
   306.6'09051–dc22

Library of Congress Cataloging-in-Publication Data
Mediating faiths : religion and socio-cultural change in the twenty-first century / [edited by] Michael Bailey and Guy Redden.
   p. cm.
   Includes bibliographical references and index.
   ISBN 978-0-7546-6786-5 (hardcover : alk. paper) — ISBN 978-0-7546-9381-9 (ebook) 1. Religion and sociology. 2. Twenty-first century. I. Bailey, Michael. II. Redden, Guy.
   BL60.M43 2010
   306.601—dc22

2010032128

ISBN 9780754667865 (hbk)
ISBN 9780754693819 (ebk)

Printed and bound in Great Britain by the
MPG Books Group, UK

Contents

List of Figures

Notes on Contributors

Michael Bailey teaches in the Sociology Department at the University of Essex. He is editor of *Narrating Media History* (Routledge, 2009) and is currently working on a co-authored study of Richard Hoggart (Blackwell–Wiley, 2011). He has held visiting fellowships at Goldsmiths, University of London; the London School of Economics and Political Science; the ESRC Centre for Research on Socio-Cultural Change; Wolfson College and the Centre for the Arts, Social Sciences and Humanities, University of Cambridge.

Ruth Barcan is a senior lecturer in the Department of Gender and Cultural Studies at the University of Sydney. Her research interests include nudity and nudism, feminist cultural studies approaches to the body, alternative therapies and New Age practices, and pedagogy. She is the author of *Nudity: A Cultural Anatomy* (Berg, 2004), co-editor of two books, and author of numerous articles in areas such as the body in culture, consumer culture, and teaching. Her new book is titled *Complementary and Alternative Medicine: Bodies, Therapies, Senses* (Berg, 2011).

Claire Chambers is Senior Lecturer in English Literature at Leeds Metropolitan University, where she specializes in South Asian writing in English and in literary representations of British Muslims. Claire is currently writing two books, the first entitled *British Muslim Fictions: Interviews with Contemporary Writers*, and the second a monograph tracing the development of artistic depictions of Muslims in Britain, 1966–present, which are supported by grants from HEFCE, the AHRC and British Academy. She has published widely in such journals as *Postcolonial Text*, *Crossings: Journal of Migration and Culture* and *Journal of Postcolonial Writing*, and is Co-editor of the *Journal of Commonwealth Literature*.

Yoel Cohen graduated in International Relations from London University and completed a doctorate in Political Sociology at City University, London. His areas of research include religion and media in Israel, and mass media and international relations. Books include *Media Diplomacy: The Foreign Office in the Mass Communications Age* (Frank Cass, 1986), *The Whistleblower of the Dimona: Israel, Vanunu, and the Bomb* (Holmes & Meier, 2003), *Whistleblowers and the Bomb: Vanunu, Israel and Nuclear Secrecy* (Pluto, 2005). He was departmental editor for Israel Media in the *Encyclopaedia Judaica* (second edition). He is a professor and chairman of the School of Communication, Ariel University Center, Israel.

Ann Hardy is a senior lecturer in Screen and Media Studies at the University of Waikato, New Zealand. Her primary research fields are New Zealand media, especially the history of film, and exploration of the intersections of religion and media in contemporary culture. Recent publications include 'From *mokomokai to upoko tuhi*: Changing Representations of Maori Cultural Property in Film', *Screening the Past*, 24 (2009), and 'Nation-Branding and the Imagined New Zealand', in Monica Emmerich and Stewart Hoover (eds), *Media, Spiritualities and Social Change* (Continuum, 2010).

Andreas Hepp is Professor of Communications at the Faculty of Cultural Studies, University of Bremen, Germany. He is head of the IMKI (Institute of Media, Communications and Information) and of the IPKM (Institute of Media History, Media and Communication Studies). His main research areas are media and communication theory, media sociology, transnational and transcultural communication, cultural studies, media change, methods of media culture research, audience studies and discourse analysis. Recent book publications include *Media Events in a Global Age*, co-edited with Nick Couldry and Friedrich Krotz (Routledge, 2010) and *Connectivity, Networks and Flows: Conceptualizing Contemporary Communication*, co-edited with Friedrich Krotz, Shaun Moores and Carsten Winter (Hampton Press, 2008).

Stephen Hunt is a reader in the Sociology of Religion based at the University of the West of England, Bristol. His specialized research areas include Pentecostal and charismatic movements, Christianity and sexuality, and the political mobilization of Christian groups. His authored volumes include *A History of the Charismatic Movement in Britain and the United States of America: The Pentecostal Transformation of Christianity* (Edwin Mellen, 2009); *Religion in Everyday Life* (Routledge, 2006); *The Alpha Enterprise: Evangelism in the Post-Christian Era* (Ashgate, 2004); *Alternative Religion: A Sociological Introduction* (Ashgate, 2003); and *Religion in the West: A Sociological Perspective* (Palgrave and the British Sociological Association, 2001). Edited books include *Contemporary Christianity and LGBT Sexualities* (Ashgate, 2009); *Sociology and Law: The 50th Anniversary of Emile Durkheim (1858–1917)* (with M. Marinov and M. Serafimova) (Cambridge Scholars, 2009); *Christian Millenarianism* (New York University Press and Hurst Publishing, 2001); and *Charismatic Christianity: Sociological Perspectives* (with M. Hamilton and T. Walter) (Palgrave, 1997).

Jay Johnston is a senior lecturer in the Department of Studies in Religion at the University of Sydney, Australia. Her publications include *Angels of Desire: Esoteric Bodies, Aesthetics and Ethics* (Equinox, 2008). Current research projects include (i) concepts of angelic subjectivity and subtle bodies in contemporary continental philosophy, (ii) the use and iconography of magical and astrological images in the Mediterranean region from antiquity to the Renaissance, and (iii) wellbeing spirituality and alternative health (with Dr Ruth Barcan).

Veronika Krönert is Researcher in Media and Communication at the IMKI (Institute of Media, Communication and Information), University of Bremen, Germany. Her research spans media and religious change, everyday life and cultural identities, media events, cultural studies, qualitative methodologies and transcultural media analyses.

Aini Linjakumpu is University Lecturer of Politics in the Department of Social Studies at the University of Lapland in Rovaniemi and Adjunct Professor at the University of Tampere, Finland. Her main research interests are political Islam and the Middle Eastern politics and their relationship to communities, new political actions, network politics and politics of emotions. In addition, Linjakumpu has been a leader of two Northern-related research projects combining historical, artistic and contemporary approaches. She is the author or editor of eight books, and has published numerous articles and book chapters.

Knut Lundby is Professor of Media Studies at the Department of Media and Communication, University of Oslo. He holds a doctoral degree in Sociology of Religion from the same university. Lundby was the founding director of InterMedia, University of Oslo, which is an interdisciplinary research centre on design, communication, and learning in digital environments. He has been involved with the international research community on Media, Religion and Culture since the early 1990s and is the editor of *Rethinking Media, Religion, and Culture* with Stewart M. Hoover (Sage, 1997). He is directing the international 'Mediatized Stories' project, from which he has edited *Digital Storytelling, Mediatized Stories: Self-representations in New Media* (Peter Lang, 2008) and *Mediatization: Concept, Changes, Consequences* (Peter Lang, 2009).

Anna E. Nekola received her PhD in Musicology at the University of Wisconsin–Madison and is now Visiting Assistant Professor of Music and English at Denison University. Her research interests centre on disputes over the moral and cultural value of popular musics, and she recently co-authored the article 'Cultural Policy in American Music History: Sammy Davis, Jr., vs. Juvenile Delinquency', which appeared in the January 2010 *Journal of the Society of American Music*. She also maintains an active performance career as a professional oboist and reedmaker.

Holly Randell-Moon teaches Critical and Cultural Studies at Macquarie University, Sydney, Australia. She has published widely on race, religion and secularism in such journals as *Australian Critical Race and Whiteness Studies*, *Borderlands*, *Transforming Cultures* and *Australian Religion Studies Review*.

Guy Redden teaches Cultural Studies at the University of Sydney. He has previously lectured at Prince of Songkla University, Thailand; the University of Queensland, Australia, where he earned his PhD; and Lincoln University in the

UK. He has published widely about the commodification of religion and alternative cultures. He is a former editor of *M/C: A Journal of Media and Culture*.

Thijl Sunier holds the VISOR chair of 'Islam in European Societies' at the VU University Amsterdam. His research interests include interethnic relations, and comparative studies of Turkish youth in France, Germany, Great Britain and the Netherlands. Presently he is preparing research on styles of popular religiosity, religious leadership, and nation-building and Islam in Europe. He is a member of the Amsterdam School for Social Science Research (AISSR) and Chairman of the board of the Inter-Academic School for Islam Studies in the Netherlands (NISIS). He is editor of the anthropological journal *Etnofoor* and Chairman of the board of the Dutch Anthropological Association (ABV).

Karen W. Tice is an associate professor of gender and women's studies and education at the University of Kentucky. Publications include *Tales of Wayward Girls and Immoral Women: Case Records and the Professionalization of Social Work* (University of Illinois Press, 1998). Other writings cover expressions of religiosity in beauty pageants and makeover shows. She is currently finishing a book manuscript titled *Queens of Academe: Beauty, Bodies, and Campus Life, 1920–Present*.

Joy Kooi-Chin Tong is post-doctoral research associate at the Centre on Religion and Chinese Society, Purdue University. She received her PhD from the Sociology department, National University of Singapore (2009). Her research interests include Christianity in Chinese societies, Islam in Southeast Asia, entrepreneurship and globalization. Her works on religion to date include 'Women, Piety and Practices: A Study of Women and Religious Practice in Malaysia', *Contemporary Islam*, 2/1 (2008) (with Bryan Turner), and 'McDonaldization and the Mega-Church: A Case Study of City Harvest Church in Singapore', in *Religious Commodifications in Asia: Marketing Gods* (Routledge, 2008).

Rob Warner is Professor of Religion, Culture and Society and Dean of Humanities at the University of Chester. Recent publications include *Secularization and Its Discontents* (Continuum, 2010) and *Reinventing English Evangelicalism, 1965– 2000: A Theological and Sociological Study* (Paternoster, 2007). Current research projects include *Christianity and the University Experience* and *Believing Women in Contemporary Christianity: Responses to the Institutions and the Bible*.

Katharine L. Wiegele is an adjunct assistant professor of Anthropology at Northern Illinois University in DeKalb, Illinois, USA. Wiegele's book *Investing in Miracles: El Shaddai and the Transformation of Popular Catholicism in the Philippines* (University of Hawaii Press, 2005, and Ateneo de Manila University Press, 2007) won a 2007 National Book Award in the Philippines (given by the Manila Critics Circle and the National Book Development Board). Wiegele received a PhD in Sociocultural Anthropology from the University of Illinois at Urbana-Champaign in 2002. Her interest in the Philippines began in 1988 when she served as a Peace Corps Volunteer in the country. Since then she has lived in the Philippines for nearly four years, in Pangasinan, Batangas, Laguna and Metropolitan Manila.

Permission and Acknowledgements

Permission

The advertisement for iWorship, *CCM* magazine, September 2003 (Fig. 10.1) is reprinted by permission of Integrity Music, Inc.

Acknowledgements

The editors would like to thank all of the contributors for delivering their manuscripts in a timely fashion. Thanks go also to Sarah Lloyd, Sophie Lumley and Bethan Dixon at Ashgate for their patience and invaluable support.

Finally, the editors are grateful to Anthony McNicholas for his initial input into the editorial process.

Chapter 1
Editors' Introduction
Religion as Living Culture

Michael Bailey and Guy Redden

A large majority of the world's population continue to identify as followers of religions.[1] The word 'continue' is used advisedly here, because although few would doubt the importance of religion in world history, over recent decades few within the social sciences have viewed it as an important dimension of the present.[2] Tacit secularism has informed inquiry across disciplines, despite heated technical debate about the secularization thesis within the sociology of religion. A.E. Crawley summarized the sentiment of social science secularism aptly back in 1905 when he declared that 'religion is a mere survival from a primitive age'.[3] In this view it is little more than a remnant of previous socio-cultural formations – of traditional superstitions to be overcome by modernity.

While Crawley went on to predict that the extinction of religion was 'only a matter of time', a distinctive feature of the secularization theories developed from the 1960s onwards was that they did not reduce the process to decreased levels of religious belief and participation *per se*.[4] Although putative declines in reported belief and practice in liberal democracies have played their part in the argument, the theories were compatible with the persistence of widespread religious affiliation among populations. They had to be. Their main point was that religion ceases to be *socially significant* in the modern world because religious ideation becomes supplanted by technical expertise in supplying the operating principles for social practice. In other words, the integrative influence of religion over primary institutions of the state wanes even though it may 'continue' to have an important place in the personal lives of individuals and families.

---

[1]   United Nations, 'Population by religion, sex and urban/rural residence: each census, 1985–2004', Demographic Yearbook, 2005, at http://unstats.un.org/unsd/demographic/products/dyb/dybcensus/V2_table6.pdf, accessed 1 October 2010.

[2]   Malory Nye, 'Religion, Post-Religionism, and Religioning: Religious Studies and Contemporary Cultural Debates', *Method and Theory in the Study of Religion*, 12 (2000): pp. 447–76.

[3]   Rodney Stark, 'Secularization, R.I.P.', *Sociology of Religion*, 60/3 (1999): p. 250.

[4]   Bryan Wilson, *Religion in Sociological Perspective* (Oxford: Oxford University Press, 1982), p. 149.

However, by the late 2000s the supposition that actually existing religion is merely a marginal, private affair has become problematic. The global awareness of the rise of Islamism and related conflicts since the September 11 attacks in the US acts as a headline reminder of both the role of religion in politics and the way it can act as a marker of ethnocultural identity. Meanwhile, although the debate is by no means finished,[5] secularization theory has been roundly criticized.[6] Peter Berger, one of the most prominent of secularization theorists, effectively recanted in the late 1990s, identifying the 'desecularization of the world' in the face of burgeoning religious movements around the globe.[7] Fundamentalist variants of all the major religions have spread and orthodox religions remain globally popular in renewed forms such as Pentecostalism.[8] New religious movements and alternative spiritualities proliferate, and there is evidence to suggest that participation in their less conventional (and countable) forums offsets much of the decline in traditional worship in countries with developed 'spiritual marketplaces'.[9] Overall, those who accept the existence of 'secularizing effects' tend to decouple them from anything like a normative theory of secularization's linear, inevitable spread. Rather, the accent is on more open-ended processes of adaptation and reformulation as religion responds to secular forces that are themselves not uniform.[10]

This volume seeks to contribute to the understanding of this environment – one in which religion remains a vital aspect of the present that is related to broader social dynamics, and is increasingly recognized as such. It brings together scholars from a range of disciplines around the challenge of thinking of religion as living culture again – that is, after the hiatus in which it was dealt with little seriousness outside of religious studies and sociology of religion, specializations that themselves developed in proportion to the effective expulsion of matters religious from other fields of social and cultural study. This first involves acknowledging

---

[5]   For one reformulation see Steve Bruce, *God Is Dead: Secularization in the West* (Oxford: Blackwell, 2002).

[6]   See Asad for a conceptual critique and Greely for a more empirical one: Talal Asad, *Formations of the Secular: Christianity, Islam, Modernity* (Stanford, CA: Stanford University Press, 2003); Andrew M. Greeley, *Religion in Europe at the End of the Second Millennium* (New Brunswick, NJ: Transaction, 2003).

[7]   Peter Berger, 'The Desecularization of the World: A Global Overview', in Peter Berger (ed.), *The Desecularization of the World: Resurgent Religion and World Politics* (Grand Rapids, MI: Eerdmans Publishing, 1999), pp. 1–18.

[8]   Paul Freston, *Evangelicals and Politics in Asia, Africa and Latin America* (Cambridge: Cambridge University Press, 2001).

[9]   Paul Heelas and Linda Woodhead, *The Spiritual Revolution: Why Religion is Giving Way to Spirituality* (Oxford: Blackwell, 2005).

[10]   Martin Geoffroy, 'Theorizing Religion in the Global Age: A Typological Analysis', *International Journal of Politics, Culture and Society,* 18/1–2 (2004): pp. 33–46; Yves Lambert, 'Religion in Modernity as a New Axial Age: Secularization or New Religious Forms', *Sociology of Religion*, 60/3 (1999): pp. 303–33.

that religion, while having special features such as appeal to superempirical agents, is not a realm distinct from the rest of culture. It is mediated, administered, lived, contested and adapted by socially situated agents, just like other forms of culture – and in relation to them. Secondly, analysing religion as culture also involves reconsidering its social significance in light of other contemporary social, cultural, economic and political issues, and the theories that have been developed with reference to them.[11]

It is somewhat ironic that founding figures in social studies, viz. Durkheim and Weber, did view religion as socially significant culture in no less than its capacity to integrate ideologically entire social systems (Durkheim) and to catalyze socio-historical formations (modern capitalism for Weber).[12] However, implicit in both arguments is the association of religion with particular arrangements that are superseded by modernity – primitive societies in Durkheim's case and early capitalism in Weber's. In taking religion seriously each thinker simultaneously helped to lay the foundations for secularization by identifying religion with originary points separated from the rationalized and functionally differentiated modern world.

In the face of religion's continued vitality in 'global modernity', determinations of its significance need to be opened up to multiple perspectives. The currency of received oppositions such as those between the sacred and the profane deserves questioning. As Asad argues, such distinctions may arise more from conceptual schemas of Western thought than they do from the logic of world religions. Whether the latter integrate institutions and practices across whole societies is a debatable measure for the relevance of religion in pluralized milieux. Its imbrication with social differences of class, race, nationality, ethnicity and gender may be just as important an influence on identities and public life.[13]

However, a limiting factor that bears upon any interdisciplinary analysis of contemporary religion is that religious studies and the sociology of religion were somewhat sequestered from the cross-disciplinary interest in the cultural aspects of social life that became known as the 'cultural turn' of the 1980s and

---

[11] In making these distinctions, we are also implying that, while religious identity can be a highly individualized experience, religious experience is always more than a subjective – or cognitive – mentality; hence the reason for our emphasizing other socio-cultural relations and processes. Cf. Meredith B. McGuire, *Lived Religion: Faith and Practice in Everyday Life* (New York: Oxford University Press, 2008).

[12] Emile Durkheim, *The Elementary Forms of the Religious Life*, 2nd edn (London: Allen & Unwin, 1976); Max Weber, *The Protestant Ethic and the Spirit of Capitalism,* 2nd edn (London: Allen & Unwin, 1976).

[13] For a fuller discussion of the changing relationship between different faith communities (viz. Anglicanism, Catholicism, Judaism, Islam, Hinduism and Sikhism) and civic society within the UK, see Zaki Cooper and Guy Lodge (eds), *Faith in the Nation: Religion, Identity and the Public Realm in Britain Today* (London: Institute for Public Policy Research, 2008). For a more philosophical analysis of these issues, particularly the question of religious citizenship within liberal democracies, see Jürgen Habermas, 'Religion in the Public Sphere', *European Journal of Philosophy* 14/1 (2006): pp. 1–25.

1990s.[14] Cultural theorists working under rubrics such as postmodernism and poststructuralism destabilized models of a universal, progressive modernity of the kind assumed by secularization, but they had little interest in exploring their radical ideas in relation to religion. One of the legacies of this is that those working in cultural studies frameworks can construe almost any phenomenon as amenable to cultural analysis, but, in practice, they do not tend to admit religion to the cathedral. This is somewhat odd, as if anything the cultural turn that followed structuralism was about the discovery that the social is replete with the production and exchange of meanings.[15] If religion – with all its constructions of the meaning of life and how to act accordingly – is not meaning-making *par excellence*, what is? The truth is that it continues to be an 'embarrassment' to many secularist academics.[16] So it is that Rita Felski suggests that everyday life, the sphere of mundane practice that is of particular interest in cultural studies, is viewed as thoroughly secular in the field.[17]

Yet, for billions, religion does play a role in how life is lived, and scholars who attend only to the 'secular' or 'religious' aspects of diverse issues related to those lives risk conveying an impoverished understanding of the phenomena they study. In proposing this, it is not our intention to dismiss the specialized study of religion. Tim Fitzgerald is one who has argued against religious studies in its current form, which he sees as being organized around a reified category of religion that constructs it as different from everything else, especially matters of state.[18] This, Fitzgerald argues, acts to create distorted discourses that separate out the religious from the secular in ways that are not borne out in practice. In these terms, religion should be researched within the frameworks of other disciplines to ensure that its imbrication with the rest of social and cultural life is an initial premise of inquiry. However, although the intent of this argument is commendable, we propose that the best means to loosen divisions is to promote exchange across already existing disciplines. Religion is distinctive in its cultural forms, even if it never stands apart,[19] and religious studies and the sociology of religion generate

---

[14]   Mike Featherstone, *Consumer Culture and Postmodernism* (London: Sage, 1991), p. 112.

[15]   Stuart Hall, 'The Work of Representation', in *Representation: Cultural Representations and Signifying Practices* (London: Sage and Open University Press, 1997), pp. 1–74.

[16]   John Frow, 'Is Elvis a God? Cult, Culture, Questions of Method', *International Journal of Cultural Studies*, 1/2 (1998): pp. 197–210.

[17]   Rita Felski, 'The Invention of Everyday Life', *New Formations*, 39 (1999): p. 16.

[18]   Timothy Fitzgerald, *Discourse on Civility and Barbarity: A Critical History of Religion and Related Categories* (Oxford: Oxford University Press, 2007).

[19]   The lack of consensus over a definition of religion and whether it is a cultural universal opens up questions about the forms religiosity can take in changing environments. Do we worship celebrities? Does advertising offer us heaven on earth? See Benthall for a recent take on the problem of defining religion and parareligion through a set of recurring features that can be instantiated in different combinations: Jonathan Benthall, *Returning

detailed knowledge of its terrain. As Stewart Hoover notes, there has already been a notable turn towards culturalism – a context-sensitive focus on lived cultures, everyday life, and meaning construction, reception and negotiation – among those who study media and religion.[20] The problem is the limited number of forums through which those conducting such work can share broader theoretical resources and findings with those working outside of the domain of religious studies. Such opportunities are grossly disproportionate to the social pervasiveness of religion.

Along these lines this volume brings together scholars from religious studies, sociology, communication studies, media studies, cultural studies, gender studies, literary studies, history, anthropology, international relations and musicology to explore religious culture through cross-disciplinary rubrics of mediation, youth, consumption and lifestyle and politics. The intent is to see how a range of conceptual resources and approaches can be brought to the empirical study of religious issues as they appear across contexts. This arrangement is designed less to build up substantive knowledge of any particular object of study than it is to highlight the ways that religion can be tied up with key dimensions of the present. Chapters raise critical concerns including governmentality, post-feminism, neo-liberalism, globalization, consumer culture, diaspora, new media and the politics of representation. The interest is to show that, whatever the situation, religion is part of contemporary sense-making and practice, and as such is an emergent property of socio-cultural change. In other words, that it is living culture.

In taking this approach *Mediating Faiths* is designed to complement other ongoing explorations that are bringing religion back into frames from which it has largely been excluded. The 'theological turn' in recent critical theory is one notable example. Since Derrida considered the spectre of faith in his later work a number of noted theorists, including Žižek, Kristeva, Badiou, Taylor and Rorty, have addressed religion.[21] Another example is the increasing amount of work that has examined the links between religion, media and popular culture.[22]

---

to Religion: Why a Secular Age is Haunted by Faith (London and New York: I.B. Tauris, 2008).

[20]   Stewart M. Hoover, 'The Culturalist Turn in Scholarship on Media and Religion', *The Journal of Media and Religion*, 1/1 (2002): pp. 225–36.

[21]   Alain Badiou, *Saint Paul: The Foundation of Universalism* (Stanford, CA: Stanford University Press, 2003); Charles Taylor, *A Secular Age* (Cambridge, MA: Harvard University Press, 2007); Richard Rorty and Gianni Vattimo, *The Future of Religion* (New York: Columbia University Press, 2007); Slavoj Žižek, *On Belief* (London: Routledge, 2001); Julia Kristeva, *This Incredible Need to Believe* (New York: Columbia University Press, 2009).

[22]   Stewart M. Hoover and Knut Lundby (eds), *Rethinking Media, Religion, and Culture* (London: Sage, 1997); Hent de Vries and Samuel Weber (eds), *Religion and Media* (Stanford, CA: Stanford University Press, 2001); Stewart M. Hoover and Lynn Schofield Clark (eds), *Practicing Religion in the Age of the Media: Explorations in Media, Religion, and Culture* (New York: Columbia University Press, 2002); Jolyon P. Mitchell and Sophia Marriage (eds), *Mediating Religion: Conversations in Media, Religion and*

The concept of mediation that lies behind our title refers not only to the expanded symbolic realm created by media technologies in which religious communications consist, but to the broader sense that apprehension of and practice in the world is mediated by material, cultural and social elements. Mediation in this sense is the intersection of multiple, co-determining factors amid any set of relations in which religiosity is implicated. Including but moving beyond media in the restricted sense of communications channels, the chapters collected present mediation as an ongoing social process of meaning-making through which religious discourses articulate with other contemporary forms. These relationships demand reconsideration of settled notions of the place and value of the sacred. In various ways throughout the chapters, the authors raise questions about the changing relations of authority over religious symbolization and practice that arise as religions interact with the rest of media and society. This happens through the ways that agents bind the religious to concerns of the everyday and to broader public spheres in the course of action and expression.

While not advancing any particular theoretical programme, this orientation can be explained with reference to Stuart Hall's development of Gramsci's concept of articulation.[23] Articulation describes the way that ideological elements form combinations with each other, social formations and subjects. The model leads to a particular way of reading in which the value of an ideological element is to be ascertained by its contingent relations with others. Religion is Hall's primary example: 'Its meaning – political and ideological – comes precisely from its position within a formation. It comes with what else it is articulated to'. In this view, it has no fixed political connotations, but is related to power structures in particular ways by particular movements, which inflect it, develop it and engage with it to construct narratives that transform people's awareness of themselves and their potential behaviour. Accordingly he notes 'the extraordinary diversity of the roles which religious formations have actually played' in the developing and modern world. For instance, he sees the 'funny language' of Rastafarianism in Jamaica as deriving from, but subverting the Bible, such that it became a

---

Culture (Edinburgh: T. & T. Clark Publishers, 2003); Peter Horsfield, Mary E. Hess and Adan M. Medrano (eds), *Belief in Media: Cultural Perspectives on Media and Christianity* (Aldershot: Ashgate, 2004); Birgit Meyer and Annelies Moors (eds), *Religion, Media, and the Public Sphere* (Bloomington, IN, and Indianapolis: Indiana University Press, 2005); Lynn Schofield Clark (ed.), *Religion, Media, and the Marketplace* (New Brunswick, NJ: Rutgers University Press, 2007).

[23] Stuart Hall, 'On Postmodernism and Articulation', in David Morley and Kuan-Hsing Chen (eds), *Stuart Hall: Critical Dialogues in Cultural Studies* (London: Routledge, 1996), pp. 141–4. Hall incidentally is one of the more influential intellectuals who has recently called for religion to be taken seriously again in the humanities and social sciences. See Laurie Taylor, 'Culture's revenge: Laurie Taylor interviews Stuart Hall', Newhumanist. org 121/2 (2006), at http://newhumanist.org.uk/960, accessed 2 September 2010.

conduit for the reconstruction of black history, a cultural resource that transformed experiences of poverty and colonialism into political subjectivity.

In this spirit, via Christian beauty competitions in the US to environmentalist Thai Buddhist monks protesting deforestation by ordaining trees, and almost any other contemporary religious culture one could mention, we propose that the significance of religion be interpreted through its place in socio-historical formations, not against universalist benchmarks that themselves prove to be creations of very particular histories.

Part I: New Media Religion

Throughout the volume contributors examine how religiosity is manifested in multiple ways with diverse consequences. Any material object, practice or representation effects signification upon being perceived. Communal worship, meditation and even vows of silence convey meanings and subjective effects that are shaped by the communications forms and physical environments in which they consist.

People often tend to think of media in terms of the most recent physical means for communicating messages. In our times these are electronic and digital. This section comprises chapters that show how changes in the media environment are directly implicated in how religion is expressed. However, in order to avoid the risk of fetishizing only the 'very latest' media technologies it is first necessary to acknowledge that religious communication and experience has always been mediated and that for as long as there has been recorded human history there have been new media of one kind or another. For instance, the 'very latest' in religious art, drama and music conveyed the Christian gospel to the illiterate European laity for generations while monks laid cultural foundations for the print revolution by fastidiously hand-copying manuscripts in their scriptoria.

The case of the European Reformation illustrates how mediation, in the sense we have proposed above, is much more than a matter of message formats. It is also the social relations that form around them and the cultures transmitted through them. Upon the publication of Gutenberg's Bible surely few at the time would have seen the potential mass dissemination of the word of God as leading to the decreased authority of the Catholic Church and the secularization of learning. However, as Elizabeth Eisenstein has argued, the capacity of printed media to store, index and distribute information promoted the specialization in and comparison between bodies of knowledge that underpinned both the Reformation and the Renaissance.[24] The heterodox monk Martin Luther was the first star author

---

[24]   Elizabeth L. Eisenstein, *The Printing Press as an Agent of Change: Communications and Cultural Transformations in Early Modern Europe* (Cambridge: Cambridge University Press, 1979).

of the print age, new media entrepreneurs ensuring that his word was sold like any other for which there was demand.[25]

Without the benefit of hindsight we can be less certain where the current electronic media 'revolution' might lead. Nonetheless, the increased volume of media messages and the proliferation in formats through which religion is communicated are certain, even if their effects may vary by context. This presents religious organizations with the strategic challenge of spreading their views amid changing media ecologies. Evangelical and Pentecostal movements appear to be the winners in this scenario because of their entrepreneurial willingness to adopt new avenues such as cable and satellite television.[26]

However, others are more ambivalent about mediated public spheres that may favour particular modes of representation (such as entertainment and critique) and that may be subject to governmental regulation, commercial power and a range of other voices. The spread of religious representations is no guarantee that they can be controlled by those who consider themselves to be the custodians of creeds. As Bryan Turner notes with reference to films such as *The Da Vinci Code* and *The Last Passion of Christ*, popular media 'contribute to the circulation of religious phenomena, but at the same time they challenge traditional, hierarchical forms of religious authority and interpretation'.[27] With its bias towards decentralized and cheap cultural production, much generated by private users, the Internet in particular has the potential to further open up the range of interpretations. It allows the public expression of personal belief and of religious ideation that circumvents state-regulated or commercialized media.[28]

---

[25]   Benedict Anderson, *Imagined Communities: Reflections on the Origin and Spread of Nationalism* (London and New York: Verso, 1991), p. 39.

[26]   See Stewart M. Hoover, *Mass Media Religion: The Social Sources of the Electronic Church* (Newbury Park, CA: Sage, 1988); Steve Bruce, *Pray TV: Televangelism in America* (London: Routledge, 1990); Quentin J. Schultze and Robert H. Woods (eds), *Understanding Evangelical Media: The Changing Face of Christian Communication* (Downers Grove, IL: IVP Academic, 2008).

[27]   Bryan S. Turner, 'Religious Speech: The Ineffable Nature of Religious Communication in the Information Age', *Theory, Culture & Society*, 25/7–8 (2008): p. 228.

[28]   For more about online 'participatory culture' see Henry Jenkins, *Convergence Culture: Where Old and New Media Collide* (New York and London: New York University Press, 2006). For work about religion and the Internet see Brenda E. Basher, *Give Me That Online Religion* (New Brunswick, NJ: Rutgers University Press, 2004); Lorne L. Dawson and Douglas E. Cowan, *Religion Online: Finding Faith on the Internet* (London and New York: Routledge, 2004); Heidi Campbell, *Exploring Religious Community Online: We Are One In The Network* (Oxford and New York: Peter Lang, 2005); Morten Hojsgaard and Margit Warburg, *Religion and Cyberspace* (London and New York: Routledge, 2005); chapters 13 and 14 in Christopher Deacy and Elizabeth Arweck (eds), *Exploring Religion and the Sacred in a Media Age* (Farnham: Ashgate, 2009), pp. 219–51; chapters 19–23 in Mitchell and Marriage, *Mediating Religion*, pp. 213–82.

Stephen Hunt's contribution charts the changing fortunes of Christian broadcasting in Britain over the last 30 years. Hunt shows how religious broadcasting on the major terrestrial channels has changed in nature and scope. The broadcast 'religious voice' has been transformed from a privileged discourse intended to 'bind the nation' under the original paternalistic public service model of the BBC, to being one voice among many after the market reform of broadcasting. Mainstream religious programmes tend to be more secular, covering matters of general morality, with critics arguing they are indistinguishable from normal current affairs. New media, satellite, cable and the Internet offer new opportunities, but also generate conflicts and paradoxes. Broadcasting in Britain is highly regulated, in terms not only of ownership but also of content. As well as facing commercial realities, Christian broadcasters have to navigate regulations regarding funding, recruitment, and freedom and curtailment of speech, if their commitment to Christian mission is to be compatible with the conditions applied to broadcasting licences. Questions arise as to how the broadcasters convey distinctive Christianity in a highly pluralist culture.[29] They make concessions in order to have voices at all, and may principally reach confirmed Christians rather than converting members of the public.

In her chapter, Aini Linjakumpu considers the emergence of 'alternative' Islamic discourses made possible by the decentralizing and globalizing influences of the Internet. In reducing the communications advantage that large organizations have over small ones and individuals, and in favouring recursive discourses that respond to other mediations, the Internet is an important platform for alternative media.[30] Violent manifestations of Islam currently take centre stage in many discussions of the religion, but there are alternatives within the mainstream. Islam has never had a centralized authority and in the past people looked to local scholars for guidance. In annihilating space, the Internet has allowed Muslims to seek advice, guidance and interpretations anywhere. This is especially important for those who live in societies where there is little freedom of speech and where it is difficult to form political organizations independent of the state. The Internet allows freer exchange of ideas, leading to lifestyle-oriented discussion on topics such as 'Queer Islam' and 'Everyday Islam'. The latter includes the use by young Muslims of social networking sites, chat rooms and blogs, to circumvent restrictions on dating, for example. In these ways, Islam is being reconfigured from within in a way that was not possible prior to the development of the Internet.

In the next chapter, Knut Lundby discusses the results of a project initiated by the Norwegian government, who wished to review religious education in the interest of social cohesion. This contribution concerns the use of new media in exploring the meaning and place of religion in the lives of twenty-first-century Norwegian

---

[29]   See, for example, Michael Bailey, 'Media, Religion and Culture: An Interview with Michael Wakelin', *Journal of Media Practice*, 11/2 (2010): pp. 185–9.

[30]   Chris Atton, *An Alternative Internet* (Edinburgh: Edinburgh University Press, 2005).

youths, all members of the Church of Norway. Though most people belong to the Church, attendance at services is low and declining, and open discussion of religious faith is not normal in Norwegian culture. The project was an attempt to draw upon the potential of new media to embrace otherwise 'unspoken' aspects of lives and to articulate the ineffable. Respondents created 'Digital Faith Stories', short, multimedia productions themed around the role of faith in their sense of identity and personhood. For these young people, 'faith' meant 'faith in oneself' rather than in any sense of the transcendental, and belonging to the Church meant just that – a sense of belonging to something, of solidarity. The results were very similar to a study on the same subject in Britain, which found that faith existed for British youth in relation to family, friends and the self. This suggests a reflexive approach to narratives about oneself and the significance of one's life that is consistent with the detraditionalization of belief in late modernity.

The question of how religious groups make use of and respond to the media is not always about the advancement of an assumed strategic interest for good publicity. The desire to control media use can also be a matter of a group's attitude towards the world beyond their constituency. Some religious traditions embrace the media and the modern world. For others, such as the Israeli Haredi community of ultra-orthodox Jews, the subject of Yoel Cohen's chapter, both are something to be shunned. He outlines the attempts of Haredi rabbis to police the use of the Internet on the basis that it threatens traditional family and religious values. The first reaction of the leadership, as it had been with every development in media from newspapers onwards, was to outlaw the use of the Internet by members of the group. This has proved difficult to maintain not least because the Internet is a valuable source of religious knowledge. Earlier bans on television and the cinema have been widely respected among the Haredim, but the ubiquity and utility of the Internet has meant that rabbis have had to reach an accommodation with this aspect of modernity, and attempt instead to control the use of it in the same way that they eventually did with newspapers.

Part II: Consumption and Lifestyle

Chapters in this section raise questions about the yoking of the sacred to apparently secular concerns with self-improvement and personal preference. Authors engage with theories of neo-liberalism, post-feminism, consumer culture and late modernity in considering how religious ideation is tied up with elective projects of self-fashioning such as those concerning health (Ruth Barcan and Jay Johnston), appearance (Karen Tice) and entertainment (Anna E. Nekola). Related to this sense that religion caters for broader lifestyle concerns of its socio-cultural environment, is the question of how religious organizations adopt strategies of 'intentional contemporaneity' to frame their appeal. Veronika Krönert and Andreas Hepp assess how the brand-like management of religious symbols constitutes a bid to grab attention amid popular culture, and Rob Warner shows how successful churches stress the convenience and experiential value of participation.

Religion is conventionally viewed as a communal affair that integrates individuals into collectivities. For functionalists following Durkheim this may be its principal social purpose. However, relations of individuality and collectivity have uneven histories. Theorists including Ulrich Beck, Anthony Giddens and Zygmunt Bauman suggest that late modernity is distinctive in the sense that society becomes increasingly organized around the category of the individual, such that in many spheres of action people have 'no choice but to choose'.[31] While critiques of such theories of individualization stress that not all citizens are in the same position to effect choices,[32] commentators including Wade Clark Roof have noted generational patterns towards what might be called 'personal quest spirituality' among baby boomers.[33] Whether manifesting in chosen affiliation with particular religions or with the eclectic consumption of options in the New Age spiritual marketplace, for many seekers the accent is on elective involvement rather than upholding a received tradition.

Neither everyday religious life nor the discourses that enjoin followers to observe piety in their lifestyles are new, but their mediation has changed. In the 1960s Thomas Luckman noted how the expression of religiosity merged with other aspects of lifestyle media to create forms of 'invisible religion'. Market models of religious symbolization and participation have developed alongside recognition that many people are at liberty to pursue religious meanings in terms that speak to their lifestyles. Berger was one of the first to note that some churches adopt marketing-style discourses through which they differentiate their angle on the sacred from others, effectively creating a brand image aimed at informing the choices of potential churchgoers.[34] New Age practices offer a more literal marketplace

---

[31] Ulrich Beck, *Risk Society: Towards a New Modernity* (London: Sage, 1992); Anthony Giddens, *Modernity and Self-identity: Self and Society in the Late Modern Age* (Stanford, CA: Stanford University Press, 1991); Zygmunt Bauman, *The Individualised Society* (Cambridge: Polity Press, 2001).

[32] Mike Savage, *Class Analysis and Social Transformation* (Maidenhead: Open University Press, 2000).

[33] Wade Clark Roof, *Baby Boomers and the Remaking of American Religion* (Princeton, NJ: Princeton University Press, 2001).

[34] For a fuller analysis of this phenomenon, especially in relation to the United States, see Schofield Clark (ed.), *Religion, Media, and the Marketplace*; Richard Cimino and Don Lattin, *Shopping for Faith: American Religion in the New Millennium* (San Francisco, CA: Jossey-Bass, 2002); Laurence Moore, *Selling God: American Religion in the Marketplace of Culture* (New York: Oxford University Press, 1994); Colleen McDannell, *Material Christianity: Religion and Popular Culture in America* (New Haven, CT: Yale Univrsity Press, 1985); for similar analyses but in relation to other global contexts, see Pattana Kitiarsa (ed.), *Religious Commodifications in Asia* (London: Routledge, 2008); Roberta Motta, 'Ethnicity, Purity, the Market and Syncretism in Afro-Brazilian Cults', in Sidney M. Greenfield and Andre Droogers (eds), *Reinventing Religions: Syncretism and Transformtion*

of commodified workshops, therapies and media that do not necessarily demand loyalty of the kind traditionally associated with religious involvement.[35]

In their chapter, Barcan and Johnston examine the articulations between spirituality and health. Religious healing has many manifestations, but there are grounds to consider whether, in some contexts, therapy is becoming not just a latent, but a manifest function of religion.[36] Some might question whether alternative health practices are in fact religion, quasi-religion, or something else altogether. However, practice in the world does not obey the logic of neat analytical distinctions. The therapies they examine are sometimes explained through recourse to metaphysics of the divine, in forms such as sacred healing power latent in the higher self, or the intervention of higher beings such as angels into physiological processes. Others may be explained in terms of a more naturalistic vitalism. While the concepts of healing the self entailed in many therapies echo the normative subjectivity of neo-liberal self-responsibility, Barcan and Johnston argue that when the complexities of alternative therapies are taken into account they appear to have ambiguous rather than simple relations to what Jackie Stacey calls 'the recognisable metaphors of western individualism (control, autonomy and personal output).'[37] Looking at these practices within body-models generated by a range of religious or spiritual disciplines opens up potentially very different understandings of them.

Krönert and Hepp present a case study of the 2005 Catholic World Youth Day celebrations held in Cologne, which they analyse as a media event. Their interest is to show how mediatization – defined as an increasing spreading of 'technical communication media' throughout different social and cultural spheres – plays a part in religious change. They argue that forms of our present media cultures structure the production and representation of religion around specific sacred brands ('the Pope', for example), making religious contents pointedly communicable in fragmented media landscapes. Drawing upon the work of Beck, such a 'branding of religion' on the side of media production and representation is related to individualized belief at the level of the consumers who appropriate the media. Clear 'brands' and 'symbols' offer material for personal 'religious bricolage'. However, this reaching out of religious institutions into the mediated public sphere is more than just a mixing of the religious with the mediated public sphere. It raises issues about who has what kinds of authority to control religious symbolization and its interpretation.

---

in Africa and the Americas (Oxford: Rowman & Littlefield Publishers, 2001); Sudeep Dasgupta, 'Gods in the Sacred Marketplace: Hindu Nationalism and the Return of the Aura in the Public Sphere', in Meyer and Moors (eds), *Religion*, pp. 251–72; Carlton Johnstone, 'Marketing God and Hell', in Deacy and Arweck (eds), *Exploring Religion*, pp. 105–22.

[35]   Guy Redden, 'The New Age: Towards a Market Model', *Journal of Contemporary Religion*, 20/2 (2005): pp. 231–46.

[36]   Bruce, *God Is Dead*.

[37]   Jackie Stacey, 'The Global Within', in Sarah Franklin, Celia Lury and Jackie Stacey (eds), *Global Nature, Global Culture* (London: Sage, 2000), p. 116.

In light of the fact that Christianity has always issued 'decrees for the flesh', Karen Tice asks how we might make sense of faith-based initiatives for beauty, fitness, diet and self-help. She traces the recent normalization of prayer and witnessing in conventional US beauty pageants and the creation of Christian beauty pageants to promote evangelical missions, examining how these initiatives fracture and reconfigure conventional binaries of body and soul, material and spiritual, religion and popular culture, and the sacred and the profane. Fuelled by contemporary neo-liberal discourses of consumerism, post-feminism and self-responsibility, a new vanguard of Christian body entrepreneurs has merged evangelicalism, bodily makeovers and popular culture in novel ways. As one manifestation of WWJD ('What Would Jesus Do?') culture of everyday religion, the case demonstrates how living truth is constructed as those with particular social interests fill the room for interpretation that exists within religious creeds.

In his chapter Rob Warner examines the experimental reconfigurations and cultural assimilations of populist neo-Pentecostalism. Case studies from three experimental churches in York, UK consider to what extent church seeding and operational initiatives exhibit a relativizing of religious traditions in the quest for pragmatic acculturation. On the basis of empirical data, Warner argues that intentional contemporaneity, particularly in terms of music and multimedia, legitimates cultural expectations of religion as commodified entertainment, and validates the participant as an autonomous religious consumer. In the reflexive project of the self, religious identities may be in the process of becoming more provisional, contingent and individually constructed. Moreover, such transitions, driven by the rhythms of popular culture, have the unintended but inevitable consequence of producing transitions in theology and ethics.

The links between evangelical Christianity and contemporary lifestyles is also the subject of Anna E. Nekola's chapter, which raises questions about the market in religious commodities and individualism. The focus is on popular music, 'Worship Music', in the USA. Music of course has always been a significant part of religious practice, but here the author argues that the popularity of the worship genre, which began in churches but is now consumed anywhere – at home, on the move, in the car – is exacerbating tensions within evangelical Christianity over the place of the Church and community in worship. To producers of this kind of music, it allows evangelicals the opportunity to worship anywhere, but others are concerned that Christianity has always been about more than individual worship, that Christians have worshipped in congregations and modern, individualistic trends mean that people are isolated rather than empowered.

Part III: Youth

How to renew and enlarge religious membership is a permanent concern for most faiths and their spiritual leaders. If a religion is to survive and reproduce itself from one generation to the next, it must necessarily ensure that its belief system and everyday rituals achieve a precarious balance between the traditional and the popular, custom and innovation, the 'residual' and the 'emergent'.[38] Hence, in recent times, even traditional monotheistic religions have developed and adapted programmes of worship and spiritual pedagogy that people can more easily identify with as they negotiate the many contradictions that tend to characterize modern societies. The melange of competing, and sometimes conflicting, public discourses and private pleasures can be especially confusing for young people, who tend to be acutely susceptible to fads, peer pressure and the popular appeals of the ever-multiplying culture industries. More crucially, while it has always been the case that religiosity varies over an individual's lifecycle, recent research would suggest that increasing numbers of young people no longer participate in an official religion or readily identify with such things as spiritual authority, pastorship, discipline and reverence. This is certainly the case in the context of Europe and Christianity, prompting some religious leaders to lament that we have entered a post-Christian era in which young people are adrift in an immoral sea of materialism and hedonistic narcissism.[39]

Of course, one could argue this has long since been the case. Furthermore, the issue of how best to secure the spiritual obedience of future generations is not just a concern for senior figures in the local church, synagogue or mosque. The question of how to instil certain moral values and practices in young people has long been a concern for most parents, especially parents who feel that the social and cultural traditions that marked their own childhood have started to wane. Sending one's children to Sunday School – a practice commonly referred to as 'religion by deputy' – or teaching them to say prayers at bedtime has a long and peculiar history, certainly in Britain.[40] And let us not forget the various functionaries of the state – not least the media – that occasionally give us cause for panic about the moral condition and the future direction of society more generally. Phrases such as 'anti-social behaviour', 'hoodies', 'yob-culture', 'chavs' and 'binge-drinking' are just a handful of the expressions that spring to mind when one thinks of the many public discourses associated with youth culture in the present instant. In short, 'youth culture' is one of the oldest and most enduring of folk devils, which

---

[38]   For a fuller analysis of worldwide religious traditions and transformations, see Steven Engler and Gregory P. Grieve (eds), *Historicizing 'Tradition' in the Study of Religion* (Berlin: Walter de Gruyter, 2005); Linda Woodhead *et al.* (eds), *Religions in the Modern World: Traditions and Transformations* (London: Routledge, 2002). See Raymond Williams, 'Base and Superstructure in Marxist Cultural Theory', in *Problems in Materialism and Culture* (London: Verso, 1980), for a fuller discussion of 'residual' and 'emergent'.

[39]   See Stephen J. Hunt, *Religion in Western Society* (Basingstoke: Palgrave, 2002), pp. 76–81; Cooper and Lodge (eds), *Faith in the Nation*.

[40]   Thomas Walter Lacquer, *Religion and Respectability: Sunday Schools and Working Class Culture, 1780–1850* (New Haven, CT: Yale University Press, 1976).

is what makes it such an important category of analysis for sociologists, historians, and the like.[41]

There is, however, a problem with treating religion and youth in fixed, functionalist terms. For a start, not all young people experience religion as something that is purely and simply the cultural logic of a dominant culture, reason of state or parental dogma.[42] Though still a minority, significant numbers of young people are turning to religion in search of something out of the ordinary. Not surprisingly, this search for a more authentic way of life is particularly evident within new religious movements, which have proved particularly attractive to teenagers, especially those that offer alternative forms of worship and spirituality.[43] Also, much recent sociological research has focused on the way in which youth culture can be spiritual and transformative without being necessarily religious, for example, as seen within the New Age movement or contemporary clubbing culture.[44] Though written over 30 years ago now, Dick Hebdige's analysis of the 'Rasta hymnal' was exemplary for the way it drew the attention of academics to the complex intersections between religion and popular culture.[45] Finally, there is an additional complication insofar as religion is widely seen as one of the causes – not a solution – to some of the problems presently associated with youth culture. The conversion of an angry minority of young male Muslims to radical

---

[41] See Michael Brake, *Comparative Youth Culture: The Sociology of Youth Culture and Youth Subcultures in America, Britain and Canada* (New York: Routledge, 1985); Stan Cohen, *Folk Devils and Moral Panics* (London: Paladin, 1964); Stuart Hall and Tony Jefferson (eds), *Resistance Through Rituals: Youth Subcultures in Post-War Britain* (London: Routledge, 1993); Dick Hebdige, *Subculture: The Meaning of Style* (London: Methuen & Co, 1979).

[42] Graham Murdock has argued that this selective viewpoint is one of the reasons why British Cultural Studies has overlooked the popular appeal of religion for so long: Graham Murdock, '"The Re-Enchantment of the World": Religion and the Transformations of Modernity', in Hoover and Lundby (eds), *Rethinking Media*, pp. 85–101; see also Lynn Schofield Clark and Stewart M. Hoover, 'At the Intersection of Media, Culture and Religion: A Bibliographic Essay', *op. cit.*, pp. 15–36.

[43] See Dereck Daschke and W. Michael Ashcraft (eds), *New Religious Movements* (New York: New York University Press, 2005); Christopher Partridge (ed.), *Encyclopaedia of New Religions: New Religious Movements, Sects and Alternative Spiritualities* (Oxford: Lion Publishing, 2004); Gordon Lynch, *After Religion: 'Generation X' and the Search for Meaning* (London: Darton, Longman & Todd, 2002); Lynn Schofield Clark, *From Angels to Aliens: Teenagers, the Media and the Supernatural* (Oxford and New York: Oxford University Press, 2003); see also Roland Howard, *The Rise and Fall of the Nine O'Clock Service* (London: Mowbray, 1996), for an intriguing account of one of the most controversial examples of charismatic Christianity in the UK in recent times.

[44] Lynch, *After Religion*; Rupert Till, 'Procession Trance Ritual in Electronic Dance Music Culture', in Deacy and Arweck (eds), *Exploring Religion*, pp. 169–88.

[45] Dick Hebdige, 'Reggae, Rasta and Rudies', in Hall and Jefferson (eds), *Resistance Through Rituals*, pp. 135–54.

Islam – largely as a result of them feeling socially marginalized and the outrage surrounding the violent conflicts in Afghanistan, Iraq and Palestine – is the most obvious and pressing example.[46]

In the opening chapter, Thijl Sunier looks at emerging forms of post-migration religiosity, religious belonging, religious representation and practices among young Muslim men and women living in Western Europe. On the one hand, Sunier calls into question the simple dichotomies such as secular/non-secular, modern/traditional, integrated/non-integrated, radical/democratic, anti-western/ pro-western that characterize much present research and the public debate on Muslims in Europe. On the other, he suggests we treat young Muslims not as victims of a cultural clash or pre-constituted religious identities, but as active agents of their own cultural environment. By elaborating the concepts of 'style' and 'styling', as 'signifying practices' and 'enactments of meaning', Sunier's analysis puts emphasis on the types of performativity and aesthetics of religion that appeal to young Muslims in the twenty-first century.

It has been argued that, under the influence of globalization, the primary challenge to religious faith is not cognitive, but rather the commodification of everyday life. As discussed above, the principal issue facing religious leaders here is how to retain the loyalty of the next generation amid fierce competition from 'Madonna, Microsoft and McDonalds'. Joy Tong's chapter addresses these related issues by looking at two of the largest charismatic megachurches in Asia – City Harvest Church and Faith Community Baptist Church – that are notable for their success in recruiting thousands of young followers over the last decade. The two churches' proactive engagement with media is particularly fascinating in this regard as they both have aimed at creating world-class quality media performances and 'pastors–entertainers'. The combination of rational structures and emotional expressivity, and the interplay of media and commodification, raises some interesting questions: how do mega-churches construct a modern and authentic experience that excels in the religious marketplace? What constitutes its spirituality? Above all, to what lengths will religions go in an effort to recruit a younger membership?

---

[46]   According to a recently published editorial in a special issue of the *New Statesman* on Islam (15 February 2010), the latest British Social Attitudes Survey reveals only a quarter of Britons feel positive towards Muslims. More than half of Britons strongly object to a mosque being built in their locality. In spite of this prejudice, surveys published in the same special issue show that the overwhelming majority of British Muslims (77 per cent) felt themselves to be British and an even greater majority (99 per cent) expressed a strong objection against terrorist attacks. For further evidence of Islamophobia and cultural segregation among young Muslims, see John R. Hinnells (ed.), *Religious Reconstruction in the South Asian Diasporas* (Basingstoke: Palgrave Macmillan, 2007); Geoffrey Brahm Levey and Tariq Modood (eds), *Secularism, Religion and Multicultural Citizenship* (Cambridge: Cambridge University Press, 2009).

Part IV: Politics and Community

This section looks at some recent examples of the ways in which religious movements have become entangled in socio-political relations and processes: the involvement of various religions in welfarism and the wider global struggle to make poverty history; the rise of religious extremism, right-wing evangelicals and radical Islam in particular; and the related issues of immigration, race and multiculturalism. Though not specifically mentioned in this volume, other examples include: the growing influence of creationism within the US, the ongoing debates surrounding the rights of gays and lesbians, the bioethics of abortion or genetic engineering, and the increasing numbers of private religious schools and faith 'academies' in Australia and the UK. And let us not forget the much older and more deeply rooted religious politics associated with, say, the Middle East, former Yugoslavia or Northern Ireland.

Of these, the 'Muslim question' has become a key issue in many Western democracies. While one may not necessarily concur with the main thrust of his argument that religious identity is set to be the primary source of international conflict in the current era, Samuel Huntington's 'clash of civilizations' thesis is a compelling and chilling narrative that has set the tone for much political and public debate following the collapse of Soviet communism and the subsequent thawing of cold-war relations.[47] One doubts whether even he could have anticipated the terrible events of 9/11, the equally brutal response of Western democracies and the so-called 'war on terror', the attendant intensification in fundamentalism (of all persuasions, not just Islam), and the escalation of ethno-religious conflict more generally. On the other hand, critics such as Edward Said have argued that Huntington's hypothesis is an overstated gimmick that has been used by 'self-appointed combatants' to legitimate a United States-led geopolitics for the twenty-first century.[48] Either way, the current political climate is one in which religious traditions and communities of faith have an important role to play, particularly where international relations are concerned, and we ignore them at our peril.[49]

Of course, religion and politics have been inextricably intertwined since time immemorial. For example, one could argue that Jesus is best understood as a non-violent revolutionary who was crucified as a political criminal for offending the Roman authorities. For over fourteen centuries, Muslims have looked to *Sharia*,

---

[47]   The theory was first mooted at a lecture Huntington gave at the American Enterprise Institute in 1992, and was later expanded and published in book form: *The Clash of Civilizations and the Remaking of World Order* (New York: Simon & Schuster, 1996).

[48]   Edward W. Said, 'The Clash of Ignorance', *The Nation*, 4 October 2001, at http://www.thenation.com/article/clash-ignorance, accessed 1 October 2010; cf. Pippa Norris and Ronald Inglehart, *Sacred and Secular: Religion and Politics Worldwide* (New York: Cambridge University Press, 2004), especially Chapter 6.

[49]   Habermas, 'Religion in the Public Sphere'.

that is, Islamic religious law, for spiritual and political guidance.[50] Indeed, most European countries have an historic association with the religious and political doctrine of royal absolutism, better known as the divine right of kings. One only need look to British history, particularly from the Reformation onwards, to see how religion has played an important role in shaping and influencing political and public debate, and effecting social and cultural change.[51] For example, though the relationship between the Church of England and the state has been one where distinct functions have been observed since 1531 – the Church as the trustee of Christian utterance and the state as the guarantor of justice and the nation's economic welfare and security – Church of England bishops still have the right to sit in the House of Lords where they can publicly voice concerns about issues other than religious ones, as Margaret Thatcher knows only too well.[52] This articulation between religion and politics is even evident in such countries as the United States where there is a constitutional separation of church and state. Indeed, the role of religion in public life, and its revitalization as a political force, is especially pervasive in the United States, to the point where faith communities really can influence social policy and the outcome of political elections.[53] In other words, it has never been clear what things belong to Caesar and what things belong to God.

---

[50]   See Antony Black, *The History of Islamic Political Thought* (Edinburgh: Edinburgh University Press, 2001).

[51]   The following are just a handful of references that provide an impressionistic survey of the role of religion in British socio-political life: David Hempton, *Religion and Political Culture in Britain and Ireland: From the Glorious Revolution to the Decline of Empire* (Cambridge: Cambridge University Press, 1996); Grace Davie, *Religion in Britain since 1945: Believing Without Belonging* (Oxford: Blackwell, 1994); Callum Brown, *Religion and Society in Twentieth-Century Britain* (Harlow: Longman, 2006); Mark Chapman, *Doing God: Religion and Public Policy in Brown's Britain* (Harlow: Longman, 2008); Philip Lewis, *Islamic Britain: Religion, Politics and Identity Among British Muslims* (London: I.B. Tauris, 2002).

[52]   Among the many critics of Thatcher's economic reforms during the 1980s, perhaps the most vociferous were liberal Church leaders, many of whom took exception to Thatcher's dismantling of the welfare state and the consequent rise in unemployment and 'selfish individualism'. One of the most damning criticisms of Thatcherite policies was the publication of the *Faith in the City* report in 1985. For a fuller and more detailed analysis, see Michael Alison and David L. Edwards, *Christianity and Conservatism* (London: Hodder and Stoughton, 1990); Henry Clark, *The Church Under Thatcher* (London: SPCK, 1993); Adrian Hastings, *A History of English Christianity 1920–2000* (London: SCM Press, 2001).

[53]   Not surprisingly, there is a vast body of literature (of varying quality and objectivity) that examines the role of religion in American politics and society, particularly in relation to the influence of evangelism on education policy, the culture wars between liberal Americans and the conservative right, the influence of American–Jewish political lobby upon US foreign policy, and the relationship between religion and race. See, for example, Kenneth D. Wald and Allison Calhoun-Brown, *Religion and Politics in the United States* (Oxford: Rowman & Littlefield, 2007); Steven Brint and Jean Reith Schroedel (eds),

Not surprisingly, there is an extensive and rapidly expanding body of literature that examines the contribution of religion to political life in multifarious ways and various global contexts, for example: in relation to religious denominations, party allegiances and voting behaviour; the association between religiosity, civic unrest and social reform; attempts by certain political elites to repress religious organizations and religious values (as was the case in Communist Europe, and still is the case in China) in an effort to suppress political rebellion; the insidious use of ethno-religious identities to promote nationalist ideologies and political violence; the relationship between faith-based aid agencies and internationalism; or the above-mentioned use of the supposed 'clash of civilizations' thesis for spurious political ends and the contemporaneous rise of Islamic militancy.[54] Such accounts raise interesting and important questions that problematize some of the more simplistic propositions put forward by secularists and modernists, particularly those on the left who still associate religion with such theses as 'the opium of the masses', 'the chiliasm of despair' or 'the sigh of the oppressed'.[55] They also bring into question the widely-held assumption that public debate is best left to politicians, pundits and the electorate *qua* secular citizens.

It is in recognition of this agonism that increasing numbers of political and cultural commentators have started to rethink the division between the religious

---

Evangelicals and Democracy in America: Religion and Politics (New York: Russell Sage Foundation, 2009); Kenneth J. Heineman, *God Is A Conservative: Religion, Politics, and Morality in Contemporary America* (New York: New York University Press, 2005); Valerie Martinez-Ebers and Manochehr Dorraj (eds), *Perspectives on Race, Ethnicity, and Religion: Identity Politics in America* (Oxford: Oxford University Press, 2009); Robert S. McElvaine, *Grand Theft Jesus: The Hijacking of Religion in America* (New York: Three Rivers Press, 2009); R. Murray Thomas, *God in the Classroom: Religion and America's Public Schools* (Lanham, MD: Rowman & Littlefield, 2008); David Domke and Kevin Coe, *The God Strategy: How Religion Became a Political Weapon in America* (Oxford: Oxford University Press, 2008).

[54] See for example, Norris and Inglehart, *Sacred and Secular*; Rik Coolsaet (ed.), *Jihadi Terrorism and the Radicalisation Challenge in Europe* (Brussels: Royal Institute for International Relations, 2008); Lucian N. Leustean and John T.S. Madeley (eds), *Religion, Politics and Law in the European Union* (London: Routledge, 2009); Shmuel Sandler, *Bringing Religion into International Relations* (New York: Palgrave-MacMillan, 2004); Jonathan Fox and Shmeul Sandler (eds), *Religion in World Conflict* (London: Routledge, 2007); John Anderson (ed.), *Religion, Democracy and Democratization* (London: Routledge, 2007); Naveed Shahzad Sheikh and Naveed S. Sheikh, *The New Politics of Islam: Pan-Islamic Foreign Policy in a World of States* (London: Routledge, 2007); John Hinnells and Richard King (eds), *Religion and Violence in South Asia* (London: Routledge, 2006); Sarah Diamond, *Not by Politics Alone: The Enduring Influence of the Christian Right* (London: Routledge, 2000).

[55] Though published over 20 years ago, Kenneth Thompson's *Belief and Ideology* (London: Tavistock Publications, 1986) offers a succinct and informative study of religion and ideology from various sociological and Marxian perspectives.

and the secular in an effort to confront the mounting ethical dilemmas that most nation-states currently face.[56] Radicals, social democrats and Tory paternalists alike (a holy trinity if ever there was one) have begun to look to their not-too-distant religious pasts for spiritual and political inspiration. For example, in his search for an exit out of that heartless wasteland otherwise known as 'democratic state capitalism', Simon During argues that Christianity is best understood as 'capitalism's lost other'. Citing the 'quasi-theological' work of such European theorists as Slavoj Žižek and Alain Badiou, During argues that 'theo-politics' (as opposed to leftist cultural theory) is the best means of rejuvenating both public engagement and a progressive politics for the future.[57] More crucially, injecting religion with a more progressive sense of spirituality might also provide an effective antidote to the many fundamentalisms to have emerged in recent times and their tendency to preach reactionary dogma, intolerance and apocalyptic fatalism. Similarly, in the recently published polemic by Terry Eagleton, the so-called 'Ditchkins' (a witty conflation of the 'anti-God brigade's' key luminaries, Richard Dawkins and Christopher Hitchens), we hear a passionate lament for religion's many virtues, not least its championing of social justice for the socially excluded, sympathy and compassion for the suffering of others (not to be mistaken for bleeding heart liberalism, by the way), selfless and unconditional love (*agape*), the idea of the human good and, above all, speaking truth to power.[58] For Eagleton, all these ideas can be understood as a political resource for resisting the cultural logic of late capitalism and the possible remaking of humanity.

Claire Chambers's chapter examines representations of the ethical issues surrounding representations of Islam and specific Muslim communities in recent British fiction. She argues that, while there was a growth of artistic interest in Islam (as it is practised in Britain) following the Honeyford and Rushdie affairs of the mid- to late 1980s and the first Gulf War of 1991, such novelists as Hanif Kureishi (in *The Black Album*) and Zadie Smith (in *White Teeth*) have used Islam rather reductively, as a marker of 'fundamentalism' in a broad sense. Other, less high-profile novelists, such as Farhana Sheikh and M.Y. Alam, portrayed groups of young Muslims grappling with issues surrounding identity in late twentieth-century Britain. In other words, while Islam was an important concern, it remained subservient to other issues, such as gender, class, sexuality and regional identities.

---

[56] Habermas, 'Religion in the Public Sphere'; see also Cooper and Lodge (eds), *Faith in the Nation*, particularly the Introduction and Michael Kenny's concluding remarks, pp. 3–15 and 61–68.

[57] Simon During, *Exit Capitalism: Literary Culture, Theory, and Post-Secular Modernity* (London: Routledge, 2010), pp. viii and 131–61; Slavoj Žižek, *The Fragile Absolute or, Why is the Christian legacy worth fighting for?* (London: Verso, 2000); Badiou, *St Paul*; see also Mike Kenny, 'A new chapter for the centre-left', at http://www.lwbooks.co.uk/ReadingRoom/public/kenny.html, accessed 3 September 2010.

[58] Terry Eagleton, *Reason, Faith and Revolution: Reflections on the God Debate* (New Haven, CT, and London: Yale University Press, 2009).

Yet creative interest accelerated in the years following the 2001 Burnley, Oldham and Bradford riots, the attacks on America later that year and the onset of the so-called war on terror, and British writers have begun to examine Islam with greater complexity.

The next chapter, by Ann Hardy, theorizes the centrality of mediated communication to religious groups in the modern world but also looks at the reciprocal shaping effects of media involvement on the groups themselves, particularly in relation to tensions around the location and exercise of spiritual and worldly forms of authority. More specifically, she focuses on how a number of conservative Christian groups in New Zealand have been stirred into political action in the face of recent liberal social legislation. In particular, Hardy looks at examples of what happens when evangelical sects that normally forbid both voting and contact with the attempt to influence an election outcome, as the Exclusive Brethren tried to do in the 2005 New Zealand general election with a million-dollar media drive to discredit the incumbent Labour Party: a strategy previously undertaken by cognate groups in Australia and the United States.

Drawing on the work of Michel Foucault, Holly Randell-Moon argues that religion is mediated through specific historical and cultural discourses as well as influencing cultural and social formations at particular political moments. Using the intersections between religion, culture and politics under the John Howard-led Coalition Government in Australia as a case study, her chapter examines how Australian culture, history and government policy are mediated through a discourse of 'Christian values'. In particular, she argues that religion is an important area for investigation into the processes by which particular political, economic and social events such as neo-liberal welfare reform are imagined and made culturally meaningful. By analysing a number of speeches by key members of the Government Randell-Moon shows how the Government's discursive framing of Christianity as beneficial to a unified Australian national identity has a corresponding legislative effect in the privatization of welfare services contracted to predominantly Christian church welfare and charity agencies.

Finally, Katherine Wiegele's chapter describes how novel uses of mass media and urban public space by El Shaddai, a new Catholic charismatic movement in the Philippines, has generated new social and ritual forms since its inception in the mid-1980s. Based on 13 months of ethnographic fieldwork, her research is anchored in the everyday experiences of residents in squatter neighbourhoods as well as in larger national contexts, such as the nationally broadcast weekly rallies these residents attend. What Wiegele illustrates is that the new social forms created by this movement are implicated in new spiritual understandings and ritual forms. The group's weekly massive rallies are also a form of demarginalization for the invisible urban poor, who now become a visible critical mass with political relevancy. Wiegele also shows how popular Catholic movements are also intertwined with a controversial relationship with the institutional Catholic Church: for example, El Shaddai's quasi-physical mass-mediated space is one from which critique of the institutional Church is possible.

PART I
New Media Religion

Chapter 2

Transformations in British Religious Broadcasting

Stephen Hunt

The last three decades have undoubtedly seen the radical transformation of Christian broadcasting in Britain and in such a way that is seemingly to the detriment of the previously dominant national sphere of religious broadcasting, once the preserve of terrestrial channels. The British Broadcasting Corporation (BBC) and later the Independent Television (ITV) company – as its sole and heavily state-regulated competitor – are now challenged by an aggressive 'religious' market exemplified by specialized independent radio and satellite channels. In particular, the new medium of satellite Christian broadcasting, as with other themed programming,[1] constitutes a part of major global industries in an ever-expanding international communication sphere, operating independent of established boundaries of national public terrains.[2] At the same time, the competition between the older terrestrial channels in religious broadcasting with the new medium is further compounded by the former's widening definitions of what constitutes religious broadcasting, given its departure from its essential 'Christian' roots. Paradoxically, widening choice has led to satellite broadcasts enjoying their own 'Christian' monopoly of sorts in the context of religious transmission.

This chapter traces these principal transformations, which provide not only indices of changes concomitant with new technological developments and a growing competitive environment, but offer evidence of the ever-advancing culture of pluralism, secularity, the consumerist society and widening expressions of religiosity in Britain today. It is a terrain that subscribes to the global development of the religious market as a specialized genre and where the globalization of religion has led to a massive global trade in online religious 'commodities'.[3] It is a

---

[1] P. Sepstrup, *Transnationalization of Television in Western Europe* (London: John Libby, 1990); I. Volkmer, 'Governing the "Spatial Reach"?: Spheres of Influence and Challenges to Global Media Policy', *International Journal of Communication*, 1 (2007); pp. 56–73.

[2] M. Serazio, 'Geopolitical Proselytizing in the Marketplace for Loyalties: Rethinking the Global Gospel of American Christian Broadcasting', *Journal of Media and Religion*, 8/1 (2009): pp. 40–64.

[3] T. Pradip, 'Selling God/Saving Souls', *Global Media and Communication*, 5/1 (2009): pp. 57–76.

world where religiously based broadcasts display their own brands in a competitive yet dwindling religious marketplace that is limited to a fairly well-demarcated audience constituted by a dedicated but nonetheless marginalized Christian life-sphere and where transmissions are hedged around by rigid regulation.

'In the Public Interest'

Since the creation of first radio, and then television at a later date, British broadcasting has traditionally allotted a privileged position to the Christian churches. The initial director general of the BBC, John Reith (1889–1971), took a paternalistic line with a vision to educate, inform and entertain an entire nation, free from political interference and commercial pressures. It was Reith, a devout Presbyterian Scot, who ensured that the culture of Christianity was regularly heard on the medium of the radio. He was known to state on numerous occasions that the BBC should aspire to become 'the nation's church' and it was under Reith that the BBC adopted the motto derived from the biblical verse 'Nation Shall Speak Peace Unto Nation'.

Reith's paternalism was to become eulogized for many years as a result of the standards that he attempted in 'good taste'. To a degree his influence was additionally guaranteed due to the fact that until the late 1960s there was only one radio company, the BBC (which had three channels), while its television channel competed with only one independent rival, ITV. Historically, both agencies voluntarily conceded to an operation within the remit of the 'public interest' and 'public good' in providing religious broadcasting and in overseeing its content. This ensured that, from early on, the BBC in particular took pride in being ecumenical, tolerant and uncontroversial.

In this conventional spirit a large part of the religious or, more precisely, Christian output for terrestrial television and radio of the past meant the broadcasting of church services. A slender advantage was given to the Church of England with the opportunity to broadcast then allocated to the various mainstream denominations and some minor evangelically orientated constituencies in rough proportion to their size.[4] This ensured that broadcasts were generally ecumenical and middle-of-the-road with not so much an inclination towards liberal variants of Protestantism as a careful evasion of anything appearing to be proselytization or criticism of competing Christian expressions. Despite ongoing attempts to embrace 'representation' and 'fairness', terrestrial religious broadcasting has fought a rearguard battle in the environment of an increasing secular and pluralist society, alongside the advent of offerings from specialized satellite Christian channels. The 'public good' on terrestrial television continues to this day to dovetail with the

---

[4]   S. Bruce, *Religion in Modern Britain* (Oxford: Oxford University Press, 1995), pp. 55–6.

broad requirements of 'representation' and 'fairness', although, as explored below, this has come to have different connotations.

Another of the major factors behind the altering face and nature of Britain's religious broadcasting is that the nation has become simply less 'religious'. By various indexes Britain is now a post-Christian society. In religious terms, it is also a pluralistic one, reflected in the nation's increasing multiculturalism. Studies continue to show low and reducing interest in the Christian faith by the population at large. Although the churches may rejoice in the latest national census, which showed that 72 per cent of people in Britain defined themselves as 'Christian', it would seem to be little more than a vague cultural reference point.

What the World Thinks of God, which was the subject of a documentary on BBC2 television in 2004, more than hinted that Britain is now one of the most religiously sceptical countries in the world. The programme was based on a large-scale survey published by the Home Office, which asked participants to state 'which things would say something important about you, if you were describing yourself?'[5] For the population as a whole, religion came ninth, after 'Family', 'Kind of work you do', 'Age and life stage', 'Interests', 'Level of Education', Nationality', 'Gender' and 'Level of income'. The significance of religion was admittedly much higher for the small minority of evangelical Christians from the Afro-Caribbean community and devout members of the world religions among other ethnic minorities, yet the findings were clear enough.

There are further indications of declining levels of religiosity. Ofcom is the independent regulator and competition authority for the British communications industries with responsibilities across television, radio, telecommunications and wireless communications services. Its survey in 2007 into viewing habits indicated that only 10 per cent of viewers placed any value on religious programmes.[6] Earlier, as part of its review of public service broadcasting in 2004, Ofcom asked viewers what types of programming they most valued on the terrestrial channels.[7] Of the 17 areas identified, religious broadcasting came 16th in terms of which genres people ranked as having personal importance (only regional programming was ranked lower) and it also came 16th in terms of which programme types people ranked as having societal importance (only arts and classical music programming came lower).

Though still relatively large, the audiences of religious broadcasting on terrestrial television steadily declined from their peak and in line with the turn down in Christian belief and observances. In the 1970s ITV's *Stars on Sunday* was

---

[5]   N. O'Beirne, *Religion in England and Wales Home Office Research Study 274*, Findings from the 2001 Home Office Citizen Survey, 2004.

[6]   Ofcom, 'Religious Programmes: A Report of the Key Findings of a Qualitative Research Survey', 2005, at www.ofcom.org.uk/research/radio/reports/bcr/religious-programmes.pdf, accessed 27 September 2010.

[7]   Ofcom Review of Public Service Television Broadcasting: Phase 1: Is television special?, 2004.

watched by between 12 and 15 million people.[8] Its successor, *Highway*, attracted
7.8 million viewers in 1987 and 7 million in 1992. The BBC's *Songs of Praise*,
essentially an outside broadcast of a church service, was watched by almost 7
million people in 1987, declining to between 5 and 5.5 million in 1992. In 1968
40 per cent of respondents deliberately tuned in to watch religious programmes
and over half reported they paid attention while the programmes were transmitted.
By 1987, this was found to have dropped, with only 7 per cent of those surveyed
saying they switched on.[9] True, it might be argued that the later declining viewing
figures are also evident in other programming genres given the increasing choice
permitted by the advent of satellite television stations, but there were nevertheless
profound implications for terrestrial religious broadcasting.

The decline in the popularity of religious broadcasting meant that the ratings
'war' had become a crucial factor. Throughout the 1980s, programmers pressed
for the fixed 'God Slot' to be abandoned. At first they were repelled by demands
from church leaders, but by 1993 religious broadcasting was switched out of its
primetime space. Typical of such developments, in 2001, the widely used Alpha
course, a popular evangelizing programme used by one in four British churches,
was given air time with a 10-week national documentary on ITV. *Alpha: Will it
Change Their Lives?* was hosted by the respected television personality Sir David
Frost. While initially planned for peak-time viewing, it was broadcast extremely
late on Sunday evenings and therefore returned relatively low viewing statistics.
Around 2.3 million people tuned into the first programme. Viewing figures settled
down to under one million. Undoubtedly its late coverage said something, perhaps
most obviously that the television company anticipated that the programme would
only generate a very limited appeal.[10]

Widening Definitions of Religion

Not to be thwarted by such indications of religious decline, the BBC still dedicates
approximately 112 hours per year to televised religious broadcasting and 400 hours
to the radio network, much more than other themed programmes, with the likely
exception of those featuring gardening and cooking, can sustain. In 2006, which
can be taken as a fairly typical year, BBC programmes retained some traditional
radio formats including such favourites as the *Daily Service* – broadcast every
morning; *Thought for the Day* – the daily words of wisdom from an invited guest;
and *Prayer for Today*. Yet despite retaining religious programming, it is clear

---

[8]   This constituted about 75 per cent of the audience for the most popular programme,
the soap opera *Coronation Street*; quoted in Bruce, *Religion in Modern Britain*, p. 56.

[9]   B. Gunter and R. Vinney, *Seeing is Believing: Religion and Television in the 1990s*
(London: John Libbey/ITC, 1994), p. 53.

[10]   ITV also attracted doubts over whether it could breach the code of conduct for
balance with the Alpha series.

that what is defined as 'religious broadcasting' has broadened substantially to feed consumer demand and to appeal to perceptions of opinions of both majority and minority religious groups, effectively squeezing out specifically 'Christian' content of programmes.[11]

Such developments were enhanced by legislative changes widening the definition of religious broadcasting. Section 264(6) of the Communications Act 2003 requires that public service television broadcasting in Britain must include services of a suitable quality and range, dealing with a number of subjects including 'religion and other beliefs'. For the purposes of the Act a 'belief' is defined as 'a collective belief in, or other adherence to, a systemized set of ethical or philosophical principles or of mystical or transcendental doctrines'.[12] Therefore broadcasting covering religion and 'other beliefs' is now part of the remit of all public service channels. The Green Paper of 2006, which examined a new 10-year charter for the BBC, suggested that one of the future roles of the BBC should be to provide a range of programming reflecting diversity within, as well as between, faiths and beliefs.[13] Such programming, it was advised, should include coverage of acts of worship and key events in the religious calendar, as well as drama and current affairs programming that explore religious issues and other belief systems in different ways, for different audiences.[14]

Legislative changes and recommendations have continued to encourage programme producers to find new, innovative and informative ways of tackling issues of religion, spirituality, ethics and values through all the different programming genres. Religious output by the BBC has thus come to be more *about* religion and less specifically religious. Indeed, criticisms of the corporation as early as the 1970s and 1980s purported that so-called religious programmes were already more about social affairs broadly defined. Certainly, the remit has widened in the production of numerous religious discussion programmes. In the not untypical year of 2006 this included the radio programme *Belief* hosted by Joan Bakewell, who talked to artists, thinkers and other public figures about what they believe and why; and *Beyond Belief*, a weekly discussion that explored religion and its place in today's world. To these programmes were added television airings that were more of a general educational interest but also tended to entertain. In 2006 this included *An Island Parish*, a six-part series that chronicled life in the parish of the Isles of Scilly, and *Extreme Pilgrim*, which featured a Church of England vicar who set off on three pilgrimages to explore Zen Buddhism, Hinduism and ascetic Christianity.

---

[11]   Gunter and Vinney, *Seeing is Believing*.

[12]   Section 264(13).

[13]   Green Paper, Select Committee Report, 2006. It recommended that the BBC's board of governors be replaced by two agencies that effectively split its functions: an executive board responsible for 'delivery' and a new BBC trust to monitor 'performance'.

[14]   Department for Culture, Media & Sport, *Review of the BBC's Royal Charter: A Strong BBC, Independent of Government*, March 2005, pp. 40, 41.

Independent Christian Broadcasting

The increasingly pluralist nature of religious programming on terrestrial channels ran parallel to the expansion of the freeing of the airways to competitors in alternative broadcasting. It was, however, a slow and tortured development. Hitherto, neither the BBC nor its regulators allowed airtime to be sold. Although the proliferation of local radio stations slightly opened up the British broadcasting media, the impossibility of starting an independent television or radio station and the inability to buy airtime remained; and even the market-driven Conservative government of the 1980s initially showed little enthusiasm for altering the policy. Yet its foremost consideration in opening up the airways to 'free' market principles was to impact in far-reaching respects.[15]

The 1990 Broadcasting Act reversed previous restrictions on ownership of ITV franchises, whereby a single company could hold only one franchise and overseas ownership was forbidden. Hence the growth, albeit slowly, of local radio stations under licence. Most of these were musical channels. Whatever their ilk, they carried little or no religious broadcasting. The Act also regulated independent broadcasting (that is, non-BBC output), making all religious bodies 'disqualified persons' for the purposes of holding a licence to broadcast. It was only at the discretion of the Radio Authority and the Independent Television Commission (ITC), which regulates commercial broadcasting in Britain, that certain types of licence could be granted to disqualified religious bodies. The licences potentially available to religious groups were local analogue radio licences, satellite (TV and radio) licences and cable (TV and radio) licences. This meant, in essence, that only one section of the community, namely those of a religious faith, remained banned from holding digital radio and national broadcasting licences.

Radio ownership rules have been debated since moves towards deregulation began 30 years ago, culminating in the 1996 Telecommunications Act, which eliminated national ownership limits and fundamentally liberalized local restrictions.[16] Yet the Act extended the automatic disqualification for religious ownership to all digital licences, including local and national radio, TV, and the new multiplexes. The Communications Act of 2003 maintained the general disqualification of religious broadcasters. This prevented Christians and other religious persons, bodies and broadcasters from holding a Channel 3 or 5 licence, a national sound broadcasting licence, a public teletext licence, an additional television service licence, a television multiplex licence and a radio multiplex licence. In addition, an officer in a religious body such as a church elder, a vicar or a member of the Parochial Church Council, was prevented from having control

---

[15]   One stance was to insist that the BBC took at least 25 per cent of its programming from independent production companies.

[16]   M. Ward, 'Dark Preachers: The Impact of Radio Consolidation on Independent Religious Syndicators', *Journal of Media and Religion*, 8/2 (2009): pp. 79–96.

of any companies related to the above.[17] Moreover, as a result of the Act, religious programmes on non-specialist channels (for example, ITV1) were, in effect, subject to more restrictive regulation than secular programmes. For instance, the ITC Programme Code prohibited 'recruitment' through religious programmes. This effectively saw an end to the full broadcasting of evangelistic rallies by those such as Billy Graham.

There are two permanent, Christian radio channels, Premier Radio in London and United Christian Broadcasters Ltd (UCB) based in Stoke on Trent, that both have a national focus; and yet it is still not possible to tune in to either on a car radio anywhere in the country. Premier Radio became the only Christian broadcaster to win a permanent local radio licence in Britain. Premier commenced broadcasting in June 1995 and subsequently had its licence renewed until 2011. It has built up a fairly loyal listenership, despite the difficulty of having to market three frequencies on AM to cover Greater London. Premier has transmitted on MW in London since January 2007. UCB's flagship station UCB UK has been available in the Greater London area on DAB. Like most of the others, these stations are forced to use the Internet to gain national coverage. There also several Christian broadcasters on satellite, for example United Christian Broadcasters and The Vision Channel.

The relatively newfound freedom in radio broadcasting has aided independent Christian broadcasters, but not to a great extent. In Britain, there are currently fewer than 10 radio stations that may be classified as 'Christian'. Allocation for national AM and FM frequencies has been assigned following award to the highest bidder. Thus, the future possibility of a national Christian station seems a remote one. The net result is that Christian radio has become fragmented and localized. In short, Christian radio in Britain is either limited to local FM or MW frequencies, or must be transmitted nationally only on platforms such as digital TV (satellite, digital terrestrial, cable).

Because of these limitations Christian would-be broadcasters have considered alternatives to the very high capital investment, and limited audiences, for temporary licences. One is to produce programmes for placing on existing mainstream stations where the opportunities for reaching a non-churched audience are much greater. Clearly this means establishing workable networks and a potential popularity, and ensuring the quality of the programmes to be such that the local station would wish to take them. There is also the possibility of syndication though services like Audiopot and Internet radio.[18]

The Christian constituency has its 'cause' groups and they have reacted strongly to the limits circumscribing Christian radio broadcasters. Broadcasters, particularly of an evangelical disposition, continually lobby the government to relax regulations preventing application for digital licences to broadcast across

---

[17]   The Act does, however, allow religious broadcasters to apply to Ofcom for digital programme service licences.

[18]   T. Kridel, 'Rethinking Religious Radio', *Broadcasting & Cable*, 137–8 (2007): pp. 18–25.

Britain. They advance the conviction that the ban is discriminatory. Peter Kerridge, managing director of Premier, the largest UK Christian radio station, which claims up to 200,000 listeners, has claimed that: 'There is effective discrimination going on. All we are asking is to be allowed to compete'.[19] More indirect are the actions taken by the Evangelical Alliance (EA), the largest umbrella organization for evangelically inclined churches and agencies in Britain. It has various grievances. One is that would-be Christian broadcasters have been labelled as 'disqualified persons' by the 2003 Broadcasting Act and that religious persons are immediately not just disadvantaged, but also totally excluded from the developing competitive digital radio market. The question advanced by the EA is, 'why can't tax-paying, law-abiding people who happen to hold office in a church or a religious charity, be treated the same as those who profess no faith or hold their spiritual life as private?' Moreover, it is pointed out that the disqualifications put the Archbishop of Canterbury, the Chief Rabbi and any officer of a church into the same Broadcasting Law category as murderers and rapists.[20]

Satellite Television and the 'Electronic Church'

Christian television channels have expanded alongside their radio counterparts. Nearly all such channels transmit on direct-to-home-style Sky satellite receivers, with Virgin Television offering the major alternative. Compared to terrestrial transmission, the cost of satellite broadcasting is relatively cheap. In 2006 there were 11 TV channels operating on satellite. A few of them also stream their signals on the Internet. GOD TV, based in Sunderland, is the longest established of the currently running TV channels on Sky and the only one that is also on the major cable TV systems in Britain. Revelation TV, in London, produces several live programmes from their studios. Premier.tv, also based in London, is a web-only TV channel, boasting over 700 programmes, much of its unique content produced from its own studios.

Despite these developments, satellite Christian television is circumscribed by other limitations. Financially, US channels fare a great deal better than British-based ones. The American practice of asking viewers to donate money to a channel to sustain it on air is still considered more culturally acceptable than in Britain, and as a result additional money is raised this way. There is no advertising revenue model that works for Christian TV channels in Britain, the traditional method of running commercial TV. In effect, the law prevents British-based Christian TV channels from asking for finances on air. Christian TV channels aimed at a British audience tend to overcome this law by situating themselves offshore in European

19   Quoted in S. Bates, *The Guardian*, Monday, 30 July 2001, p. 17.

20   See J. Peter Wilson, Broadcasting Campaigns Consultant for Evangelical Alliance, at http://www.crossrhythms.co.uk/articles/life/Why_Christian_Broadcasting_is_Difficult_in_This_Country/7226/p1/, accessed 4 September 2010.

countries that permit asking for money on air. At present, of the religion channels on Sky, only two, Revelation TV and UCB TV, are truly British-based and so are restricted for asking for funds by law; the other nine are free to do so, despite all of them giving the appearance of being British-based channels for a British target audience (or a European/international audience including Britain).

There is further limitation. Perhaps the worst charge against Christian broadcasters is that many of their programmes are simply not of a good quality. Greg Watts, Premier's former adviser, has claimed that the station's output was mediocre: 'The thinking at Premier [was] that because we pray before programmes, we don't need to think much about quality. God will do it all. Well he doesn't.'[21] Moreover, into the milieu of satellite television have come narrowly defined television evangelists originating in the US and over-represented West African churches of a similar style. Large-name and charismatic televangelists like Kenneth Copeland, Benny Hinn and Oral Roberts have developed a theology that states or at least suggests that God desired Christians to be wealthy. This includes the teaching of the 'law of return'. Since this involved giving financial subscriptions to the ministries in return for God's material blessing, there are invariably claims of the exploitation of their more vulnerable followers.[22]

When satellite television became available many liberal churchmen feared conservative-style televangelism, particularly its North American variant, which they saw as a reflection of neither 'public interest' nor 'good taste', and were repelled by the thought of the dominance of a style of televangelism that they regarded as populist, right-wing, big business and hucksterish. Fears were also expressed by the British liberal media. The *Guardian* newspaper in 2001 carried an article by Stephen Bates that included a journalistic parody of the American media influx:

> Discover, in one extraordinary week, the skills you need to live a triumphal life', claims an advert … 'Meet the Greatest Risk-Taker Of All', exclaims a US television presenter with a smart suit and bouffant hairstyle. Somehow you know whom he is going to be talking about ….[23]

Some anxieties regarding the dangers of independent Christian broadcasting were, in fact, realized. Religious broadcasters with local analogue licences in Britain have been censured for conduct breaches. In 1999, the Christian Channel was fined £20,000 for contravening advertising codes relating to political impartiality after a complaint about an advert for a rally by the US healing evangelist Morris Cerullo that claimed 'Satanic hordes [had] occupied the principal palaces of power in Europe'. The Universal Church of the Kingdom of God, an offshoot of the Brazil-

---

[21] Quoted in Bates, p. 17.

[22] K. Downey, 'Getting to God Online', *Broadcasting & Cable*, 138–40 (2008): pp. 16–24.

[23] Quoted in Bates, p. 17.

based Universal Church, has extensive media interests, including Liberty Radio in London. In 1997, the church was criticized by the Advertising Standards Authority for its poster, which read: 'Constant headaches, depression, insomnia, fears, bad luck, strange diseases … these are just a few symptoms caused by demons'.[24]

The Ghetto of Christian Broadcasting

In Britain, the dominance of American and other evangelicals on the Sky Religion channel and its rival is a far cry from the *The Daily Service*, the Anglican Evensong and the general decorum of denominational and mainstream Christianity, and certainly marks a departure from the more religiously pluralist tone of mainstream broadcasting. It may well be that the attraction of the traditional offerings of the BBC and ITV to the British population at large has always been more nostalgia for distant cultural heritage than any true commitment to the faith. Yet even on the terrestrial channels the nature of religious broadcasting is changing. Those who watch such channels are now largely left to disentangle marginalized Christianity from the wider agenda of programming concerned with educating and entertaining or where it is likely to be subsumed under some other genre.

Specifically Christian programmes are not popular. In homes that have access to Sky Television, religious broadcasts by terrestrial channels suffered an audience fall-off of 84 per cent since satellite programmes commenced.[25] At the same time, the BBC has been accused of being 'anti-religious' and 'biased' against religion or, alternatively, allowing the subject too much airtime. In a January 2006 interview with the Catholic magazine *The Tablet*, Mark Thompson, director general of the BBC, asserted that religious broadcasting had proved to be the most controversial subject of his tenure. He attributed this to 'a post- 9/11 sensitivity to religious belief'.[26]

Speculatively, in a culture of consumer choice, where religion is of a personal, highly individual concern, those who seek Christian programming are more than likely to turn to the specialized Sky Religion channel or suchlike. Thus the advent of Christian satellite programmes may be the preserve of those who are more religious in a conventional sense and now partake of a distinct 'commodity'. It is difficult to gauge its popularity. In 1991 a survey showed that only 1–2 per cent of those with satellite TV had watched what was on offer. Since Sky does not publish viewing figures it is impossible to know if more recent viewing has significantly increased or decreased. This is a far cry from developments in the USA.

---

[24]   Quoted in ibid.

[25]   Quoted in letter to Michael Grade, Chairman, BBC from Keith Porteous Wood, Executive Director, 'Protest about religious broadcasting seminar', at http://www.secularism.org.uk/41655.html, accessed 4 September 2010.

[26]   Ofcom, *Religious Programmes: A Report of the Key Findings of a Qualitative Research Study Conducted by Counterpoint Research*, May 2005, p. 143.

In the USA Christian believers can now choose to have only Christian programmes transmitted into their homes. Ninety-six per cent of evangelicals consume some form of Christian media each month according to the Barna Research Group.[27] Sky Angel, one of the nation's three direct-broadcast satellite networks, carries 36 channels of Christian radio and television, nothing besides. Many evangelical programmes and networks are linked to conservative Christian political or legal organizations that use broadcasts to help generate funding and mobilize their base supporters who tune in en masse. Evangelically inclined Christians in the USA, then, appear to wish to dwell solely in what Mariah Blake has referred to as an 'alternative universe'.[28]

For Hadden and Shupe, the principal reason the electronic church is important in the USA, the reason it has captured the concern of America, is not found in audience size or budgets or airtime.[29] Rather, the significance is observable in the potential clout of its exponents in reshaping American culture. Evangelists have taken advantage of a contemporary medium but have helped establish a particular kind of Christianity that reflects the aspirations of the American way of life. In this respect, Yancey suggests that the electronic church has necessarily developed a popular Christianity with the illusion of a 'superculture'.[30] The contrast with Britain could not be more stark.

Conclusions

The USA, of course, is known for its religious 'exceptionalism' that runs counter to the declining impact of Christianity in the majority of western countries. By various criteria the USA is a far more religious society than Britain. It is likely that specifically Christian viewing, largely through satellite TV, may become something of a ghetto in Britain, failing to reach beyond its dedicated audience and in no position to reshape its culture. In Britain, the like of Sky's Religion channel may do little more than convince its followers of their distinctive Christianity, a unique commodity in a highly pluralist environment and what may be understood as an increasing tendency to brand religious broadcasting.[31]

The fact that British Christian, specifically evangelical constituencies appear cocooned in their own worldview is undoubtedly saying something significant. In

---

[27] Quoted in M. Blake, 'Air Jesus', *Columbia Journalism Review*, posted 5 May 2005, at http://www.alternet.org/media/21940, accessed 27 September 2010.

[28] Ibid.

[29] J. Hadden and A. Shupe, *Televangelism* (New York: Knopf, 1988).

[30] P. Yancey, 'The Ironies and Impact of PTL', *Christianity Today*, 21 September 1979, p. 33.

[31] See M. Einstein, *Brands of Faith: Marketing Religion in a Commercial Age* (New York: Routledge, 2008), and D. Morgan, *Religion Media and Culture* (New York: Routledge, 2008).

short, it is a 'superculture' of sorts, furnishing a unique lifestyle among many, but one that must be continually bolstered by a media environment that reaffirms a worldview in a largely secular society that still continues to regulate and proscribe what that culture has to offer. It is also a form of broadcasting of dubious quality, fragmented and viewed disparagingly from outside. Christian satellite might be truly transnational, inasmuch that a great deal is beamed from overseas, yet in Britain it serves a marginalized enclave light years away from the past distant world that attempted to speak of what was understood to be in the 'public interest' and that such an interest was directed from and to the 'nation's church'.

Chapter 3

Alternative Islamic Voices on the Internet

Aini Linjakumpu

Alternativity within Islam: Authority in Question

Research related to Islam and Islamic actors often concentrates on the highly politicized dimensions of Islam. Over the last few years, Islamic terrorism and extremism have received considerable media coverage, and they have occupied centre stage of public debate. Aggressive and narrow interpretations of Islam have been common and there has only been limited space for criticism or counter-arguments towards, for example, Islamic doctrine, traditions or culture. Mainstream Islam, representing the conventional and traditional ideas of the religion, has remained the main option for the majority of Muslims, much to the frustration of 'different' Islamic actors that wish to create a more pluralist Islamic. The aim of this chapter is to explore these 'hidden' and 'minor' Islamic voices as alternatives to the mainstream understanding of Islam. More specifically, I want to examine these alternative Islamic voices in the context of the Internet and the phenomena of *queer* and *everyday Islam*.

Alternativity cannot be studied without the idea of authority: whose voice is considered the most powerful? Who can speak on behalf of Islam? Even though it is widely recognized that there are no formal clerical structures in Islam, authority has tended to come from religious scholars. However, in recent years, these traditional forms of authority and knowledge have become increasingly dispersed.[1] The main contextual element here is globalization, which, according to Peter Mandaville, 'can be seen to represent a further shift in the extent and intensity of debate about the meaning and nature of the authoritative in Islam'.[2] In other words, globalization represents a tendency towards transnational Islam and

---

[1] See, for example, Frédéric Volpi and Brian S. Turner, 'Introduction. Making Islamic Authority Matter', *Theory, Culture & Society*, 24/2 (2007): pp. 1–19; Mohammed Arkoun, 'Rethinking Islam Today', *The ANNALS of the American Academy of Political and Social Science*, 588/1 (2003): pp. 18–39; Mohammed Arkoun, 'The Answers of Applied Islamology', *Theory, Culture & Society*, 24/2 (2007): pp. 21–38; Mohammed Ayoob, *The Many Faces of Political Islam* (Ann Arbor, MI: University of Michigan Press), pp. 1–41; Bryan S. Turner, 'Religious Authority and the New Media', *Theory, Culture & Society*, 24/2 (2007): pp. 117–34.

[2] Peter Mandaville, 'Globalization and the Politics of Religious Knowledge', *Theory, Culture & Society*, 24/2 (2007): pp. 101–15.

decentralized authority. Hence the emergence of different alternative Islams in which we can see the pluralization of Islamic doctrine as well as Islamic practices and worldviews.[3] Of course, the globalizing tendency of Islam is intertwined with the deterritorialization of religion more generally.[4] That is to say, there exists a process of disconnection between religion and culture in which original cultural markers in a given socio-cultural context are fading. It is with this in mind that Mandaville further characterizes present-day Islamic authority as a 'heterarchy', a system 'governed collectively by multiple units having roughly the same status or level of authority'.[5] In short, 'being a good Muslim' is no longer dictated by local religious scholars, and understandings of Islam are created by many, potentially contradictory influences. In this context, it should be noted that the focus of the chapter is not related to any specific locations in the Muslim world or to local variations of Islam. This is due partly to the limitations of space, but even more importantly due to the need to focus on deterritorialized dynamics on the Internet, which is inherently transnational in its character.

The Meaning of the Internet in the Context of Authority

Why, then, Islam and the Internet? Gary Bunt argues that 'Islam does not need computers'.[6] As a religion, Islam – like Christianity, Buddhism or Judaism – can certainly function without the Internet; it is not dependent on virtual connections. However, the situation is somewhat different when we speak of Muslims and the relations between Muslim people, organizations and nation-states in a global constituency. Modern information technology, including the Internet, has also changed the social and political conditions by which power relations and forms of authority are produced; in particular, it provides a voice for marginalized groups.[7] For example, according to Saskia Sassen, cyberspace can create new types of political subjectivities that are not normally found within more formal socio-political structures.[8]

The Internet has played a major role in spreading Islamic material and interpretations. The written religious tradition and its presence in the life of ordinary people have been limited in Islamic states. The number of written sources

---

[3]   Ibid.

[4]   Olivier Roy, *Globalized Islam: The Search for a New Ummah* (London: Hurst & Company, 2004), p. 38.

[5]   Peter Mandaville, *Global Political Islam* (London: Routledge, 2007), p. 306.

[6]   Gary R. Bunt, *Islam in the Digital Age: E-Jihad, Online Fatwas and Cyber Islamic Environments* (London: Pluto Press, 2003), p. 1.

[7]   Ananda Mitra, 'Marginal Voices in the Cyberspace', *New Media & Society*, 3/1 (2001): pp. 29–48.

[8]   Saskia Sassen, 'Local Actors in Global Politics', *Current Sociology*, 52/4 (2004): pp. 649–70.

has been low and access to texts has not been widely available. The Internet has created a significant change in this sense: religious texts and interpretations have been opened up to very different groups of people in new ways and on a new scale. On the one hand, there is a wider range of sources that Muslims can utilize. There is also an increasing number of people who can create and disseminate their own understanding of Islam through the Internet. For Muslims, the Internet is no longer just an archive or 'bulletin board' as in the early days, but it allows an efficient, versatile and cheap publication and communication platform.[9]

In the context of this contribution, the globality of the Internet has an especially relevant position. Earlier, communication and political activity were restricted mainly to local and national contexts. The means of communication could not provide suitable or 'productive' channels for transnational communication or connections between Muslim people. The Internet is able to connect remote Muslims and also non-Muslims together. Like other people and communities, Muslims are also able to connect globally through the Internet. The borderlines between the diaspora and countries of origin become blurred, and at the same time the Internet allows connections between Muslims and non-Muslims. Individual Muslims are thus a part of a transnational media sphere.

The Internet is especially relevant in politically or culturally closed societies. In many cases, Muslim states – especially in the Middle East and Africa – do not have clear regulations on the freedom of speech, and thus there is no proper possibility to participate in open discussions in any sphere of public life, be they religiously articulated or not. In addition to the political sphere, many Islamic religious and cultural practices have not encouraged open socio-political participation and communication either. In this sense, the hypothesis of this article is that the Internet provides a powerful forum for alternative Islamic expression that might be aimed against mainstream ideas and ideologies in different Islamic domains.[10]

The Choice of Data

In the Muslim world, the use of the Internet is developing even though the level of access and availability of connections are still low. However, an increasing number of governmental offices, organizations and individuals are present in the virtual reality. The study of the Internet and Islam is not a novel one. In many cases, though, public interest has been directed towards the use of the Internet as a

---

[9]   Jon W. Anderson, 'Wiring Up: The Internet Difference for Muslim Networks', in Miriam Cooke and Bruce B. Lawrence (eds), *Muslim Networks from Hajj to Hip Hop* (Chapel Hill, NC: University of North Carolina Press, 2005), pp. 252–63.

[10]   See Bunt, *Islam in the Digital Age*, pp. 1–2.

form of Muslim politics and as a forum for religious organizations, i.e. phenomena referring to mainstream or extreme tendencies within Islam.[11]

For this contribution, several hundred Islamically articulated homepages or portals were explored focusing especially on pages related to civil society and its activities somehow representing 'alternative Islam'. Therefore, governmental sites, Islamic universities and official Islamic organizations are excluded. Different information portals representing mainstream Islam have also been left out, as they could be seen 'as a reproduction of what is available to hear within a local mosque'.[12] Furthermore, 'purely' political organizations have been excluded (such as the Muslim Brotherhood, Hamas, and Palestinian groups). Political organizations occupy Islamic discourse and are therefore one of the main alternative voices explored here.

Some sites are multilingual and directed to non-Muslims and non-Arabic Muslims. The focus here has explicitly been on English sites. In global Islamic discourses, English is currently the central language of communication. Traditionally Arabic has been the hegemonic language of Islam: Islam's sacred texts are in Arabic and the core area of Islam has been located in the Arabic-speaking countries, even though the majority of Muslims live in Asia, and the biggest Muslim country is Indonesia. Today, knowledge of Arabic is not self-evident; in the non-Arabic Muslim countries the use of Arabic is not as obvious as previously. There are also increasing numbers of diaspora Muslims and converts who do not have a natural connection to the language, and their first and possibly only lingua franca could be English. This development could be defined as the formation of 'Islamic English'.[13]

Who, then, represents alternativity in the context of cyber Islam? Alternative Islam also means alternativity of actors: new actors also change and reconstruct the very idea of Islam. In this way, the Internet shows its most powerful element: it can open up the possibility of socio-political participation for new groups of people. NGOs, networks and communities collecting different types of people, have a major influence in creating alternative Islamic discourses. Furthermore, some academic institutions and think-tanks have Islamic goals with an alternative tone in their programmes. The Center for the Study of Islam & Democracy[14] and The International Centre for Islam and Pluralism[15] are examples of think-tanks whose intention is to disseminate information about a moderate and modern understanding of Islam.

---

[11] Gary R. Bunt, 'Islam Interactive: Mediterranean Islamic Expression on the World Wide Web', in B.A. Robertson (ed.), *Shaping the Current Islamic Reformation* (London: Frank Cass, 2003), pp. 164–86.

[12] Ibid., p. 166.

[13] Peter Mandaville, *Transnational Muslim Politics: Reimagining the Umma* (London: Routledge, 2004), p. 164.

[14] At http://csidonline.org/, accessed 6 September 2010.

[15] At http://www.icipglobal.org/, accessed 6 September 2010.

Web-based communication and actions also enable individual commitment. In the context of this contribution, influential individuals are often also behind institutional websites, which may be based on a single person's ideas even though their scope is wider than that. In addition, there are several websites produced by (or dedicated to) one person. Scholars, whether living in the diaspora or in Muslim countries, have traditionally included persons who have tried to promote open discussion within Islam. Artists, authors and representatives of popular culture form an increasingly important group of people in terms of alternative Islam. Gender, sex and sexual orientation are also important denominators of actors. This category gathers very heterogeneous actors ranging from ordinary people to different sexual minorities.

In the context of alternative Islam on the Internet, undoubtedly the most apparent and overarching theme is the renewal of Islam. *Ijtihad*, i.e., the independent interpretation of Islamic law, is seen as a primary goal. Demands for the depoliticization of Islam have also been articulated in numerous ways by different organizations. The idea of those actors is to separate politics and religion in public life, and to prevent situations in which Islam is being politicized. In the post-9/11 era, the issue of Islamic terrorism has been a burning topic among Muslims, and therefore the denunciation of violence also has appeared as a key objective.

The Internet is widening the sphere of potential actors and their geographical locations in the context of global Islam. The existence of these actors characterizes the trends of change and transformation within Islam. There have been many opinions declaring the death of the liberalized forms of Islam. However, it is important to focus not only on certain types of political projects (like liberal or progressive Islam) within Islam, but also on the overall process related to alternativity in Islam. Change within Islam is not only attached to political groups or organizations, but also to a style of living and the roles of academics, professionals, artists and ordinary people. Although the objectives of actors would be different, they are combined loosely together by the ethos or idea of alternativity.

Two different, though related, phenomena – *queer Islam* and *everyday Islam* – will be analysed more deeply in the next sections. *Queer* Islam refers to the construction of communities of Muslim sexual minorities: how those communities are formed and what aspects they contain. *Everyday* Islam, in turn, represents a sort of 'banal' dimension of Muslim life: how everyday practices of ordinary Muslims have an influence on the public, socio-political existence of Islam. Both phenomena are good examples of how authority structures of Islam are being challenged through Internet communication and activities. In the examined cases, the religious status of actors is heterogeneous. Some actors are religiously relatively competent, whereas some actors do not possess any specific qualities in terms of religious knowledge. However, they all consider themselves Muslims, not just 'sporadic' persons living in Muslim communities.

Hidden Networks of Alternativity: Queer Islam

In Islamic cultures, as in most religious cultures, sexuality is one of the most normative of issues. It is rigorously controlled by religious and cultural norms, and it determines essentially Islam and Muslim communities.[16] Sexual liberation has, however, also entered Muslim cultures, and Islam has become a target of struggles over meanings and definitions. Questions about sexual minorities are part of this larger debate. In most Muslim countries, homosexuality is not considered lawful, and it is not tolerated in cultural terms either. Therefore, homosexuals and other sexual minorities have mostly remained a hidden phenomenon. The Internet provides a forum for communities and individuals to express their feelings and emotions related to sexual orientation:

> I was 16 when I first realized that I was sexually attracted to some of the boys in my high school classes. I had no idea what I could do with that feeling. All I knew about homosexuals were the jokes and negative stories that people told about them. I thought a homosexual was someone who sexually abused children – until I saw the word 'homosexual' for the first time in an English encyclopaedia, and found a definition of myself. After that, I started searching the Internet for information about homosexuality. Eventually I came across two Iranian Web sites where I could communicate with other gays.[17]

Women's sexuality has been previously largely ignored as an issue in Islamic cultures, and woman–woman sexuality has remained thoroughly submerged.[18] Through the Internet the question has now been powerfully articulated and at the same time it has found a transnational dimension. Many Muslim female queer communities – for example, US-based organization *Al-Fatiha* – have been running since the late 1990s on the Internet.

Increased awareness is not only related to other Muslims, but also non-Muslim queer groups and activities in various parts of the world. Queer-awareness or 'recycling' queer-discourse accommodates the creation of an imagined community of like-minded individuals,[19] in part, regardless of religious background. The

---

[16]   See Leila Ahmed, *Women and Gender in Islam* (New Haven, CT: Yale University Press, 1992). Cf. Hammed Shahidian, 'Gender and Sexuality among Immigrant Iranians in Canada', *Sexualities*, 2/2 (1999): 189–222.

[17]   Amir, 'I'm Here, President Ahmadinejad', *Washingtonpost.com*, 30 September 2007, at http://www.washingtonpost.com/wp-dyn/content/article/2007/09/28/AR2007092801322_pf.html, accessed 6 September 2010.

[18]   Stephen O. Murray, 'Woman–Woman Love in Islamic Societies', in Stephen O. Murray and Will Roscoe (eds), *Islamic Homosexualities: Culture, History, and Literature* (New York: New York University Press, 1997), pp. 97–104.

[19]   Evelyn Blackwood, 'Transnational Sexualities in One Place: Indonesian Readings', *Gender & Society*, 19/2 (2005): pp. 221–42.

existence of queer-awareness provides an opportunity to imagine being a part of a larger, potentially transnational like-minded community. For sexual minorities the ordinary forms of community-building are difficult, but the Internet can be used to build their own virtual communities. Communities are not necessarily culturally or legally feasible outside the Internet, and thus virtual networking may be the only possibility.

The examples address emancipatory thinking: the issue is about recognition of sexual identity and claiming respect for our own sexual choices.[20] The aim is to get rid of the feelings of shame, the fact that queer sexuality is inferior or reprehensible.[21] The demand for recognition as well as growing awareness of others in a similar situation is an instrument of emancipation, and hence a conscious starting point for the battle. The term 'Queer Jihad' has been used in some cases to describe a fight for sexual minority rights:

> Queer Jihad is the queer Muslim struggle for acceptance: first, the struggle to accept ourselves as being exactly the way Allah has created us to be; and secondly, the struggle for understanding among Muslims in general.[22]

Historically, Islam has been a vigorously communal religion, but the deterritorialization of the Islamic world has meant disengagement of many Muslim individuals from traditional communities and their activities and connections at a local level. Religiousness becomes a sphere of personal experience: religious experience integrates the individual and God together. Individualization and the privatization of Islam have had an effect particularly on religious interpretations. Internet communities and individuals claim the right to a reassessment of religious sources, and at the same time they attack the mainstream views of Islam.[23] This refers to the 'queer reading' of religious sources, where sources are tried to recontextualize and to show the incompetence of earlier interpretations.[24] The aim is to find a suitable, individual interpretation, rather than to expect traditional, mainstream Muslim actors to do it.

In addition to the issue of identity, queer Islam is also related to the issue of human rights in the contexts of states and the international community. Although

---

[20]   See, for example, Aswat, 'Mission', at http://www.aswatgroup.org/english/about. php?category=24, accessed 6 September 2010.

[21]   Stephen O. Murray, 'The Will Not to Know: Islamic Accommodations of Male Homosexuality', in Murray and Roscoe (eds), *Islamic Homosexualities*, pp. 14–54.

[22]   'About Queer Jihad', at http://www.well.com/user/queerjhd/aboutqj.htm, accessed 6 September 2010.

[23]   See, for example, Safra Project, at http://www.safraproject.org, accessed 6 September 2010.

[24]   Andrew Yip, 'Queering Religious Texts: An Exploration of British Non-Heterosexual Christians' and Muslims' Strategy of Constructing Sexuality-affirming Hermeneutics', *Sociology*, 39/1 (2005): pp. 47–65.

the primary reference of queer Islam is often shaped by religion and religious authority, the conventional political sector is also involved in the discourses of sexual minorities. In particular, the human rights discourse is present in individual and collective perceptions. For example, the Lebanon-based organization *Helem* has worked with human rights issues. The objective of *Helem* is to struggle against the Lebanese penal code that states that 'unnatural sexual intercourse' is punishable by up to one year of imprisonment.[25]

Achieving rights as members of a sexual minority opens the debate on the functions and value-judgements of state and society. The issue is not just that queer Muslims have the right to subjective existence; there is a link to citizenship and claims to social and political agency. The positioning of queer Muslims as citizens is related also to awareness of the actions of governments and authorities in relation to sexual minorities. Raising awareness and increasing criticism of police- and court abuse gives the opportunity for tacit resistance to different mechanisms of power. In these situations, networking is obvious: support is sought from others or via alternative struggles. Sexual minorities in non-Muslim countries are also relevant in terms of Muslim queer awareness and actions. This also relates to diaspora organizations that have been active with Muslim refugees who have been forced to leave their country of origin for sexuality-related reasons.[26]

Queer Muslims are thus part of a broader international entity, where different kinds of Islam and alternative voices are networked, or are at least aware of each other. Transnational networking, in which the Internet operates as both medium and mediator of concrete activities, discourses and meanings, also occurs between Muslim organizations and Western human rights movements.[27] In this context, for example, Human Rights Watch and Amnesty International are major actors with which these queer organizations get involved.

All in all, queer Islam would exist to an extent even without the Internet; as a rule, however, it could be estimated that in the absence of cyber reality the problematics of sexual minorities would remain in the shadows. The Internet has been a concrete tool through which these questions have been articulated, and at the same time queer Muslims have been able to find others like them. The Internet helps the formation of queer communities, and it is for many the only channel through which to express their sexual identity, or communality. In the formation of queer Islam, internal differences of Islam inevitably emerge and are increasingly recognized and 'reinforced': issues related to sexual minorities constitute a clear dividing line between Muslims.

---

[25]   Helem, at http://www.helem.net/node/115, accessed 29 September 2010.

[26]   See, for example, Al-Fatiha, http://www.al-fatiha.org, accessed 6 September 2010.

[27]   Blackwood, 'Transnational Sexualities'; Brian Whitaker, *Unspeakable Love: Gay and Lesbian Life in the Middle East* (Berkeley, CA: University of California Press, 2006).

The Banalization of Islam: Everyday Islam

Alternativity within Islam may be an active approach, but on the other hand it can also be neutral or even passive compared with politically oriented approaches and discourses. In this context, the idea of *banal* or *everyday* Islam is relevant. In Islamic extremism and in many ways also in mainstream Islam, religion appears as a holistic subject determining all aspects of human life. The banalization of Islam means, on the contrary, the detachment of political and extremist activities from Islam's core content: Islam is normalized as an everyday issue and is not considered a meaning system changing the whole world. As Hossein Godazgar proposes, 'Islam constitutes only one factor in Muslims' "everyday" activities and trends'.[28]

The Internet helps the process of banalization because it is not necessarily easy to maintain nobility or a strictly authentic communication in virtual reality. The Internet allows for direct and informal discussion and communication. This occurs in particular in chat rooms and blogs: an actor can be anyone, and forms of expression are free and informal. This type of communication does not require any special knowledge or a lifelong or intense commitment, as for instance in the case of Al-Qaeda or similar groups.

How does the banalization of Islam occur on the Internet? In Islam, interactions between males and females have traditionally been defined by the content and orthodoxy of Islam. Sexuality has remained taboo in many Muslim cultures for a long time, and it has been difficult to approach openly. The Internet has opened up a very busy world related to dating, marriage and finding partners among both Muslims, and Muslims and non-Muslims. For example, MuslimFriends.com, Qiran.com and Muslima.com focus on cyberdating, and discussions related to marriage, dating and sex. Muslimyouth.net is, in turn, a multifaceted platform for young people:

> By profiling the real experiences of Muslim youth in a public forum, muslimyouth.
> net aims to confront the cultural stigma attached to common social issues such
> as mental health, drug abuse and sexuality. The forum and chat rooms will allow
> young Muslims to talk openly and anonymously about the issues that affect
> them without fear or community reprisal.[29]

In the same way that queer Muslims build 'parallel communities' through the Internet, the Internet also expands Muslims' social circles in the sphere of heteronormative dating. According to traditional religious thinking, dating before marriage is not allowed. With the help of virtual dating this rule can be either directly or indirectly circumvented: computer-mediated communication lacks

---

[28] Hossein Godazgar, 'Islam versus Consumerism and Postmodernism in the Context of Iran', *Social Compass*, 54/3 (2007): pp. 389–418.

[29] 'About Muslimyouth.net', at http://www.muslimyouth.net/about, accessed 6 September 2010.

a concrete human connection. On the other hand, there is an attempt to lift the secretiveness surrounding sexuality in Internet communication: sexuality and sexual pleasure are understood as an essential part of human life, and they should be openly discussed. In an Islamic context, this means loosening and modifying the traditional social ties and norms.

In addition to sexuality, other issues of ordinary life can be mediated through the Internet. For example, consumption, tourism, homecare and beauty attract intense attention. Conversations and communications in relation to homecare or day-to-day life incidents and events create the image of Muslims whose identification with Islam does not cover all activities of life. In these cases everyday life appears in many respects religiously neutral; it could also be argued that focusing on non-religious issues distracts one's interest and use of time from religion.

Consumption is associated with a range of dimensions in the context of the Islamic world. On the one hand, there is so-called 'Islamic consumption', which aims to politicize consumption-related activities. On the other, consumption that merely seeks satisfaction or aesthetic pleasure is relevant in terms of alternative Islam and the banalization of Islam. The latter violates the Islamically articulated, politicized consumption. Consumption appears in this case as a non-ideological issue, related to the satisfaction of immediate human needs and desires. In this case religious authority cannot necessarily reach an individual's life and experiences, since a Muslim could 'withdraw' from the religious collectivity into individuality. For example, discussions at different Muslim forums represent consumption as an everyday practice without any specific relation to the religion, for example:

> ... anyway back on topic, what advice can you guys/ girls give to novices buying their first car. What are the things to look out for and to notice. What questions do you need to be asking?[30]

Godazgar refers to consumerism in which 'consumption may be viewed as a matter of gratifying desires and wants through luxury and unnecessary services and goods'. Consumerism does not lean on religious legitimacy, neither is it ethically convincing, and, at the same time, it is 'far removed from religion's serious, significant, profound and lasting messages'. In Islamic discourse consumerism often appears readily as Westernization and cultural invasion, and even a new colonialism. Consumerism also threatens the unity of the Islamic community because it is based on individual thoughts and actions.[31]

The people referred to here are Muslims − they can be seen and identified in some way as Muslims − and their collective experiences might be built upon

---

[30]   At http://www.ummah.com/forum/showthread.php?253561-Buying-your-first-car-tips-warnings-useful-links-advice!, accessed 6 September 2010.

[31]   Godazgar, 'Islam versus Consumerism', p. 390; see also Mona Abaza, 'Shopping Malls, Consumer Culture and the Reshaping of Public Space in Egypt', *Theory, Culture & Society*, 18/5 (2001): pp. 97–122.

the basis of Islam yet their everyday activities do not appear unconditionally religious. This challenges those lifestyles where all parts of life are articulated through Islam. When this connection is detached, the socio-political meaning of Islam decreases and it no longer defines all conditions of human existence. This means a disengagement from authorities of power: when there is nothing specific to be controlled, there is no need or reason to be exposed to constant scrutiny.

Conclusions

How should we interpret the meaning of alternative communication on the Internet concerning Islam and its relation to mainstream and extreme trends? In many cases, the very existence of communication and different forms of Internet activity is important. The Internet may be the only possible communication medium for many Muslim people to convey their non-mainstream ideas. The Internet is particularly powerful in increasing the common consciousness of people sharing a particular situation, revealing that they are not alone in the existing political, social or cultural circumstances. Furthermore, an individualization of religious experience and understanding is also taking place.[32]

The dispersion of power and authority in the Islamic world takes a concrete form in Internet communication. Formal or traditional authorities are unable fully to control the transnationally dispersed Internet, on which in principle anybody can reposition him-/herself to a place of religious authority. In addition, the increasing heterogeneity of Muslim life as well as the ever greater and more intense exposure to foreign or new cultural influences disrupts the hegemony of traditional lifestyles.

The idea of virtual *umma* in the case of alternative Islam should not be seen as too overarching or totalizing, as in extreme Islam. For example, the mission of Al-Qaeda is based on a vision of a global, homogenous Islam without borders and on a common understanding of Islamic doctrines. Alternative Islam is, in turn, a transnational, non-coherent network of ideas, meanings and discourses. In this sense, the global *umma* is not a concrete community produced through practical political actions, but merely an inspiring idea of the 'spiritual core' of Islam.

The discourse on extreme tendencies of Islam has strongly emphasized the unique nature of Islam: it covers all dimensions of life. Accordingly, the identity of a Muslim person is defined by Islam alone. If one is a Muslim, one cannot be anything else. Alternative forms of Islam, in turn, put emphasis on the idea of multilayered identities; Muslim identity is not considered exclusive, but can exist along with other forms of identity. Themes related to sex, gender and sexual minorities have broken through the confines of private life, which has been the major denominator of extremist as well as mainstream Islamic discourses. Private life has remained 'the guardian of Islamic lifestyle' in a situation where many

---

[32] Cf. Roy, *Globalized Islam*, pp. 175, 181.

other issues have been secularized or de-Islamized. Alternative Islam has made private life public and open to new ideas and practices.

The dispersion of authority in Islam is apparent in Internet communication. The logic of authority cannot be defined as legal–rational, but instead is dispersed and devolved;[33] the official authorities no longer explain who is in power in Islam. Therefore, it is not possible to achieve a coherent, unified, disciplinary and homogenous Islam; neither is this appreciated by many actors in alternative Islam. In this way, internal differences in Islam are being recognized and 'confirmed'.

The articulation of alternative Islam creates wide and multiple 'contact surfaces' with Muslims as well as non-Muslims in relation to Islam. In other words, there will be more and more articulated discussions within Islam about Islam. Differences between people are being recognized, and there is a growing interest to advance discussion and debate about them. The global articulation of the extreme trends of Islam now coincides with alternative voices enforcing a geographical and juridical dispersion of Islam. In any case, the Internet is now playing a considerable role in reconstructing the global Muslim public sphere, since it provides a communication forum not feasible elsewhere.

---

[33]   Turner, 'Religious Authority', p. 124.

Chapter 4

Mediatizing Faith: Digital Storytelling on the Unspoken[1]

Knut Lundby

Introduction: The Changing Media of Religion

Religion cannot be analysed outside the forms and practices of mediation that define it.[2] Media in a broad sense, from written texts and pictures to modern audiovisual- and multimedia, are not external to religion. Media are inherent, as a condition. Mediation is part of religion. Religions have been transformed by adopting new media technologies ever since the invention of the printing press.[3] Now, at the beginning of the twenty-first century, public religion faces new challenges in having to adjust to new technologies, styles and formats.[4]

'New media', then, should be expected to make a difference. However, there is no New Media Religion as such. Although religion as living culture is a matter of communication shaped by its forms of mediation, religious expressions draw upon the socio-cultural heritage and environment in which the new media are applied.

The concept of mediation refers here to acts and processes of communication via a technical medium, which may affect the message as well as the relationship between those who communicate.[5] New media offer new means of mediation. Mediation as the use of media in socio-cultural communication is an inherent

---

[1] This research is carried out in cooperation with Birgit Hertzberg Kaare. Our case study is part of a larger research project, 'MEDIATIZED STORIES. Mediation Perspectives on Digital Storytelling among Youth', funded by the Research Council of Norway 2006–2011, at http://www.intermedia.uio.no/mediatized/, accessed 7 September 2010. Karoline Tømte and Sissel Nyegaard-Larsen provided invaluable help as research assistants. I am also grateful to Gordon Lynch for references on religion in youth cultures in the UK and the USA.

[2] Birgit Meyer and Annelies Moors, 'Introduction', in Birgit Meyer and Annelies Moors (eds), *Religion, Media, and the Public Sphere* (Bloomington, IN: Indiana University Press, 2006), p. 7.

[3] Elisabeth Eisenstein, *The Printing Press as an Agent of Change: Communications and Cultural Transformations in Early-Modern Europe* (Cambridge: Cambridge University Press, 1979).

[4] Meyer and Moors, *Religion, Media, and the Public Sphere*, pp. 19–20.

[5] Stig Hjarvard, 'The Mediatization of Society. A Theory of the Media as Agents of Social and Cultural Change', *Nordicom Review*, 29/2 (2008): p. 114.

and normal practice of religion. However, when the adoption of new media technologies and formats *transform* religious meanings and practices, this is to be regarded as a process of 'mediatization'.[6] The concept of mediatization points to social change brought about by the all-embracing media of late modernity, and more specifically to the transformations of social and cultural activities.[7] There is also a mediatization of religion to be observed.[8] This approach helps to detect how the media today fundamentally change the nature or religion and spirituality, Stewart Hoover holds.[9]

This chapter explores new mediation practices in a church setting. Young church members create personal digital stories about their lives and their relation to religious tradition. The research question is, do their articulations with new digital narrative tools[10] indicate transformations towards 'mediatizing faith'?

The Unspoken

The context of this study is the Lutheran *Church of Norway*, which is still a state church to which most of the population belong. Eight out of ten Norwegians are members, and almost three in four newborns are christened in this church. However, most Norwegians do not attend church beyond transition rites of life and death. Among adults, the pietistic division between those 'inside' and those 'outside' may still matter.[11] Passive members of the church may be satisfied that those active few act on their behalf. This 'vicarious religion'[12] keeps access open to the church and the rites 'in case'.

Although the question of religion under the influx of Islamic immigration and the so-called New Secularism has become a greatly debated topic in the Norwegian public sphere, most Norwegians do not talk about their own personal faith and religious traditions. Faith is a matter of a general belonging to the church rather than of expressed beliefs: a cultural–religious tradition of what I term

---

[6]   Knut Lundby (ed.), *Mediatization: Concept, Consequences, Changes* (New York: Peter Lang, 2009)

[7]   Knut Lundby, 'Introduction: "Mediatization" as a Key', in Lundby (ed.), *Mediatization*, pp. 1–18.

[8]   Stig Hjarvard (ed.), *The Mediatization of Religion: Enchantment, Media and Popular Culture*, Northern Lights 16 (Bristol: Intellect, 2008).

[9]   Stewart M. Hoover, 'Complexities: The Case of Religious Cultures', in Lundby (ed.), *Mediatization*, pp. 130–37.

[10]   Knut Lundby (ed.), *Digital Storytelling, Mediatized Stories: Self-representations in New Media* (New York: Peter Lang, 2008).

[11]   Knut Lundby, 'Closed Circles: An Essay on Culture and Pietism in Norway', *Social Compass*, 35/1 (1988): pp. 57–66.

[12]   Grace Davie, 'Is Europe an Exceptional Case?', *The Hedgehog Review*, 8 (2006): pp. 23–34.

the Unspoken. This chapter explores how young participants in the Church of Norway, a new generation of church members, mediate this Unspoken through digital storytelling.

It is not regarded proper among 'ordinary' Norwegians, as for most people in the Nordic countries, to talk about emotions, particularly in relation to religion. This Unspoken is nothing new. A study of people's memories of their own confirmation found this tendency all the way back to the generation born in Norway in the 1880s.[13] This attitude towards religion may be even older. Faith, then as now, may rather be expressed through forms of belonging: social relations and identifications, where individuals confirm their belonging to a larger collectivity. The folk church provides the institutional frame and the Christian tradition offers symbolic support for such cultural–religious belonging. It offers meaning without the need for words. Church buildings throughout the country have great significance for most people – the local population may care for their church building although they rarely visit the church for services. This sense of belonging to the Church of Norway seems remarkably widespread and stable, despite the erosion of membership.

However, there are changes within this fairly stable pattern. From life stories in extensive interviews with 72 Norwegians Inger Furseth documents a move *From Quest for Truth to Being Oneself*. Within the frames of the collective religious traditions there is a shift towards the self, towards religious individualism. The tendency is strongest among the young.[14] There is a turn towards the subjective, although not as massive and uniform as Heelas and Woodhead[15] claim, Furseth concludes.[16]

Religious practices among youth in Norway follow the same downward trends as elsewhere in Europe.[17] However, the voluntary participation in church confirmation has actually risen slightly during the last few years, even with a visible secular–humanist alternative available. Two out of three 15-year-old Norwegians are still confirmed in the Church of Norway. In the capital of Oslo, 38 per cent of the age

---

[13]   Birgit Hertzberg Johnsen, *Konfirmasjon og erindring. Konfirmasjonens betydning i et livsløpsperspektiv* [Confirmation and Remembering: The Meaning of the Confirmation Rite in a Life Course Perspective], Arkiv for kirkehistoriske tradisjoner (Oslo: University of Oslo, 1993).

[14]   Inger Furseth, *From Quest for Truth to Being Oneself* (Frankfurt aM: Peter Lang, 2006), pp. 295–311.

[15]   Paul Heelas and Linda Woodhead, *The Spiritual Revolution: Why Religion is Giving Way to Spirituality* (Malden, MA: Blackwell, 2005).

[16]   Furseth, *From Quest for Truth*, p. 312.

[17]   Pille Valk, Gerdien Bertram-Troost, Markus Friederici and Céline Béraud (eds), *Teenagers' Perspectives on the Role of Religion in Their Lives, Schools and Societies: A European Quantitative Study* (Münster: Waxmann, 2009).

group in this more multicultural population did choose confirmation in the church. Among the 15-year-old church members in Oslo the figure was 59 per cent.[18]

Belonging, in late modern settings like contemporary Norwegian society and especially among the young, has, in general, become a fluid and continuous confirmation of social bonds, grounded in reflexive processes. These are global tendencies. A study on spiritual agency in late-modern Catholic Mexico, titled 'Dealing with the Unspeakable', found people speaking 'the unspeakable in terms of Narcissistic self-representations' and expressions of their 'autonomous self … in the form of everyday informal social interactions.'[19] This condition of 'elective belonging'[20] also creates the context for the young storytellers in this study. They chose to explore the church as a site for performing identities. [21]

The 'Digital Faith Stories' Project

This case study is of 16- to 18-year-olds in a suburban congregation outside the capital of Norway. Living in an 'over-served' area, these young people have many options and are used to choice in this market of possibilities. Those joining the project were all, to some extent, involved in youth programmes in the local church. However, their level of activity was fluid and dependent on shifting social relations with friends and youth leaders in the congregation. The youths were invited to use multimedia applications to create short stories related to their own faith, life and religious tradition. This 'Digital Faith Stories' project was an experiment within a large-scale reform of religious education in Norway, decided upon by the parliament, the *Stortinget*, in 2003.[22]

Parliament encouraged new forms of mediating faith within the various belief communities, funded by the government, a motivation for which is the right of all

---

[18]   Figures from 2007. The growth on a national basis was 0.4 per cent from 2006 to 2007 and another 0.4 per cent from 2005 to 2006. Source: *Årbok for Den norske kirke 2009* [Annual book of the Church of Norway 2009] (Oslo: Church of Norway National Council, 2009).

[19]   Juan Carlos Henríquez Mendoza and Victoria Isabela Corduneanu, '"Dealing with the Unspeakable", a Discusssion on Spiritual Agency in Late-Modernity', paper to the IAMCR conference, Mexico City, 2009.

[20]   Mike Savage, Gaynor Bagnall and Brian Longhurst, *Globalization and Belonging* (London: Sage, 2005).

[21]   Knut Lundby and Birgit Hertzberg Kaare, 'The Sacred as Meaning and Belonging in Digital Storytelling', in Inger Furseth and Paul Leer-Salvesen (eds), *Religion in Late Modernity: Essays in Honor of Pål Repstad* (Trondheim: Tapir akademisk forlag, 2007), pp. 69–86.

[22]   Knut Lundby, 'Transforming Faith-Based Education in the Church of Norway: Mediation of Religious Traditions and Practices in Digital Environments', *Studies in World Christianity*, 12/1 (2006): pp. 5–22.

children to spiritual development according to Article 27 of the UN's Convention on the Rights of the Child. The *Stortinget* wanted the reform to support identity formation with resources from the collective faith tradition, and to help the young to master life and understand their own cultural–religious heritage. This was intended to provide a basis for respect and tolerance in a more multicultural and multi-religious society.

The reform has taken the most visible form within the Church of Norway, as this church encompasses the great majority of the country's children and youth. Its programme aims at socialization and identity-formation related to the Christian tradition of the church.[23]

The Digital Faith Stories project was based in the congregation at Haslum outside Oslo, an area with a high level of income and education. The medieval church building acts as a visible symbol for the local people. The confirmation programme in the local church is attractive to the youth.

The project was testing a methodology that could possibly be applied as one among many others in the new religious education of the church. The youth minister directed the project and had two part-time co-leaders, with competence in church–youth relations and digital technologies, in his team. Recruitment of storytellers was slow and difficult. Those approached tended to check whether or not their friends would come. It was also hard for them to commit themselves to the expected follow-up productions. A few participants from neighbouring congregations were invited. Four rounds of production took place between autumn 2005 and spring 2007, the period covered in this research. Each round of productions was finalized with a DVD compilation of the digital stories from the set.

However, the specific idea and format of a 'Digital *Faith* Story' was not firmly established – it actually had to be developed. The Haslum project took the principles of Digital Storytelling and amended them for their purpose of 'faith stories'.

Paradigmatic Principles of Digital Storytelling

'Digital storytelling' is a workshop-based practice in which people are taught to use digital media to create short audio–video stories, usually about their own lives, as defined by John Hartley and Kelly McWilliam in their collection *Story Circle: Digital Storytelling Around the World*.[24] Of course, there are many forms of digital storytelling, in film and television and on the Internet. Here the term is applied to a method and movement to give people a voice through computer tools. The approach is inspired by the format outlined at the Center for Digital Storytelling

---

[23]   See www.kirken.no/?event=doLink&famID=11298, accessed 25 June 2009.

[24]   John Hartley and Kelly McWilliam (eds), *Story Circle: Digital Storytelling Around the World* (Oxford: Wiley–Blackwell, 2009).

(CDS) in California in the early 1990s.[25] They started to apply multimedia programmes that are now available on most laptops to put still pictures and maybe music and short video clips together with a written story. The 'Capture Wales' project picked this up and brought 2-minute personal stories to Britain and the BBC.[26] John Hartley sees the Californian roots in independent film festivals and the Welsh roots in broadcasting. In both cases, there is a challenge of scalability, as the production of these digital stories is workshop-intensive. This is linked to a problem of expertise: that of the facilitator who then has to develop the expertise of the user or storyteller. This kind of digital storytelling is self-made and will remain small-scale media.[27]

The idea is that 'everyone has a powerful story to tell' and digital technology could help tell it, as they state at the Californian centre. They are short 'multimedia tales', as the initiator of 'Capture Wales' says. Seen by researchers, they are mediated self-representations[28] or topical autobiographies.[29]

The core methodology[30] is introduced to the storytellers in weekend or weeklong workshops. The development of the story and the storyline defines and leads all aspects of the process. This takes place in the 'Story Circle' aspect of the workshop. The Story Circle as a group script-review process is crucial.[31] This is the part of the workshop where the story with its plot is developed; in discussions between the narrator, the coach and the rest of the group. The multimedia technology for the subsequent production is fairly simple and easy to learn.

The completed narratives are told in the first person, by the narrator herself, as personal stories. Pre-existing visual archives, e.g. the family album and home video, inspire the stories, which usually last for a few minutes only.

Digital Storytelling according to these ideas – capitalized to distinguish it from other forms of digital storytelling – is a proliferating phenomenon throughout the world.[32] The paradigmatic principles of Digital Storytelling were brought to bear on the Digital Faith Stories project as well.

---

[25] Joe Lambert, *Digital Storytelling: Capturing Lives, Creating Community*, 3rd edn (Berkeley, CA: Digital Diner Press, 2010).

[26] Daniel Meadows, 'Digital Storytelling: Research-Based Practice in New Media', *Visual Communication*, 2/2 (2003): pp. 189–93.

[27] John Hartley, 'Problems of Expertise and Scalability in Self-Made Media', in Lundby (ed.), *Digital Storytelling*, pp. 197–211.

[28] Nancy Thumim, 'Exploring Self-Representations in Wales and London: Tension in the Text', in Hartley and McWilliam (eds), *Story Circle*, pp. 205–17.

[29] Hertzberg Johnsen, *Konfirmasjon og erindring*, pp. 44–9.

[30] Lambert, *Digital Storytelling*, Ch. 5.

[31] Hartley and McWilliam (eds.), *Story Circle*.

[32] Ibid.

Producers of Digital Objects

The young creators of Digital Faith Stories are media producers.[33] From the perspective of the project's organizers these young people are invited to perform agency in pursuit of religious culture and identity. However, the young producers themselves may follow other objectives. This case study aims to disclose the story behind their stories.

The small group of participants in the Haslum project stayed close to each other and the young leaders as a community of practice[34] through the workshop process: the leaders helped configure the participants' stories through supervision in the Story Circle and feedback from peers and leaders helped each participant to confirm for themselves whether the story drafted was appreciated by others in the group, hence confirming their relationships.

Digital tools help make personal narratives into material artefacts – DVDs with collections of Digital Faith Stories – with which others can interact. The Digital Faith Stories are digital objects.

As digital objects, these stories could easily have been shared widely on the Internet or by other means of digital distribution; however, the Haslum leaders, as well as the Norwegian Data Inspectorate, put restrictions on such dissemination for reasons of privacy on topics related to religion. The young storytellers appreciated this carefulness with their personal stories, while at the same time they were keen to master the production of a digital object that could be shared – within controlled contexts.

The young producers of the Digital Faith Stories have the copyright of their digital stories – they are completely in control of their stories. They could withdraw from the project at any time if they wanted to.

While the restrictions of the paradigmatic principles of digital storytelling – the short 2–3 minutes format – and the demands of the software place heavy restrictions on the creation process, these Digital Faith Stories have the potential to express the Unspoken.

The Produced Stories

Twenty-one young storytellers created 27 'Digital Faith Stories'. None of the stories are about explicit religious practices. Some tell about youth activities in the local church where such practices may play a part, but specific religious practices are not commented upon. What counts in these stories is the social aspect

---

[33]   Birgit Hertzberg Kaare, 'Youth as Producers: Digital Stories of Faith and Life', *Nordicom Review*, 29/2 (2008): pp. 189–201.

[34]   Etienne Wenger, *Communities of Practice: Learning, Meaning, and Identity* (Cambridge: Cambridge University Press, 1998).

of the church activities, and, for some, the confidence they are shown when they are asked to act as peer-leader.

Two participants made stories about the Digital Faith Stories workshop: they talk about the good social companionship during the process and about the skills they developed, as well as considerations on how to get across thoughts and feelings in the making of the digital stories.

Four others share positive experiences from their confirmation preparations: about finding support in that church community – for three of them by becoming co-leaders for new groups of confirmands. Only one of these four mentions 'God' or 'Jesus', which he locates in the setting of friendship and belonging to the group: through this social environment, 'I found that the confirmation period was not just about God and Jesus: I was myself part of our team. And the rest of the world for that part', said a boy in his story.

A girl spoke about her singing in the church during her sister's confirmation. Indirectly, by citing the song she performed, she proclaimed that 'you are of great value', and although you may think that you are not important, 'God, our Father accepts you.' Otherwise, explicit religious beliefs, i.e. references to a transcendental reality, are not stated. However, one boy wonders about his friend, who died in a tragic accident. In a loose reference to heaven, he thinks that, wherever his friend is now, he is sure he runs in 'endless powder' on his snowboard.

The majority of the digital stories do not have any explicit reference to the church or religious tradition. They are about friendship and social relations (as are the above-mentioned stories that relate to youth activities in the congregation). Another main theme is the ability to perform and be good at sports and dance. In short, the digital stories are about aspects of the kind of identity work that young people at this age do. They are identity works on 'being me'. This is in line with the general aim of the religious education reforms, which is to stimulate the development of one's own identity.

However, when the Church of Norway specified that through the church's religious education children and young people 'will be able to share their faith and sense of wonder',[35] what these young people share in their small films may surprise the reformers. The only direct references to 'faith' in the 27 Digital Faith Stories are to have 'faith in myself'. It occurs explicitly in three of the stories. For two girls this self-confidence is directly related to performance skills in dance and theatre: 'If you want to be good you need to have faith in yourself and forget what others think of you', says one. 'At an audition I learnt something important:' recounts another, 'that you should not lose confidence in yourself.' A boy making a story about his sporting activities states: 'Faith is important in sports. Faith in myself. Faith in the ability to succeed.'

---

[35]   The description in English of the 'Religious Education in Church of Norway', at www.kirken.no/?event=doLink&famID=11298, accessed 24 June 2009.

Cues to the Unspoken

The digital stories that were made are the public face of the narratives of these young people. In semi-structured interviews, 11 out of the 21 filmmakers shared their reasons and considerations behind their productions and offered cues to their faith as it appears in their stories. In the confident company of one researcher, the young storytellers spoke to the Unspoken as it relates to their life. These interviews disclose codes to the Digital Faith Stories.

It is the composition of the digital stories in a church setting that makes them into Digital Faith Stories, the producers explained in the interviews. Simply doing such an activity in the local congregation *makes* this a part of their belonging to the church.

Some admitted they had been worried that the project would put pressure on them to confess. They were happy when they learnt that the digital stories 'did not need to have any Christian message or anything', as one phrased it. However, the participants accepted the idea of their digital productions as 'faith stories'. They appreciated the opportunity to shape such narratives.

Almost all the interviewees think it is possible to express faith through digital stories and most consider it easier to talk about personal faith indirectly rather than in an upfront way. They explain how faith is 'hinted at' through their choices of music, pictures and symbols. Further, they think that their faith is visible through the personality they put on display in their personal stories, or in the theme they choose. For some the participation contributed to the development of personal faith, for others to a more nuanced view of the Christian tradition. At the same time, the completed digital story was regarded as valuable, both as a memory and because this digital object offers an opportunity to share concerns that are regarded as important yet not spoken much about, because it is felt to be difficult.

The young people in this study appear self-conscious in their expression of self and identity. They regard their Digital Faith Stories as something personal, but, when asked, they don't know how to express faith. Faith is for them not primarily about belief in something or somebody, like God or Jesus. For them, the word and the phenomenon of 'faith' relate basically to *my* stand in life, to *my* process. Talking about religion in belief categories is not easy for them. The Unspoken remains as something they do not proclaim. However, when asked about their relation to the church, they reply that they belong, of course. They identify themselves as belonging to the church as an institution but not in a submissive way. They regard themselves as competent and with resources they would like the church to make use of. This is their choice: if the church does not treat them well, they may leave. This activity takes place in their leisure time, during which they are in command of their time resources as well as their own creative capacity. The Digital Faith Stories project also relates to the part of this book about consumption and lifestyle.

Projects of the Self

The Digital Faith Stories are concerned with self-improvement and personal preference. They offer insight into how religious ideation is tied up with elective 'projects of the self'. The digital storytelling genre in general favours a focus on 'me', as they are meant to be self-representational, personal stories. The young storytellers at Haslum ride the wave of self-realization so prominent in their cultural environment. It is important for them, as for youth in similar situations, to express themselves in an authentic way. However, this is an assumed authenticity[36] as the storytellers always relate to their social environment.

Similar negotiations of belonging as happened during the Story Circle go on when the completed stories are shared with friends: this response from friends is more important than reactions from family or within the congregation, interviews made clear.

Young people do reflexive work on the formation of their identities.[37] Several participants in the Digital Faith Stories project in interviews did indeed describe how they experienced self-reflection during the production process. Modernity makes questions of self-representation relevant and urgent, and the new digital technologies offer tools to construct this self-representation in advanced ways that, at the same time, connect individuals in new social relations.

Digital Modalities

The interviews with young participants in the Haslum project confirm that digital media are a 'natural' part of their social and cultural environment. Participants made it clear that youths do not consider activities cool just because they are digital. However, the use of digital tools in the Haslum storytelling project made the church contemporary and relevant to their life, interviewees said. The multimedia software and the modes of production for creation of the digital stories were new and exciting for many of the participants, but they had the necessary digital literacy and could easily grasp the opportunities.

They did, in general, like this use of digital technologies, and they appreciated the variety of multimedia modalities. They found that the pictures added a lot to the written text, sometimes putting demands on the shaping of the text, and it became easier to express what they wanted to say – and more fun and interesting for those being presented the story, they stated. Music could add even more. Although this

---

[36] Birgit Hertzberg Kaare and Knut Lundby, 'Mediatized lives: Autobiography and Assumed Authenticity in Digital Storytelling', in Lundby (ed.), *Digital Storytelling*, pp. 105–22.

[37] As, for example, Anthony Giddens and Thomas Ziehe have shown.

kind of digital storytelling is quite simple, as multimedia productions the dynamics of digital multimodality are at work.[38]

Narratives as well as digital media are cultural tools that merge in digital storytelling. Ola Erstad and James Wertsch point out that new digital media may transform the role narratives play in our lives. Narratives are cultural tools that everybody applies in meaning-making activites. However, something new appears when one starts to use new tools, as in digital storytelling. New digital technologies help create new performance spaces.[39]

The shaping of Digital Faith Stories is a configuration of relevant and available elements into a set media form with the repertoire of modalities in the narrator's voice, photos in the 'personal archive', and possibly graphics, images from the Internet, music and video.

When the shaping of the story is dependent on the media form itself and the modalities that are applied, the configuration of the story appears as a process of mediatization. Digital media through the technology of digitalization has this potential of transformation. The multimodality of digital media offers more power to the configuration.[40]

The Unspoken in Generation Y

In their handling of the Unspoken, youths at Haslum relate to the Unspoken in the cultural–religious tradition of the Church of Norway. However, they also connect to wider patterns in their generation. The digitally competent interviewees in the Haslum study are part of the so-called Generation Y, born since 1982: 'Generation Y is a technological generation that take computers, emailing, text messaging and the Internet for granted.'[41] They have grown up in a globalized society where digital media have become a natural part of their environment.

---

[38]   Gunther Kress and Theo van Leeuwen, *Multimodal Discourse* (London: Arnold, 2001). See also more specific studies such as Glynda Hull and M.-L. Katz, 'Crafting an Agentive Self: Case Studies of Digital Storytelling', *Research in the Teaching of English*, 41/1 (2006): pp. 43–81.

[39]   Ola Erstad and James V. Wertsch, 'Tales of Mediation: Narrative and Digital Media as Cultural Tools', in Lundby (ed.), *Digital Storytelling*, pp. 21–39.

[40]   We have elsewhere developed this line of thought in relation to Paul Ricoeur's outline of prefiguration, configuration and refiguration in storytelling. See Birgit Hertzberg Kaare and Knut Lundby, 'The "Power of Configuration in Digital Storytelling", in Yvonne Gächter *et al.* (eds), *Erzählen – Reflexionen im Zeitalter der Digitalisierung / Storytelling – Reflections in the Age of Digitalization* (Innsbruck: Innsbruck University Press, 2008), pp. 99–110.

[41]   Sara Savage, Sylvia Collins-Mayo, Bob Mayo, with Graham Cray, *Making Sense of Generation Y: The World View of 15–25-Year-Olds* (London: Church House Publishing, 2006), p. 7.

Adult Americans are quite outspoken on religion – the religious landscape in the US is rather different from the one in Norway. However, the major American National Youth and Religion project found from nationwide surveys and in-depth interviews a similar non-articulate relation to religion. Although the character of teenage religiosity in the United States is regarded as extraordinarily conventional and active, the researchers conclude: 'Most U.S. teens have a difficult to impossible time explaining what they believe, what it means, and what the implications of their beliefs are for their lives … Religion seems very much a part of the lives of many U.S. teenagers, but for most of them it is in ways that seem quite unfocused, implicit, in the background.'[42]

British youth may have an even weaker relation to religious institutions than the Norwegians. The researchers behind the British study *Making Sense of Generation Y* try to figure out how the worldview of 15- to 25-year-olds relates to church, religion and spirituality in Britain.[43] They conducted semi-structured group interviews with 124 'socially included' young people in localities away from churches at 18 sites across the country. Sixty per cent of the interviewees defined themselves as non-Christian, 40 per cent as Christian. The research team worked on the basis of the assumption that young people use popular culture as a resource for their own religious and spiritual ideas. The stories and cultural symbols they catch from films and television soap operas and the experiences they have from popular music and clubbing helped the researchers to trace the worldviews and the fundamental questions of the young interviewees.[44]

The researchers found a worldview that they characterize as 'the happy midi-narrative'. What emerged from the group interviews was not a meta-narrative like the Judaeo-Christian or the Enlightenment ideas of progress. Neither was it an individualistic mini-narrative. 'It is communal on a small scale (me, my friends, and my family): a midi-narrative', they conclude. The aim is to be happy. This aim will be realized through me being myself, and connecting to others. Bad things can happen that prevent us from attaining this happiness. But resources of family and close friends surround each of us. The popular arts also provide us with valuable resources: information, choice and creativity. Having 'grown' through these resources, the happy ideal is after all possible. Popular arts mediate between the Actual life and the Ideal of happiness.[45]

The description of this midi-narrative among rather secularized young Britons is strikingly close to the narratives the young Norwegian folk church members share in their Digital Faith Stories and in the accompanying interviews. God, sin and fear of death are among the elements that are absent from the Happy

---

[42]   Christian Smith, *Soul Searching: The Religious and Spiritual Lives of American Teenagers* (Oxford: Oxford University Press, 2005), p. 262.

[43]   Savage *et al.*, *Making Sense of Generation Y.*

[44]   Ibid., pp. 26–31.

[45]   Ibid., pp. 38–41.

midi-narrative. Life as an ultimate value, family that are there for you, and celebrities as role models are among the themes present in be-Happy midi-narratives.

Mainstream post-rave dance clubs are quite different from the Haslum project, but there is a similar emphasis in self-realization and self-expression, with personal autonomy and authenticity. The importance of belonging and identification with the group is valid in relation to the clubbing crowd and other youth in the church. There is not much difference between Mike, after clubbing, saying, 'I've got a lot more confidence in myself',[46] and one of the storytellers at Haslum who ends her story, 'I have grown incredibly much in these three years I have been doing theatre. My self-confidence has increased, and I feel that I really have found what I want to go on with. And most important: I have confidence in myself.'

These cultural analyses move 'religion' from something substantive or transcendent to something functional, an 'invisible religion' as set out by Thomas Luckmann.[47] The Haslum findings find resonance in the conclusions in Sylvia Collins's study from 1997, *Young People's Faith in Late Modernity*, conducted in Britain. She found that faith was organized around family, friends and the reflexive self, with the creed: 'I believe in myself'.[48]

Mediatized Faith

If these are general trends among youth in late-modern societies, how could Digital Faith Stories be pointing to processes of mediatizing faith?

This occurs on a general level, as the lifeworld of these young people in Generation Y is shaped through relations to the contents of the popular media and the extensive interaction through information and communication technologies. This is, as mediation, an ongoing social process of meaning-making through which religious discourses articulate with other contemporary cultural forms. However, the media use also transforms religion and spirituality in their lives and hence appears as processes of mediatization. Mediatized religion is shaped by media forms and processes within institutional transformations.[49]

The interest of this chapter, however, is in more specific processes related to the practice of digital storytelling in the Norwegian setting. In the case of the Digital Faith Stories, we observe that the digital format and the digital modalities open up possibilities for stories that have not been told before, and that they are

---

[46] Gordon Lynch and Emily Badger, 'The Mainstream Post-Rave Club Scene as a Secondary Institution: A British Perspective', *Culture and Religion*, 7/1: pp. 27–40.

[47] Thomas Luckmann, *The Invisible Religion: The Problem of Religion in Modern Society* (London: Macmillan, 1967).

[48] Sylvia Collins, *Young People's Faith in Late Modernity*, doctoral thesis (University of Surrey, 1997).

[49] Stig Hjarvard, 'The Mediatization of Religion: A Theory of the Media as Agents of Religious Change', in Hjarvard (ed.), *The Mediatization of Religion*, pp. 9–26.

told this way because of the digital options; because of the form and technology of Digital Storytelling. They are created for this specific medium and format. Hence the Digital Faith Stories are mediatized stories.

Digital Faith Stories make into digital objects personal accounts on topics most Norwegians are hesitant to talk about, adults and teenagers alike. This is a way of 'mediatizing' faith, as the form and the format of the digital media shape the stories. Similar stories could possibly be created as digital objects in other cultural–religious settings, on *their* Unspoken.

Chapter 5

Haredim and the Internet:
A Hate–Love Affair

Yoel Cohen

The Haredi (Hebrew for 'fearful ones') community or ultra-orthodox Jews are characterized by social withdrawal from 'the dangers of modern society'. Haredim account for some 5 per cent of the Israeli Jewish population (or 400,000 souls). One of the major challenges to Haredi self-isolation has come from the mass media. Reflecting its philosophy of withdrawal from modernity, and seeking to maintain religious values in a cultural ghetto framework, Haredi rabbis have over the years issued religious decrees (*pesuk din*) against the mass media as being a threat to Jewish family values.[1] This chapter analyses the response of Israeli Haredim to the Internet.[2]

Haredi Rabbis and the Internet

In 2000, just a few years after the Internet entered Western lifestyles, the Haredi rabbinical leadership declared the World Wide Web to be a moral threat to the sanctity of Israel. More specifically, the Internet threatened the high walls that Haredi rabbis had built over the years to resist secular cultural influences. Thus there followed a ban shortly after a special rabbinical *bet din* (or religious law court) was established to deal with the spread of computers. In part the ban was directed at children who, it was feared, would surf unsuitable sites such as pornographic sites, as well as be distracted from their religious studies. Rabbis were also concerned

---

[1]   See for example, Simeon Baumel, 'Communication and Change: Newspapers, Periodicals and Acculturation among Israeli Haredim', *Jewish History*, 16/2 (2002): pp. 161–86; Amnon Levi, 'The Haredi Press and Secular Society', in Charles Liebman (ed.), *Conflict and Accommodation between Jews in Israel* (Jerusalem: Keter, 1990), pp. 21–44; Yoel Cohen, 'Religion News in Israel', *Journal of Media and Religion*, 4/3 (2005): pp. 179–98.

[2]   For a fuller discussion of early Haredi rabbinical attitudes to the Internet see Neri Horowitz, 'Haredim and the Internet', *Kivunim Hadashim*, October 2000 [Hebrew]; Orly Tsarfaty and Dotan Balias, 'Between "Cultural Enclaves" and "Virtual Enclaves": Haredi Society and the Digital Media', *Kesher* 32 (November 2002): pp. 47–55 [Hebrew]; Karine Barzilai-Nahon and Gad Barzilai, 'Cultured Technology: The Internet and Religious Fundamentalism', *The Information Society*, 21 (2005): pp. 25–40.

that increasing numbers of young people would reach undesirable material. This said, it is important to note a distinction between the so-called European Lithuanian school and the European Hassidic and Oriental–Sephardi branches of Haredim. The stricter Lithuanian school placed a ban not only upon the Internet but also upon computers as a whole, calling upon its members who owned computers to get rid of them from their houses. The statement included a cartoon depicting the snake from the Garden of Eden, which caused Adam to sin, exploding within the computer screen and bringing down the Haredi child. Hassidic and Sephardi Haredi communities, on the other hand, were more flexible. The Sephardim are generally more tolerant, and the European Hassidim are more inclined to go to work in contrast to the Lithuanians who study in *yeshivot* (talmudical colleges), surviving on stipends. Hence the Hassidim were more sensitive about the need for the Internet for business purposes and a distinction was drawn between the Internet at home, which was banned, and in businesses.

Printing the word 'Internet' for the first time in December 2007, Haredi newspapers carried announcements from 'the rabbinical committee for communication matters' allowing businesses to use the Internet. An agreement was reached with the Israeli telephone company, Bezek, to provide access for businesses to a small number of websites.[3] The committee devised three concentric circles of control. The first circle was a safety device – which only a computer technician could remove – stopping a child from going beyond the permitted sites. The second circle was a device on the computer mouse that enabled people to go only to permitted sites. A third device, on the telephone itself, stopped somebody from, say, ordering an ADSL line to his telephone. However, the system was not foolproof, as was shown in 2008 when the Belze Hassidic court became the first Hassidic branch of Haredim to allow its community a special package of some 150 websites both at home as well as in business. The problem was that seemingly appropriate sites led to others that were problematic through links, or themselves carried questionable advertising, or were originally deemed permissible but were subsequently updated with 'immoral' material. Hence the rabbinical committee for communication affairs recommended an alternative system of 'white' sites. Access would be allowed to only those sites relevant to a specific profession. The weakness with this system was that there was an inbuilt contradiction, in which some Haredi customers would be prohibited access to websites that were allowed to other Haredi customers whose businesses depended on those sites.

The Shas Bill

Haredi demands for dealing with the Internet took on a parliamentary form in 2007 when Itzhak Cohen, a member of Shas, the Sephardi Haredi political party, placed a private members bill in the Knesset, the Israel Parliament, that required Internet

---

[3]   *Haaretz*, 18 December 2007 [Hebrew].

servers not to supply pornographic material to any children or even to adults, with the exception of those adults specifically requesting to receive pornographic matter. Cohen enjoyed the backing of the Minister of Communications, Ariel Attias, who also belonged to the Shas Party. In effect, Internet servers would be required to use a screening device that prevents unsolicited pornographic material from reaching its clients. Clients would be sent two letters informing them about the filtering device, followed by a third letter announcing its installation. Only those identified as adults would be able to request that the service not be installed. A server sending out such matter, except to those requesting it, could be fined the equivalent of $75,000. The Shas bill was not so much aimed towards its own Haredi communities; its significance lay in the fact that it was a Haredi attempt to influence the Internet use of the entire Israeli population.

The bill passed its first reading in 2008, with 46 members of parliament voting for and 20 against after Shas mustered the votes of other religious political parties, both Haredi and modern orthodox, as well as feminist MKs and the Arab political parties. The bill generated opposition from both the Left and secular right-wing MKs, who suggested that censorship of the Internet should be a voluntary act, not something imposed by the state. Arguing that it was a curtailment of freedom, the Israel Association for Civil Rights threatened to appeal to the Supreme Court if the law reached a second or third reading in the Knesset. The Association also argued that the proposed law was an invasion of privacy because people requesting pornographic access would have to register. More crucially, there was a danger that a database of customers for porn-related material would be exploited for commercial purposes.

As it happened, the bill floundered after the government ministerial committee that examines upcoming parliamentary legislation decided, with the exception of the Shas minister, to oppose the bill, arguing that more pedagogic methods should be used to educate the young about the dangers of the Internet. The ministers' decision was a powerful message from the non-Haredi Israeli majority that the Haredi propensity for censorship was anathema in a progressive society. Similar anti-porn Internet legislation had been proposed in other western countries, but the fact that the bill was initiated by a Haredi party weakened its long-term chances of reaching the statute book.

Jewish Religious and Educational Websites

The discussions within the Haredim rabbinical leadership about the threat from the Internet occurred at the same time as a parallel proliferation of Jewish-related websites emerged, many of which were educational, which made it more difficult for rabbis to impose their anti-Internet line. For example, an early Haredi site was the Shema Yisrael Torah network.[4] Founded in 1992, www.shemayisroel.com is a

---

4   At www.shemayisroel.com , accessed 4 October 2010.

'closed and secure' Jewish website that provides educational material but also prevents users from going into 'forbidden' sites. The site comprises *Daf Yomi*, a religious learning tradition that involves the study of one page per day of the *Talmud* (which consists of the major corpus of Jewish law writing), enabling the reader to complete the *Talmud* over a seven-year cycle of study. The site also embraces *Halakha Yomi* (daily study of Jewish religious law), weekly scriptures, stories of Jewish faith (*hashgacha pratis*), and Jewish content suitable for children. The site was an immediate success and in 1997 was accessed over 100,000 times across a 50-day period (16 per cent being users in Israel, 50 per cent in the US, and the rest elsewhere in the Jewish Diaspora).[5] Originally free, the site has since expanded and today offers fee-paying courses that cover a broad spectrum of educational-related materials that go beyond the Haredi population: for example, 'The Making of a Kosher Kitchen', and Jewish business ethics and laws concerning usury and interest.

Similarly, the early computerization of Jewish religious sources had an influence that extended well beyond Jewish religious sites. One of the earliest attempts to computerize Jewish sources was the Bar-Ilan *Sheiltot* project, which stored in computerized form over 100,000 rabbinical *Sheiltot* – that is, rabbis' answers from the Geonic period to the present day, covering a range of questions concerning the application of Jewish law to particular situations. There are an estimated half a million *Sheiltot* contained in 300 books. Their value mostly relates to legal matters, but they also contain useful historical sources concerning Jewish communities, figures and events. In a project that began in 1963, by professors Aviezer Frankel and Jacob Shoika, the 100,000 *Sheiltot*, comprising 160 million words, were fed into a computer retrieval system at Bar-Ilan University. Its significance was that it was one of the first computer systems in the world, and the first in the Hebrew language, that was based on full text, thus enabling the inquirer to determine the key words, rather than negotiate the conventional classification system of categories and sub-categories. The Bar Ilan project also had to teach the computer Hebrew and Aramaic, the language of the Babylonian Talmud, and the Hebrew script used by Rashi, the French-born Jewish Bible commentator. What is more, even though Bar-Ilan University is affiliated with the modern orthodox community, the Haredi community has warmly embraced the project. Additional *Sheiltot* have been added over the years, and in 1994 the entire data base was placed on a CD-ROM – 'the Global Jewish database' – enabling individuals and institutions to purchase it. In short, the project has provided access to *Sheiltot* manuscripts – which had previously been limited to a few libraries or private manuscript collections – for Jews and non-Jews worldwide.[6]

---

[5]   *Jerusalem Post*, 23 March 1997.

[6]   Batsheva Pomerantz, 'Technology in the Service of Judaism', *Etrog*, 35 (April 2007): pp. 20–23; All the Torah on one disc, *Yediot Aharonot*, 12 October 2007 [Hebrew]; Aviezer Frankel, 'To Turn the Rabbinical Sheiltot into a Ball: A Few Reflections on the

In a like fashion, the 1990s saw a proliferation of attempts at applying different technologies to Jewish religious study. While these attempts did not replace traditional frameworks for Jewish education, notably the *Shiurim* (formal religious lessons delivered by the rabbi to students), they did add a new dimension to *limud Torah* (the study of Judaism). That said, the benefits of *Shiurim* being mass-mediatized have been questioned, not least because the traditional one-on-one student–rabbi *Shiur* has evolved over hundreds of years and is still one of the basic features of religious study in *yeshivot* (talmudical colleges). For example, according to Rabbi Marc Bleiwess,

> ... the discourse of Jewish study comprises partners breaking their teeth for hours trying to understand sometimes just two lines of ambiguous and deliciously profound text. Each interaction that relates to those lines – with a study partner, another student, a teacher – probes that much deeper. The solitary and usually shallow world of the net surfer rarely offers this kind of rigorous inquiry ... By reducing the effort required for serious study, the modern web may be inventing a whole new mode of Jewish discourse that loses authenticity, depth and intellectual precision whatever it gains in accessibility.[7]

Some of the reservations were allayed with the establishment in 2007 of the Web Yeshiva – ironically an outgrowth of Yeshiva Hamivtar in Efrat, where Bleiwess was director – whereby students study in a live online *Shiur* as well as learning online with a *chavruta* (a study partner). Transcending geographical boundaries, classes are available in Hebrew, English and Russian, from four in the morning to midnight.

Other Israeli Jewish websites include online listings of synagogues, kosher restaurants, burial societies, cemeteries, and the Jewish calendar. For example, the *MyKehilla* website (literally 'my community') enables synagogue communities to keep in touch with their members. Whereas in the pre-Internet era, synagogual contact with members revolved around the Sabbath and holidays when attendance at synagogue services provided a means for updating members about the community, websites like *MyKehilla* enable a synagogue to maintain weeklong contact with members. Alternatively, there are sites that offer training in cantorial music (*chazanut*) or singing the weekly Torah portion to prepare bar-mitzvah boys – who celebrate their coming of age at 13 – by reading that week's Bible portion in the synagogue.[8] Yet another site enables female Jews to calculate their *nida*, menstrual cycle, which includes that part of the month when women are deemed ritually 'unclean' and are not allowed to maintain marital relations. The Israel Government's Ministry of Religious Affairs website lists rabbinical courts for matters of marriage, divorce and religious conversion (all of which in Israel

---

Sheiltot Project, on the Occasion of the Israel Prize', *Hatzofe*, 30 March 2007 [Hebrew], p. 11.

[7]   Mark Bleiweiss, `In Defence of the Inaccessable', *Sh'ma*, November 1999, p. 3.

[8]   At www.kolkoren.com, accessed 4 October 2010.

arc the responsibility of the rabbinical courts).[9] The site even caters for *agunot*, or married women whose husbands have disappeared or refuse to give them a divorce, featuring a 'WANTED' photographic gallery of these men.

Haredi Exposure to the Internet

Haredim have lower exposure to computers and to the Internet than the rest of the Israeli Jewish population. For instance, in 2006 50 per cent of Haredi families possessed a computer at home in contrast to 90 per cent of Israelis Jews who defined themselves as secular.[10] Similarly, according to a 2005 official survey by the Central Bureau of Statistics,[11] only 10 per cent of Haredi families were linked to the Internet, compared with 61 per cent of the total Israeli Jewish population. In yet another survey, of those with neither a computer nor access to the Internet, 42 per cent of Haredim had no computer at home, compared with 29 per cent of the general Israeli population. And of those who possessed computers but were not linked to the Internet, 27 per cent were Haredi Jews. Haredim were also less inclined to be heavy Internet users (less than once per day).[12] In terms of gender, Haredi women are less inclined than Haredi men to use the Internet: in 2004 35 per cent of Haredi women used the Internet, compared with 65 per cent of Haredi men. The male–female difference was far greater among Haredim than other Israeli groups, largely because the Internet was only permitted within the Haredi community at the place of work.

Having said this, there are notable exceptions. One of the few Haredi communities to use the Internet early on was a Hassidic sect commonly known as Habad or Lubavitch. In contrast to the negative outlook of other Haredi groups about computers and the Internet, Habad see new media technologies as neutral means for distributing the Torah. Indeed, the information highway is part of the divine plan. For example, under the title 'The Computer in the Service of God', a Habad publication writes: 'the computer does not innovate things. Man is able to think without a computer, but it makes calculations much faster'.[13] Furthermore, 'everything God created was to sanctify his glory'. Hence, with the appearance of the World Wide Web, Rabbi Yosef Kazen established Chabad.org, an outgrowth of Fidonet, which was an online discussion network in the '80s.[14] The site also hosts Askmoses.com, a panel of some

---

9   At www.religions.gov.il, accessed 10 September 2010.

10   Geotopographia survey, *Mercaz Inyanim*, 23 May 2006 [Hebrew].

11   Central Bureau of Statistics, Jerusalem, 2005.

12   Survey by Netvision Institute, Tel Aviv University, September 2005.

13   Rav Yosef Ginzberg and Professor Yirmiyahu Branover, 'How Beautiful are Your Creations', in *Science and Technology in the Light of Hassidus* (Kefar Habad, Israel, n.d.) [Hebrew], p. 156.

14   Sue Fishkoff, *The Rebbe's Army: Inside the World of Chabad-Lubavitch* (New York: Schocken, 2003), p. 283.

40 rabbis and women teachers who provide a round-the-clock response to religion-related questions, averaging 200 questions per day.

Among the most popular of these sites is Habad.org, which averages over 73,000 visitors a day, increasing at times of religious holidays, reaching a peak at Chanuka with some 500,000 daily hits, and a little less on Passover, the New Year *Rosh Hashonah* holiday and Yom Kippur. The website is operated by Habad in parallel with television and video services provided by its Lubavtch Media Service, which prepares pre-packed material suitable for local use by Chabad emissaries worldwide on local media outlets. A further development was the creation in 2008 of Chabad's online school for the children of some 400 emissaries who are posted to different parts of the Jewish world; indeed, many of them are situated in small Jewish communities where there is no local Jewish school.

While Haredi rabbis have been mostly accepting of the aforementioned, the development of Haredi Internet news sites is a very different matter. By 2009 a handful of Haredi news websites were operating independently of rabbinic supervision. These include *Kikar Shabbat* (also the name of the main intersection of the Jerusalem Haredi neighbourhood of Geula-Mea Shearim), *Haredim* and *LaDaat* ('to know'). Economically successful, the sites have been targeted by outside interests: for example, in the case of *Kikar Shabbat*, by the *Globus* business news daily. While no offensive material was allowed, the sites did not subject themselves to the rabbinical censors that, for example, inspect pre-publication copies of the Haredi daily newspapers. Hence the news websites are more likely to print uncensored information about the political infighting between different sections of the Haredi community, such as between rival chassidic courts, publication of which some rabbis see as a violation of *loshon hara* (a Jewish law that prohibits political and social gossip).

Most of the websites draw upon the prototype model of www.HadreiHadarim (a play on the word Haredim, meaning the inner chamber of chambers), established towards the end of the 1990s by the journalist David Rottenberg. Originally a populist online blog that challenged rabbinical authority, appropriately called 'Hyde Park', *Hadrei Hadarim* gradually evolved into an independent news site. By 2008 it had an estimated 6000 entries per hour. However, though it is widely accepted that such websites generated more competition within the Haredi media and led to greater professionalism, some of these Haredi websites closed – but subsequently reopened – or their personnel resigned since late 2009 after leading Haredi rabbis, concerned at the threat these unsupervised sites posed to their authority, imposed a public ban on the sites on the grounds that they 'contain lies and terrible impurity'. Most Haredi leaders refuse to be interviewed by the sites, and the names of those sponsoring the sites or editing them have been hidden from public view.

Conclusions

The impact of the Internet upon the Haredim may be measured in a number of ways. A 2006 survey of 1000 religious surfers of the Kippa religious website, which includes Haredim, found that the Internet was used by 26 per cent for friends and pleasure, and by 25 per cent for electronic mail. Its value as a source of Jewish religious information is undeniable even if Jewish religious study accounted for only 6.6 per cent of regular usage.[15] Another 2006 survey found that 38 per cent of Haredim purchase goods and services on the Internet and trusted online banking transactions – but this was significantly less than the secular population.[16] And a 2007 survey found that 17 per cent of Haredim order foreign holidays on the Internet.[17] On the other hand, the Internet has been rated by many Haredim as a bad influence on their religious identity. And the more religious the surfer, the greater the inclination to acknowledge this. In fact, according to the aforementioned 2006 Kippa survey, 43 per cent of Haredi respondents said that the Internet damaged their religious community, and 56 per cent said that they would not recommend acquaintances to get an Internet connection.

Such statistics do bring into question Barzilai-Nahon and Barzilai's claim that Haredi rabbinical structures have been challenged by the egalitarian nature of the Internet.[18] If anything, there is evidence suggesting that rabbis have been largely successful in maintaining the legitimacy of rabbinical decrees in the eyes of the Haredi population. For example, according to a survey by Bezek, the Israeli telephone company, 91 per cent of Haredim were aware of the instructions from Haredi rabbinical committees for communications and 81 per cent agreed with them. One telling example that rabbinical decrees were mostly respected was the recent banning of cellphones with Internet access following the rabbinical committee for communication affairs negotiating with mobile phone companies to provide mobile phones with telephone facilities alone. Indeed, four major Israeli mobile phone companies competing for the Haredi market now offer 'kosher' Internet-free phones. Similarly, in 2009 the local rabbinate in the Haredi city of Betar, south of Jerusalem, declared that Betar would become the first Internet-free city.[19] Residents who required the Internet for business purposes would need to install an Internet-restricted connection with a filtering device. Schools in Betar were instructed not to accept children who had unlimited access to the Internet. Elsewhere, there have been instances of so-called 'modesty squads' demonstrating outside net cafés used by Haredim to surf.

---

[15]   Survey of 1000 religious surfers of the Kippa religious website, released 3 April 2006.

[16]   Geotopographia survey, *Haaretz* 23.5.2006 [Hebrew].

[17]   At www.HadreiHadarim, accessed 22 January 2007.

[18]   Barzilai-Nahon and Barzilai, 'Cultured Technology'.

[19]   *Yerushalayim*, 25 September 2009 [Hebrew]; *BeKehilla*, 24 September 2009 [Hebrew].

In short, the majority of Haredim continue to exhibit a certain ambivalence towards the Internet. For the most part, Haredi life still centres around the synagogue, the Jewish home and the study of the Torah.

PART II
Consumption and Lifestyle

Chapter 6

Fixing the Self: Alternative Therapies and Spiritual Logics

Ruth Barcan and Jay Johnston

Alternative medicine is a complex amalgam: part medical system, part spiritual formation, part pop culture. Its use in Western countries continues to grow rapidly,[1] with the result that it is both economically and medically significant. While the Complementary and Alternative Medicine (CAM)[2] phenomenon has generated hopes for an 'integrated' medical future in which CAM and biomedicine might work co-operatively with each other,[3] it is also unsurprising that such a diverse, popular, economically significant and paradigmatically disparate set of practices has attracted its share of intense criticism from both professional and lay advocates of biomedicine, who have seen it as, for example, 'pernicious',[4] or as 'superstition and pseudoscience posing as medicine'.[5]

But alternative medicine is as much a socio-cultural phenomenon as a medical one, and critiques commonly address not just the question of CAM's medical effectiveness but also philosophical, spiritual and political matters. Religious beliefs are a significant aspect of this socio-cultural framework and CAM practitioners engage with such beliefs to varying degrees. For some, the engagement is implicit in the practice – for example, those healers who claim direct contact with a

[1]   Surveys in Australia, the US and the UK consistently show that almost half the population (and 80 per cent of cancer patients) consult CAM practitioners: Alan Bensoussan and George T. Lewith, 'Complementary Medicine Research in Australia: A Strategy for the Future', *Medical Journal of Australia*, 181/6 (2004): p. 331.

[2]   Here we make use of both 'alternative' and 'CAM'. For a summary of some of the politics of terminology for these practices see Mike Saks, *Orthodox and Alternative Medicine: Politics, Professionalization and Health Care* (London: Continuum, 2003): pp. 2–3.

[3]   See, for example, Hans A. Baer, *Toward an Integrative Medicine: Merging Alternative Therapies with Biomedicine* (Walnut Creek: Altamira Press, 2004); Benjamin Kligler and Roberta Lee (eds), *Integrative Medicine: Principles for Practice* (New York: McGraw-Hill, Medical Pub. Div., 2004).

[4]   William J. Donnelly *et al.*, 'Are Patients who Use Alternative Medicine Dissatisfied with Orthodox Medicine?', *Medical Journal of Australia*, 142/10 (1985): p. 539. They support this single word 'pernicious' with 20 footnotes!

[5]   Guy Curtis, 'Paying for Snake Oil', letter to the editor, *Sydney Morning Herald*, 9–10 May 2009, News Review, p. 8.

spiritual entity, guide or angel that dispenses medical diagnosis and/or effects healing. Other practices, including forms of spiritual healing, crystal- and colour therapy, are premised upon an energetic concept of the body that has filtered into more secular frameworks from origins in religious/spiritual traditions (for example the *chakra* system of Yogic traditions). Still other modalities embrace a broader engagement with concepts that are spiritually underpinned in their conception of the interrelationship between an individual, community and cosmos, 'wholeness' being an example popular in New Age[6] discourse. Whether acknowledged explicitly or not, the vast majority of alternative medical practices engage to some degree with concepts of life, healing and/or the body that have emerged from religious/spiritual beliefs and practices.

Oddly enough, Cultural Studies has shown dramatically less interest in alternative medicine than one might have expected of a discipline in which both the body and popular culture are standard objects of analysis.[7] This is partly attributable to the discipline's residual squeamishness about addressing issues of religion and spirituality.[8] The studies it has produced, like those in the critical social sciences, have mostly addressed alternative medicine using Foucauldian approaches. They have tended to argue or assume that the 'alternatives' offered by these therapies are impossible (and hence misguided), individualistic (and hence politically compromised), purely about self-gratification (and hence socially reprehensible), and inevitably about re-securing the individual into a dominant social order. Across the socio-cultural disciplines, alternative therapies are frequently read as an instance of the ever-increasing medicalization of everyday life,[9] as part of the dominant logic of both neo-liberalism and consumerism,[10] and as congruent with

---

[6]   In general 'the New Age' is understood as an umbrella term for a diverse range of beliefs and practices that broadly reject institutionalized religion and commonly valorize individual authority (ranging from the occult arts of magic and astrology to channelling, alternative therapies, various divination techniques, UFO-based religions, neo-shamanism and inclusive of eastern spirituality; and, for some, Neopaganism). See, for example, Paul Heelas, *The New Age Movement* (Oxford: Blackwell, 1996). Alternative medicine has stood squarely within the bounds of these analyses and is generally considered a core feature of the Mind–Body–Spirit orientation attributed to New Age worldviews in all their diversity. For a survey of past debates and current scholarship on these issues see George D. Chryssides, 'Defining the New Age', in Daren Kemp and James R. Lewis (eds), *Handbook of the New Age* (Leiden: Brill, 2007), pp. 5–24.

[7]   Jay Johnston and Ruth Barcan, 'Subtle Transformations: Imagining the Body in Alternative Health Practices', *International Journal of Cultural Studies*, 9/1 (2006): pp. 25–44.

[8]   John Frow, 'Is Elvis a God? Cult, Culture, Questions of Method', *International Journal of Cultural Studies*, 1/2 (1998): pp. 197–210.

[9]   David Armstrong, 'The Rise of Surveillance Medicine', *Sociology of Health and Illness*, 17/3 (1995): pp. 393–404.

[10]   Jackie Stacey, *Teratologies: A Cultural Study of Cancer* (London: Routledge, 1997).

problematic conceptions of the whole-person.[11] In short, Medical Sociology and Cultural Studies have tended to see them as not really 'alternative' to anything, but rather an insidious *extension* of dominant logics.

This chapter focuses on two common critiques. The first is the argument that alternative therapies are complicit with a desire for control that typifies neo-liberal societies, and with the consumerist logic with which neo-liberalism is now inextricably intertwined.[12] In this critique, alternative therapies are seen as the recourse of a demographic accustomed to purchasing solutions for their medical, psychological and even social problems. The second critique is the related charge of individualism, in which alternative therapies are dismissed as at best politically naïve and at worst ethically and politically impoverished.[13] This chapter argues that, despite the validity and importance of these critiques, alternative therapies need to be read as more than just 'therapies of normality'.[14] Our aim is not to refute these critiques so much as to render them more complex. One way of doing this is to engage with the religious and spiritual ideas with which alternative therapies are commonly infused. Another is to engage more fully with them as bodily practices, and to seek the input of both practitioners and clients. Accordingly, this chapter examines some of the spiritual concepts and body models on which many therapies repose, and draws on an extensive qualitative research project involving CAM practitioners.[15] When the complexities of alternative therapies are taken into account, these practices appear to have ambiguous rather than simple relations to what Jackie Stacey calls 'the recognizable metaphors of western individualism (control, autonomy and personal output)'[16] and to invite a more complex idea of selfhood than that assumed by either biomedicine or neo-liberalism. As we argue in the second half of this chapter, the model of the self as multiple, comprised of

---

[11]   David Armstrong, 'The Problem of the Whole-Person in Holistic Medicine', *Holistic Medicine* 1 (1986): pp. 27–36; Rosalind Coward, *The Whole Truth: The Myth of Alternative Health* (London: Faber, 1989).

[12]   For example, Paul Heelas's early work critiques the consumerist dimensions of New Age practices, seeing them as ultimately incompatible with 'true' religion: Paul Heelas, 'The Limits of Consumption and the Post-Modern "Religion" of the New Age', in Russell Keat, Nigel Whiteley and Nicholas Abercrombie (eds), *The Authority of the Consumer* (London: Routledge, 1994), pp. 102–15.

[13]   For discussion and critique of such perspectives see Paul Heelas, *Spiritualities of Life: New Age Romanticism and Consumptive Capitalism* (Malden, MA: Blackwell, 2008).

[14]   Nikolas Rose, *Inventing Our Selves: Psychology, Power, and Personhood* (Cambridge: Cambridge University Press, 1996), p. 17. Rose uses this phrase to refer to the 'psy' disciplines rather than to CAM specifically.

[15]   Quotations from practitioners are drawn from a study carried out by the authors for the University of Sydney, Australia. We would like to thank all participants for their time and expertise.

[16]   Jackie Stacey, 'The Global Within', in Sarah Franklin, Celia Lury and Jackie Stacey (eds), *Global Nature, Global Culture* (London: Sage, 2000), p. 116.

energy and acting in unseen intercorporeal ways with the selves of others, and indeed with the animal, vegetable and material world, far exceeds the individual autonomous self imagined by modern psychology

The first section of the chapter explores the criticism that alternative therapies are, ultimately, complicit with a logic of control or mastery that (allegedly) typifies biomedicine and that not incidentally also serves neo-liberalism. We complicate this critique by exploring the New Age idea of illness as a form of pedagogy, spelling out points of difference between the idea of healing and that of medical cure. The second section opens out the charge of individualism by exploring the energetic model of the body that underpins many therapies. We argue that this spiritual model of the body – the so-called 'subtle' body – produces a potentially different conception of selfhood from that implied by either neo-liberalism or biomedicine, notwithstanding the contemporary 'dematerializing' of the mainstream biomedical conception of the body.[17] Before making these arguments in detail, we elaborate further the framework through which CAM is so frequently understood in the socio-cultural literature, notably that provided by Medical Sociology, especially of the Foucauldian variety, and by Cultural Studies. In particular, we provide some background to the charge that alternative therapies exemplify and participate in an ever-expanding contemporary desire for control.

Alternative Therapies and the Logic of Control

The medicalization of everyday life has been an important theme in Medical Sociology.[18] Irving Zola's foundational critique of the extension of medicine was made famous in Ivan Illich's vitriolic condemnation of medical expansionism in *Medical Nemesis*, in which Illich critiqued the spread of medicine into more and more domains of life.[19] The rise of alternative medicine, some decades later, might well seem to provide further instances of this expansionism, given that CAM's claims on the emotional, the interpersonal, the social and the spiritual far outweigh those of biomedicine. Summarizing (though only ambivalently subscribing to) this critique, the sociologist David Armstrong paints a nightmarish vision of total surveillance:

> ... holistic medicine might claim to be radical but it is only radical chic; its proponents might be well-meaning but they are the unwitting advance guard of

[17] Emily Martin, 'The End of the Body?', *American Ethnologist*, 19/1 (February 1992): pp. 121–40; Judith Fadlon, 'Meridians, Chakras and Psycho-Neuro-Immunology: The Dematerializing Body and the Domestication of Alternative Medicine', *Body & Society*, 10/4 (2004): pp. 69–86.

[18] Irving Zola, 'Medicine as an Institution of Social Control', *Sociological Review*, 20 (1972): pp. 487–54.

[19] Ivan Illich, *Medical Nemesis* (London: Calder & Boyars, 1976).

medical hegemony or the lackeys of a capitalist system. Their wider concerns with the whole-person simply mean that the whole person must be brought into visibility and control.[20]

For Armstrong the underlying holism of alternative therapies is not a welcome relief from a mechanistic biomedicine, but rather a disturbing extension of what he elsewhere calls 'surveillance medicine'.[21] More recently, analysts have noted what amounts to the extension of this very extension – whereby the gap between biomedicine and its alternatives appears to be closing from both directions – both through the (arguable) 'domestication'[22] or 'co-option'[23] of some alternative therapies by biomedicine, and through the increasing infiltration of particular alternative perspectives into some branches of medical treatment, notably cancer care.[24]

But some see the continuities as running even deeper. Jackie Stacey, for example, considers modern science and what she calls 'the self-health culture of the 1990s' to be united by 'the desire for mastery. It is the desire to see, to know and to control. It is the desire to fix meaning and to make outcomes predictable. It is the desire to prove that one has power over disease, the body and the emotions.'[25]

In a series of interviews in 1981 with people in the US about their concept of health, Robert Crawford found that the idea of health as a form of self-control was 'a consistent and unmistakable theme'.[26] The contemporary person is encouraged, he argued, in the illusion that s/he can and should predict, control and master the vagaries of illness and the body. Crawford found that his interviewees judged their own health 'failures' harshly.[27]

So does CAM exacerbate what is already an entrenched biomedical conception of health as self-discipline? Alternative medicine does undoubtedly extend and exacerbate the illusory hope or expectation that all human infirmity and illness can (or should) be controlled, especially considering its core demographic. While alternative medicine attracts a range of clients, from devotees to occasional users, its principal consumers are middle-aged white women.[28] This demographic results both from cultural factors (such as the feminization of approaches valorizing

---

[20]   Armstrong, 'The Problem', p. 32.

[21]   Armstrong, 'The Rise of Surveillance Medicine'.

[22]   Fadlon, 'Meridians, Chakras'.

[23]   Judy Singer and Kath Fisher, 'The Impact of Co-Option on Herbalism: A Bifurcation in Epistemology and Practice', *Health Sociology Review*, 16/1 (2007): pp. 18–26.

[24]   Stacey, *Teratologies*, p. 135.

[25]   Ibid., p. 238.

[26]   Robert Crawford, 'A Cultural Account of "Health": Control, Release, and the Social Body', in John B. McKinlay (ed.), *Issues in the Political Economy of Health Care* (New York: Tavistock Publications, 1984), pp. 60–103.

[27]   Ibid., p. 69.

[28]   Mary Ruggie, *Marginal to Mainstream: Alternative Medicine in America* (Cambridge: Cambridge University Press, 2004), p. 46.

emotions and intuition) and economic factors, such as the fact that the vast majority of CAM therapies lie outside of national health care schemes, where they exist. One shouldn't oversimplify, though, since CAM also attracts those at the end of the biomedical line, and its customers are an odd mixture of those who use them as therapies of both first and last resort.[29] But it is not grossly unfair to claim that a large percentage of users of alternative therapies are people who are used to treating life's problems as challenges to be solved with a combination of ingenuity, hard work and money. This attitude is especially rewarded in neo-liberal environments, where taking responsibility for one's health is part of the expectations of good citizenship.[30] Health is increasingly understood as 'a distinct goal'; it has become the 'object of intentional action'.[31] This 'general moralization of health under the rubric of self-responsibility'[32] is a 'subtle mechanism for shifting responsibility from the state to the patient'.[33] It masks a political programme aimed at 'shift[ing] the burden of costs back to labor and consumers' and avoiding the macro issues of environmental and occupational hazards.[34] Add to that the dominance of the discourse of personal 'choice' and empowerment in consumer environments, and it is clear that consumerism and neo-liberalism are influences on and contexts for the rise of alternative medicine, whose discourses resound with the themes of responsibility, choice and entitlement, and whose selection involves considerable consumer knowledge, discernment and payment.

But that is not the whole story, for alternative medicine is not simply or only about the search for 'solutions'. In order to get a fuller picture, we utilize the practitioners of alternative medicine's own stories (collected in interviews conducted over several years) to investigate issues of cure and control. It is to their therapeutic experience that we now turn.

Illness as Pedagogy

At this point, we would like to open up the notion of 'fixing' raised by Stacey's claim that both biomedicine and alternative therapies seek to 'fix meaning', taking the opportunity to explore the intersection of the two senses of 'fixing': pinning down, but also repairing or curing. 'Fixing' is not, in fact, part of the lexicon of alternative medicine. The preferred term is 'healing'. Indeed, legal restrictions in many countries actively prevent alternative medicine from promising or

---

29   Michael S. Goldstein, 'The Persistence and Resurgence of Medical Pluralism', *Journal of Health Politics, Policy and Law*, 29/4–5 (2004): p. 940.

30   Ruth McDonald *et al.*, 'Governing the Ethical Consumer: Identity, Choice and the Primary Care Medical Encounter', *Sociology of Health and Illness*, 29/3 (2007): p. 432.

31   Crawford, 'A Cultural Account', p. 67.

32   Ibid., p. 60.

33   McDonald *et al.*, 'Governing the Ethical Consumer', p. 434.

34   Crawford, 'A Cultural Account', p. 75.

advertising 'cures', in the process thus unintentionally promoting a non-medical idea of healing. Whatever physical promises they make, most therapies also understand healing far more amorphously – as an unpredictable process, achieved through the *dynamizing* of the body-self and through the *renunciation* of control, without sure knowledge or promise of outcomes. For many practitioners, healing involves, above all, *destabilization* rather than 'fixing'.

Therapeutic treatment is widely understood as a catalyzing and dynamizing process with unpredictable outcomes. The amount and nature of efficacy attributed to patient, healer and other agents (herbs, spirits, angels, remedies) varies between modalities. In some therapies, healing is conceived of as an activation of something internal to the patient, rather than the action of an external agent upon a body: 'Something's going on that awakens them to a part of themselves that they have forgotten … it's not like it's coming from outside, it's there', says Reiki practitioner Sharron. The external action of the practitioner is conceived of as catalytic rather than curative, with the healer seen as a conduit.[35] Thus, forms of energetic healing (of which Reiki is a type) have been characterized as more a form of being than *doing*,[36] which sets it apart from the action-based programmes of orthodox medicine. Moreover, many practitioners describe healing as potentially mutual – shared between practitioner and client. As Sharron puts it: 'When I'm giving a Reiki treatment the healing is mutual. I'm receiving Reiki too. So I'm getting healing for some grief, [and] so are they'.

Whereas mainstream medicine still addresses the 'biographical disruption'[37] associated with illness as a side issue (if at all), for alternative medicine it is core business. In alternative therapies, the supposedly adjunctive or companion issues associated with illness, such as psychological distress, family disruption, economic upheaval and so on, are seen as a central part of both illness and treatment. While for its critics this represents an insidious medicalization of huge areas of human life, this very expansiveness is also what loosens 'healing' from 'cure'. Healing is inherently multifaceted and may involve any or all of the following: physical, emotional or mental transformations; forgiveness (of self, or others); letting go of the past; letting go of some attachment; achieving a feeling of peace or wellbeing. Even a certain kind of death (a peaceful letting go) can be understood as a form of healing – a view that is, perhaps, the clearest indication of alternative therapies' debt to spiritual traditions, and that puts it most at odds with the survive-at-all-costs orientation of orthodox medicine (palliative care being, at best, the feminized and cloistered discipline that remediates medicine's supposed 'failure'). Indeed, alternative medicine's 'hesitancy to employ "heroic" measures that often are

---

[35]   Larry Dossey, *Healing Words: The Power of Prayer and the Practice of Medicine* (New York: HarperSanFrancisco, 1993), p. 198.

[36]   Lawrence LeShan, in ibid., pp. 197–8.

[37]   Michael Bury, 'Chronic Illness as Biographical Disruption', *Sociology of Health and Illness*, 4/2 (1982): pp. 167–82.

useless or have disastrous side effects'[38] has been identified as one of the features that make it attractive to many patients. One of the authors remembers being at a Reiki seminar many years ago at which an employee of a nursing home recounted how she had been giving many of the elderly residents Reiki treatments. She decided to desist as many of them died shortly after treatment. She was concerned not that she might have 'killed' them – after all, in orthodox terms she had done nothing to them, having only placed her hands lightly on their body – but at the mismatch between the medical paradigm under whose name the nursing home operated, and for which death is by and large defined as failure, and that of her therapeutic practice, according to which these deaths might be imagined as the peaceful release of a soul now ready to move to another plane.

Peaceful death is imaginable as healing within the alternative paradigm because healing itself is not seen as the logical and expected outcome of a known and repeatable procedure. Rather, it is often seen as an unpredictable transformation that occurs as a result of the *dynamizing* of the mind–body–spirit system:

> Some times things happen that they weren't expecting. Sometimes people come because they think Reiki might help with … an illness, but the first thing that they notice is that they feel more optimistic or that they have the stamina to stand and water their own garden or pick up their grandson. … So they might come because they hope the Reiki might get rid of their tumour but what happens along the way is that they realize what's important and these things enrich their life. (Sharron)

For Sharron, healing therefore includes a multitude of unexpected effects: '… even just a client saying, "Wow, I didn't know I could relax that much." Or a client who has a history of sexual abuse saying, "Wow, it's really nice … it feels like a hug but not dangerous."

The spiritual strains in alternative medicine construe illness itself as a lesson from 'the universe' – a form of spiritual pedagogy, if you like. It should not simply be repelled, but needs to be examined and mined for its spiritual lessons. The aim of treatment when illness is thus conceived is not simply – sometimes not *even* – to restore physical health:

> It is essential that we deal with the deeper meaning of our illnesses. We need to ask, what does this illness mean to me? What can I learn from this illness? Illness can be seen as simply a message from your body to you that says, *Wait a minute; something is wrong. You are not listening to your whole self; you are ignoring something very important to you. What is it?*[39]

---

[38]   Goldstein, 'The Persistence and Resurgence', p. 930.

[39]   Barbara Ann Brennan, *Hands of Light: A Guide to Healing through the Human Energy Field: A New Paradigm for the Human Being in Health, Relationship, and Disease* (Toronto, ON: Bantam Books, 1988), p. 7, original emphasis.

For New Age practitioners especially, illness is 'a meaningful state'.[40] The interpretive dimension of (some) alternative medicine is where the question of control reasserts itself. Metaphysical theories of illness have gained much popular traction via the New Age, and in their bluntest articulations it is indeed true that they try to fix meaning and make outcomes predictable, as Stacey contends. Louise L. Hay's enormously popular metaphysical tables, for example, are exactly the type of prescriptive schemata lamented by Stacey, consisting of a detailed list of the 'meanings' of symptoms and body parts along with corrective affirmations.[41] This conception of illness is one of the most contested of all aspects of alternative medicine.[42] Our purpose here is not to enter this important debate, but rather to point out how paradigmatically significant this point of difference is, and to note the ambiguity of the question of control implied in the idea of illness as a lesson. On the one hand, the desire to understand the 'meaning' of an illness is indeed an attempt to take control and is, as critics note, quite congruent with neo-liberal ideas of taking responsibility for one's health. On the other hand, if illness is a communication, a spiritual lesson, it follows that 'healing' is not coterminous with 'cure'. For, in the eclectic and syncretic spiritual terrain of the New Age, simple metaphysical interpretations that might promise a cure also jostle for space with other spiritual ideas that tend in a different direction, such as that of destiny or karma (according to which the individual is ultimately enjoined to relinquish control and to accept illness rather than to try to 'conquer' it) or that of a higher spiritual self (whose will or intention is understood as not always knowable or reconcilable to the embodied human self). Moreover, it is important to note that not all alternative practitioners are interested in 'decoding' illness as a message from the universe or the unconscious.[43]

The unpredictability of healing is most obvious in modalities like spiritual, psychic or prayer-based healing, where healing involves the invocation of a higher power and the handing over of control (though not, according to most practitioners, of responsibility). Researchers who have tried to assess the efficacy of these types of healing using scientific criteria for validity have concluded that success rates are statistically significant, but random and unpredictable.[44] In most alternative therapies,

---

[40]   Kim A. Jobst *et al.*, 'Diseases of Meaning, Manifestations of Health, and Metaphor', *Journal of Alternative and Complementary Medicine*, 5/6 (1999): p. 495.

[41]   Louise L. Hay, *Heal Your Body: The Mental Causes for Physical Illness and the Metaphysical Way to Overcome Them* (Concord, MA: Specialist Publications, 1988).

[42]   See, for example, Susan Sontag, *Illness as Metaphor* (Harmondsworth: Penguin, 1977), and Coward, *The Whole Truth*.

[43]   Jungian psychotherapist Robert Bosnak is, for example, an advocate of a very bodily form of dreamwork based on unpredictable transformation rather than interpretation: *Embodiment: Creative Imagination in Medicine, Art, and Travel* (Hove: Routledge, 2007). The body worker Fritz Frederick Smith also uses the metaphor of alchemy: see *The Alchemy of Touch: Moving towards Mastery* (Taos, NM: Complementary Medicine Press, 2005).

[44]   Dossey, *Healing Words*, pp. 200ff.

in fact, the client may not get what they hoped for, but they may consider the process to have been a healing one nonetheless. Healing thus has processural as well as outcomes-based dimensions. Homeopath and Reiki practitioner Wendy says:

> Someone may come with chronic fatigue and in the process of being healed they may work through all sorts of frustrations, all sorts of things that they've had to deal with in order to deal with having that disease. Senses of guilt, sense of alienation, being left out, missing out. Grief over opportunities lost. There are so many aspects of dealing with a disease … that a practitioner needs to be aware of. So that you can simply allow that process to unfold.

This idea of 'unfolding' puts alternative therapies at odds with the more pragmatic, evidence-based, solution-seeking paradigm of biomedicine. This difference is, for many clients of alternative therapies, one of the prime attractions, though modern people's relation to outcomes-based thought is likely to be quite contradictory. Modern pragmatism tends to make us seek solutions: 'The impulse to *do* when sick is understandable – to take the antibiotic with a cold's first sniffles, to rush to surgery, and so on'.[45] In the case of serious illness, however, the limits of medicine cast a shadow over this outcomes-based thinking, and we commonly hear cancer patients, for example, forced to adopt a more processural view of life; they often talk of 'taking one day at a time'. The recognition of the limitations of solutions-based thinking to certain types of bodily, emotional or mental illness is an important reason why many find alternative therapies attractive.

Across many modalities, then, healing is multiple and unpredictable; it operates right across the mind–body–spirit spectrum and is not always tied to a desired 'outcome'. It is understood to transcend both the client and the practitioner, and is frequently shared between them. It involves some form of giving over, letting go or acceptance. Moreover, healing is not reducible to the disappearance or attenuation of physical symptoms, and in some cases may not even appear to involve physical relief at all. It might manifest in the form of the relief of physical symptoms, an action (e.g. leaving a husband), a changed perspective, or a business or financial decision (selling a house, buying a house, starting a business). This marks it out from biomedical ideas of 'cure' and, moreover, makes it politically unpredictable, a point that ought to make it of interest to Cultural Studies.

Individualism and the Subtle Body

As we have seen, Stacey's claim that alternative therapies are part of a culture of control is significant, but this is not the whole story. While it is true these therapies can be employed to maintain boundaries of a 'static' and essential self against the chaos and illogic of illness, we would like to consider briefly another model

---

[45]   Ibid., p. 19.

of the self underpinning some alternative therapies that necessarily requests a suspension of discourses of mastery – that of the subtle body.[46] For underlying the difference between 'cure' and 'healing' are, argues Anne L. Scott, two different conceptualizations of the body, which themselves are, finally, caught up in different understandings of agency.[47] The difference between the two approaches is not strictly speaking a question of modality (i.e. some modalities promising cures and others promising healing) as of the paradigm within which a given practitioner chooses to exercise his or her art. The self upon which the majority of alternative therapies 'work' is built upon a temporal, energetic and processural ontology that does not clearly 'fix' the borders of self. Modalities of healing strongly influenced by this concept of self, for example spiritual healing, incorporate a concept of whole-person that is not hermetically sealed like the bounded subject of biomedicine. The subtle body 'whole-self', while no less individual and 'whole', is dynamic, fragmentary, radically permeable and inherently unknowable as a totality.

The self in subtle body models comprises numerous interpenetrating sheaths of matter-energy, most of which are understood to extend beyond the physical body. There are many complex 'maps' of these energetic bodies specific to both particular religious traditions and healing modalities. However, in contemporary wellbeing culture these bodies are commonly figured as a nexus of energy often termed the 'aura'. We have discussed this conceptualization of the body in more detail elsewhere.[48] It is, however, generally understood, in the many and different cultural and religious traditions that 'use' this concept of the body, that to recognize and register the influence and effects of one's subtle bodies, certain types of perceptive abilities are required (most usually clairvoyance). Therefore, claims by social control theorists that alternative therapies are discourses of 'control' designed to have the entirety of the subject 'brought to visibility' are inadequate, as they fail to recognize what 'visibility' might mean in a radically different ontological paradigm – one that requires the development of an entire perceptive modality that remains unrecognized (and/or feminized and derided) by dominant discourses. Paradoxically, the acquisition of different ways of seeing and 'reading' the self necessitates a suspension of control rather than orchestrating yet more refined levels of self control. It requires the acknowledgement of a relation of radical intersubjectivity between self and other – occasioned by interpenetrating subtle bodies – that can't be fixed, can't be clearly located. The boundaries of self and other (if perceptible to the individual) can't be pinned down (because they are understood to consist of a 'subtle' spiritual matter that radically interpenetrates both

---

[46]   For a discussion of the subtle body as a distinct form of intersubjectivity and its informing religious traditions see Jay Johnston, *Angels of Desire: Esoteric Bodies, Aesthetics and Ethics*, Gnostica (London and Oakville: Equinox, 2008).

[47]   Anne L. Scott, 'The Symbolizing Body and the Metaphysics of Alternative Medicine', *Body & Society*, 4/3 (1998): p. 21.

[48]   Johnston and Barcan, 'Subtle Transformations'.

self and other). Such selves are extensive, processural and radically interconnected with others and the broader world.

This model of the self calls for its own forms of responsibility – in this case to acquire the necessary perceptive skills in order to apprehend the subtle aspects of self directly – while simultaneously requiring a letting go of control, an understanding that these perceptive modalities will only make more evident the nebulous and uncontrollable boundaries of self and other. Such a giving up of control couldn't be further from what Stacey identifies as the desire for mastery. Rather, it is an acknowledgement of the self as radically intersubjective, energetic, temporal and beyond ever being known (comprehended) in its entirety. As such, the absolute boundaries of self cannot be built upon concepts of ownership, but upon a greater apprehension and acceptance of one and another's unknowable boundaries and processes. From the perspective of subtle bodies, a 'whole' individual is not a closed unit, but dynamic and fragmentary, necessarily open to the other (individual, planet, cosmos etc). To be whole is to be centred, while simultaneously 'all over the place'.

It may well be that the ethical implications of this model of the body are not fully realized within New Age discourse and that the more New Age-inflected styles of alternative medicine do emphasize the ability to take control of one's life. For example, self-help guru Louise L. Hay's prescriptive list of corrective thought patterns for healing illnesses ultimately contradicts the ontological nature of the subtle bodies that it seeks to elucidate. In one of the many paradoxes and contradictions that typify the syncretic, hybrid New Age, however, her prescriptive list contains some affirmations designed to correct an overactive need for control, and others designed to correct a perceived lack of control. Clearly, despite the widespread use in alternative therapies of a model of the body as multiple and dispersed, fantasies of selfhood, nature, wholeness and perfection interact in complicated ways, and often the types of fix sought for both self and body are based on the notion that 'reconstruction' or 'restoration' of a more complete, whole or unsullied state is both desirable and possible. In Hay's words, 'In the infinity of life where I am, all is perfect, whole and complete'.[49] Here, as commonly in New Age/alternative discourse, aspirations towards constructing and maintaining a 'whole' subject are dominant and normalized. Idealist conceptions such as this have seen alternative therapies roundly condemned within Cultural Studies – see, most famously, Rosalind Coward's critique of discourses of holism and naturalness in alternative therapies and Nikolas Rose's Foucauldian analysis of the way in which therapeutic discourse is addressed not only to those in need but 'to living itself'.[50]

---

[49]   Louise L. Hay, *You Can Heal Your Life* (Concord, MA: Specialist Publications, 1987), p. 15.

[50]   Coward, *Whole Truth*; Nikolas Rose, *Governing the Soul: The Shaping of the Private Self* (London: Free Association Books, 1999), p. 218.

However, as conceptualized in 'subtle' body models, the form of self is energetically expansive and always in a process of relation: that is, never 'complete'. Further, while alternative therapies are usually based on fantasies of natural wholeness, the concept of holism has its own (usually unarticulated) complexities. Healing is imagined as emanating from an external agent and/or from the activation of something internal to the patient. The complex location of the catalytic agent (both 'inside' and 'outside') suggests, in turn, a self conceived of as multiple and radically connected with other agents, both living and non-living.

As such, these selves exceed dominant logics of mastery and control and complicate normalized conceptualizations of wholeness and healing. The intersubjective exchanges upon which this model of the self is founded are indirectly reflected in Paul Heelas's contention that, rather than being mere superficial and selfish consumption, 'holistic, mind-body-spirituality activities' do partake in an 'ethics of humanity'. In a revision of his earlier position on the New Age as an entirety, Heelas contends that 'wellbeing spirituality' practices are a 'more subtle, whilst more effective counter-culture' then those of the 1960s and '70s *because* they are founded upon '"normal", familiar everyday' practices of consumption, which, although they are an individual endeavour, are directed towards 'social good-living'.[51]

Clearly, it is inaccurate to characterize alternative therapies as having a simple, unified relation to control and to individualism, both because of their diversity and because of the contradictions and paradoxes that arise from the selective and syncretic uptake of a vast array of differing spiritual practices into a neo-liberal, consumerist environment. This chapter has sought to temper the valuable Foucauldian critiques of wellbeing cultural practices with a nuanced reading of the way in which control and mastery play out in the experience of patients and practitioners, particularly through the framing logic of illness as pedagogy. Central to the figuration of such experiences is a concept of the self, of the body – the subtle body – that necessarily renders control impossible. Indeed, the interaction of such bodies in the context of a healing practice is often characterized by individual acknowledgment of the need to 'give up' agendas of self mastery coupled with a recognition of the centrality of intersubjective relations: relations nebulous yet palpable. In philosophical terms, such a self is one of both individual integrity and energetic extensivity. Perhaps the strongest role for socio-cultural criticism is to help actualize this philosophical potential into an active political one.

---

[51] Heelas, *Spiritualities of Life*, pp. 10, 14 and 17.

Chapter 7

Religious Media Events and Branding Religion

Veronika Krönert and Andreas Hepp

The Pope and the Media

'We Are Pope!' headlined *Bild*, Germany's top-selling tabloid the day after Cardinal Joseph Ratzinger was elected pope in spring 2005. A few months later, at the Catholic World Youth Day in Cologne, thousands of buttons with this slogan were spread among the participants – a fact that again was covered by the press. Rather than evidence of a possible 'return' of religion, we see this as an example for the present mediatization of religion that results in its 'branding': a staging of religion according to the forms and patterns of commercialized media cultures. In other words: this is an aligning of religious media representations with sacred 'brand symbols' to facilitate the mediation of religion throughout fragmented media landscapes.

In this chapter we argue that an articulation of sacred worlds around specific 'faith brands'[1] on the part of media production and representation corresponds with religious individualization in everyday life. In the context of an ongoing process of individualization, 'brands' offer landmarks for individual religious questing and open up communicative spaces for personal spiritual experiences. To support this thesis we follow a three-step argument. First, we contextualize the idea of 'branding religion' within processes of religious individualization and mediatization. Based on this and our own empirical research we shall, second, theorize the Catholic World Youth Day as a religious media event and an outstanding way of branding religion. Finally, we make some concluding remarks on the significance of mediatization as 'branding religion' within the context of present religious change.

'Mediatization' as 'Branding Religion'

All the way into the 1980s and 1990s an unquestioned reference point in the social sciences and cultural studies was the loss in the significance of religion in

---

[1] Mara Einstein, *Brands of Faith: Marketing Religion in a Commercial Age* (New York: Routledge, 2007).

(post)modern consumer societies.[2] In view of an assumed secularization process, religion was denied any major relevance in the area of media communication. While formal religion was supposed to be marginalized by an increasingly differentiated range of popular media texts, the social functions of religion were presumed to be satisfied by 'quasi-religious' media functions.[3] While long since the secularization paradigm has come in for criticism in US and Latin American media studies,[4] we have come to realize only gradually that despite its changing public role in the last decades even in Europe religion never really disappeared from the media landscapes. Hence, what we are witnessing is not a re-emergence of religion since this would simply be a mirror-inversion of the secularization thesis,[5] but rather new ways of rearticulating religion.

A viable framework for researching the rearticulation of religion is Ulrich Beck's individualization theory. Generally speaking, individualization does not mean an increasing isolation or atomization of the individual; rather it emphasizes that in the course of 'reflexive modernization'[6] the personal (yet unequally shared) responsibility and necessity to make choices becomes a dominant pattern in many social and cultural contexts. As Beck stated only recently, this is also true for religion. Relating to earlier thoughts by Peter L. Berger,[7] religious individualization means that 'the individual builds out of his or her religious experiences their own individual religious roofing, a religious "canopy"' [own translation].[8] Thus certain faith offers are appropriated in relation to one's 'own god' in a reflexive process that is driven by the decision of the individual and not primarily by social origin and/or religious organizations. However, this does not mark the end of religion, but points to the contradictory narration of 'secular religiosity'[9] that research on religious and media change has to decipher.

---

    2   Cf. Jesús Martín Barbero, 'Mass Media as a Site of Resacralization of Contemporary Cultures', in Stewart M. Hoover and Knut Lundby (eds), *Rethinking Media, Religion, and Culture* (Thousand Oaks, CA: Sage, 1997), pp. 102–16.

    3   John Fiske and John Hartley, *Reading Television* (London: Methuen, 1989).

    4   Cf. Martín Barbero, 'Mass Media as a Site of Resacralization'; Stewart M. Hoover, 'Media and the Construction of the Religious Public Sphere', in Hoover and Lundby, *Rethinking*, pp. 283–97.

    5   Cf. Friedrich Wilhelm Graf, *Die Wiederkehr der Götter: Religion in der modernen Kultur* (Munich: Beck, 2007), p. 20.

    6   Ulrich Beck and Elisabeth Beck-Gernsheim (eds), *Individualization: Institutionalized Individualism and its Social and Political Consequences* (London: Sage, 2001).

    7   Peter L. Berger, *Heretical Imperative: Contemporary Possibilities of Religious Affirmation* (New York: Doubleday, 1980).

    8   Ulrich Beck, *Der eigene Gott. Die Individualisierung der Religion und der 'Geist' der Weltgesellschaft* (Frankfurt a.M.: Suhrkamp, 2008), p. 31.

    9   Ibid.

Within this overall argumentation, the remarkable point is how Ulrich Beck brings the media into his reflections. He diagnoses a 'mass mediatization'[10] as part of a religious individualization that brings an increasing staging of religious institutions and their main representatives in the mass media. Examples he quotes are especially media events such as the funeral of Pope John Paul II, the election of Benedict XVI, or the so-called Muhammad cartoon crisis. Even if these events might not fill churches, they offer the opportunity to communicate religion *across* different territories and traditions via media that themselves are globalized. In this way they correspond not only to the fact that nowadays 'the world religions historically separated from each other are forced to compete and communicate with each other in the boundless space of a mass-mediatized public sphere' [own translation];[11] up to a certain degree they compensate, as Beck argues, the decay of religious authorities. Where religion becomes an individual construction of an 'own god', the media are the instance of communicating possible religious or spiritual references.

With this emphasis on the media as deterritorial mediators of an ever-growing plurality of faith, Beck opens up the debate on religious change in late modern societies to the media and the symbolic dimension of religious meaning-making. Although interest in the media as driving forces of religious transformation was raised already at the end of the last century when Thomas Luckmann in the Epilogue to the German translation of his classical essay on *The Invisible Religion* accounted for the key role of the media in the constitution and proliferation of an ever more dynamic religious marketplace,[12] the cultural implications were disregarded for a long time. This is where Beck's argument comes in. Whereas Luckmann treated the media primarily as communicative infrastructure for the 'distribution'[13] of otherwise independent religious and ideological offers of meaning, Beck points to the staging of religion *in* the media and addresses the question how the media enter *into* the processes of religious meaning-making, reshaping them subsequently. What becomes obvious, then, is that we have to analyse further what mediatization means in detail in relation to religion, and how the idea of branding religion comes in here.

In his reflections on *Religion in the Media Age* Stewart Hoover argues that 'in the relation between "religion" and "the media", the latter are, in many ways, in the driver's seat'.[14] This metaphorical formulation refers to what the concept of mediatization tries to theorize and what Beck and others coming from Sociology and Religious Studies do not reflect on further: the adoption of 'the media' by

---

10   Ibid., p. 55.

11   Ibid., p. 169.

12   Thomas Luckmann, *Die unsichtbare Religion* (Frankfurt a.M.: Suhrkamp, 2008), p. 180.

13   Ibid.

14   Stewart M. Hoover, *Religion in the Media Age* (London: Routledge, 2006), p. 284.

religious institutions is not a neutral act but rather a process of mutually related rearticulations.

In this sense, the concept of mediatization[15] enables us to clarify what Hoover captures with the metaphor of the 'driver's seat'. If we understand mediatization as the spreading of technical communication media throughout different social and cultural spheres, we can differentiate a quantitative and a qualitative aspect. In the *quantitative respect*, more and more media are accessible at more and more times and locations for more and more purposes. In the *qualitative respect*, increasing importance of the media in different socio-cultural contexts goes hand in hand with changes in the forms through which we communicate and relate to each other.

Both aspects of mediatization are challenging religious institutions insofar as they can no longer situate themselves outside of these processes. On the contrary, if we share with Nick Couldry[16] the assumption that the main aspect of the media age – or maybe more specific: of media cultures – is that the media are constructed successfully as the 'unquestioned centre of society', it becomes clear that religion and spirituality are also subjected to this. Any religious community or faith offer that claims to be of 'central' value for society today has to be staged in the media as it is the media that provide access to resources that represent – or at least are thought to do so – the 'centre' of society, even though this centre is increasingly fragmented and deterritorialized due to the globalization of media communication.

Yet becoming part of the centre is not a neutral act in the way that certain religious or spiritual communities use the media as strategic instruments. Rather, the media as 'technology and cultural form'[17] exert certain 'moulding forces' on the way religion and spirituality are communicated. Television, for instance, implies the need to communicate religion and spirituality visually, based on appealing symbols and practices; the Internet puts religious or spiritual statements in a broader ethical discourse pushed by increasingly individualized believers and non-believers, and so on.

In this perspective we can understand branding as *one* dominant pattern of the mediatization of religion. Basically, 'branding' describes a communicative process in which – based on a so-called 'core brand' – the product is positioned with the aim of differing in an appropriate way from competing products and

---

[15] Cf. John B. Thompson, *The Media and Modernity* (Cambridge: Cambridge University Press, 1995); Friedrich Krotz, 'Media Connectivity: Concepts, Conditions, and Consequences', in Andreas Hepp, Friedrich Krotz, Shaun Moores and Carsten Winter (eds), *Connectivity, Networks and Flows: Conceptualizing Contemporary* Communications (Cresskill, NJ: Hampton Press, 2008), pp. 13–31; Andreas Hepp, 'Differentiation: Mediatization and Cultural Change', in Knut Lundby (ed.), *Mediatization: Concept, Changes, Consequences* (New York: Peter Lang, 2009), pp. 135–54.

[16] Nick Couldry, *Media Rituals: A Critical Approach* (London and New York: Routledge, 2003).

[17] Raymond Williams, *Television: Technology and Cultural Form* (London: Routledge, 1990).

being taken into the consumers' 'relevance set'.[18] With regard to religion, Mara Einstein emphasizes:

> Within this environment of being able to select your religion, or religions, combined with unfettered access to information, religion must present itself as a valuable commodity, an activity that is worthwhile in an era of overcrowded schedules. To do this, religion needs to be packaged and promoted. It needs to be new and relevant. It needs to break through the clutter, and for that to happen it needs to establish a brand identity.[19]

What becomes obvious, then, is that, as presumed guardians of tradition, religious institutions like the Catholic Church are under considerable pressure to present themselves and their specific faith offers in a popular way in the media to hold their ground on the deterritorial religious marketplace. In this regard, Einstein points to religious 'community, stability, and a foundational belief system' as characteristic elements that may help to distinguish religion from broader consumer culture and thus can be seen as constitutive for 'a religious organization's unique selling proposition'.[20]

In a similar way Lynn Schofield Clark regards 'religious lifestyle branding'[21] as a characteristic pattern to communicate religion on the present religious marketplace. Whereas Einstein refers first and foremost to the promotional aspect of 'branding religion', Schofield Clark highlights the need to tie in with the individualized life-worlds of people:

> Branding is not so much about linking products with certain attributes that we then select when we are looking for means of self-expression. Branding ... creates a space for us to occupy, one that we actually see ourselves already occupying. The company is just claiming that space as its own ... branding works when it speaks to what we already are.[22]

However, transferring the idea of branding to the area of religion might have problematic aspects if the analogy is overemphasized. The German sociologist Hubert Knoblauch, for instance, points to the tendency implicit in market-related metaphors to narrow down questions of faith to a utilitarian logic, missing the special cultural value of religion. To avoid reductionism he stresses the importance

---

[18]   Gabriele Siegert, 'Branding – Medienstrategie für globale Märkte?', in Hans-Bernd Brosius (ed.), *Kommunikation über Grenzen und Kulturen* (Constance: UVK, 2000), p. 75.

[19]   Einstein, *Brands of Faith*, p. 12.

[20]   Ibid., pp. 35–6.

[21]   Lynn Schofield Clark 'Identity, Belonging, and Religious Lifestyle Branding', in Lynn Schofield Clark (ed.), *Religion, Media and the Marketplace* (New Brunswick, NJ: Rutgers University Press, 2007), p. 27.

[22]   Ibid., p. 11.

of taking into account also the struggles over symbolic power and legitimization involved in these overall transformation processes.[23] Taking these arguments together with Lynn Schofield Clark's reflections, we conceptualize branding religion less in terms of marketing religion with regard to profit maximization but rather as a narrative strategy (and its appropriation) to communicate religious topics within the patterns of commercialized media cultures. In such an extended understanding, the idea of branding religion captures two main aspects of the present mediatization of religion:

1. First, mediatization implies certain 'moulding forces' on different religions to communicate themselves across different media. Only if a faith offer spreads out successfully over increasingly fragmented media landscapes does it have a chance of being recognized as being part of the centre of society. Thus the core meaning has to be communicated widely across a broad range of media products – and staging religion and spirituality around sacred brand symbols might be an opportunity to facilitate this.

2. Second, due to this mediatization religious institutions lose the symbolic sovereignty over the sacred space and thus their exclusive spaces of communication like churches and parochial media. As religion gets under pressure to show up in the media, it has to present itself in the symbolic forms of a commercialized media culture. Thus branding refers to the necessity of religious self-presentation in the commercialized space of present media cultures.

However, *religious* 'branding' is distinctive because even in largely individualized, mediatized and commercialized contexts, the core meaning of religion is its transcendent or sacred claim.[24] So, branding religion means presenting religion in the 'profane' communicative space of commercialized media culture, without losing the sacred aura constitutive of religion. Keeping this in mind, a concept like branding religion helps to shed light on how media-related rearticulations of religion interfere with overall social and cultural transformations in the course of individualization. This becomes clear if we look at how the Catholic World Youth Day was articulated as a religious media event at the different levels of creating religious meaning.

---

[23]   Hubert Knoblauch, 'Spirituality and Popular Religion in Europe', *Social Compass*, 55/2 (2008): pp. 140–53.

[24]   Cf. Johanna Sumiala-Seppänen, Knut Lundby and Raimo Salokangas (eds), *Implications of the Sacred in (Post)Modern Media* (Gothenburg: Nordicom, 2006).

The World Youth Day as a Religious Media Event: Staging and Appropriating Branded Religion

Religious media events are a helpful example in studying the various implications of what we conceptualized as branding religion. To account for this we shall present a case study on the 20th World Youth Day, held in 2005 by the Catholic Church in the German city of Cologne. The World Youth Days go back to a youth meeting in Rome in 1985 on the occasion of the United Nations' International Youth Year. Since then they have been celebrated every second or third year at an international level, not only as a local gathering with up to a million participants or more, but also as a translocal media event that reaches far beyond the hosting country into other global regions with a majority of Catholic inhabitants.

Taking the example of 2005, we investigated the mediatization of the Catholic World Youth Day based on a broad range of empirical data on the production, representation and appropriation of the media event in Germany and Italy:[25] undertaking interviews with Catholic representatives in charge of the cultural production of the media event; quantitative and qualitative content analyses of the World Youth Day coverage in television, newspapers and various religious and non-religious journals; participant observation of the mediatization *in situ*, i.e. the media use on site; and finally interviews with young Catholics on the appropriation of the media event. In all, our research follows a 'transcultural perspective' with respect to Germany and Italy: while it is clear that certain aspects of Catholicism differ across national cultures, we analysed the World Youth Day in its transcultural character against the background of Catholicism as a deterritorialized belief community. Referring to Néstor García Canclini, 'deterritorial' in this sense means that territoriality is no necessary reference point for the articulation of these communities, as it is for example for the imagined community of the nation as the basis of the modern state.[26]

Contextualizing the World Youth Day as a religious media event within the broader research on media events, it is striking that from the outset the discussion referred to questions of religion. Most prominently, in their seminal work on media events Daniel Dayan and Elihu Katz see a deep link between media events and religion: being 'presented with *ceremonial reverence*, in tones that express sacrality and awe', media events 'play a part in the civil religion'.[27] 'Like religious holidays', media events 'mean an interruption of routine, days off from work,

---

[25]   Cf. Andreas Hepp and Veronika Krönert, 'Religious Media Events: The Catholic "World Youth Day" as an Example for the Mediatization and Individualization of Religion', in Nick Couldry, Andreas Hepp and Friedrich Krotz (eds), *Media Events in a Global Age* (London: Routledge, 2010), pp. 265–82.

[26]   Néstor García Canclini, *Hybrid Cultures: Strategies for Entering and Leaving Modernity* (Minneapolis, MN, and London: University of Minnesota Press, 1995).

[27]   Daniel Dayan and Elihu Katz, *Media Events: The Live Broadcasting of History* (Cambridge, MA, and London: Harvard University Press, 1992), pp. 12, 16.

norms of participation in ceremony and ritual … and of integration with a cultural center'.[28] In a similar way Eric Rothenbuhler[29] in his early work on media events considers the Olympics as a ritual media event with a quasi-religious dimension. Here he meets with Knut Lundby's[30] research on the 'sacralized moments' in the opening ceremony of the Winter Olympics.

All these approaches share a focus on the quasi-religious function of what we want to call 'ritual media events', arguing that today's media events have a transformative role in relation to social forms and functions that sacred ceremonies had before. While this argument still is important, it falls short in view of an exceptional mass-mediated religious celebration like the Catholic World Youth Day. For sure it includes ceremonial moments of traditional religious celebrations (liturgy, for example, or prayer), which according to the above-mentioned definition by Daniel Dayan and Elihu Katz create a 'sacred aura' and thus constitute the ritual core of a media event. However, this describes the World Youth Day only in part. Intentionally *staged as a media event*, it also comprises aspects we know from popular film or television events.

In this sense, we can characterize the World Youth Day as a 'hybrid religious media event', integrating both aspects of 'ritual media events' and of entertainment-orientated 'popular media events', marked by consumer culture.[31] It is against the background of this hybridity that the branding of religion becomes concrete.

Producing the Media Event: The Articulation of a Hybrid 'Brand Space'

The notion of hybridity directly points to the tensions between the claims for centrality of the Catholic Church and the interests of the media organizations that characterize the cultural production of the World Youth Day as a media event. The interviews we conducted with the press spokesman of the World Youth Day organization office, with a priest responsible for liturgical planning and also with different media journalists all indicate that from the beginning the World Youth Day was planned *also* as a media event.

Every part of the programme with a sacred claim was orchestrated carefully and under significant control of the Catholic Church. Much knowledge and a great deal of the resources of the Catholic Church have been devoted to the creation of a mystic aura. To quote the priest responsible for the central liturgies: 'If people get the impression that everything has been said here, then we have missed the

---

[28]   Ibid., p. 16.

[29]   Eric W. Rothenbuhler, 'The Living Room Celebration of the Olympic Games', *Journal of Communication*, 38/3 (1988): p. 78.

[30]   Knut Lundby, 'The Web of Collective Representations', in Hoover and Lundby (eds), *Rethinking*, p. 161.

[31]   Andreas Hepp and Nick Couldry, 'Media Events in Globalized Media Cultures', in Couldry, Hepp and Krot (eds), *Media Events*, pp. 1–20.

essential, because it should also stay mystical … if the last person thinks he has fully understood, that isn't religion.'

What this statement illustrates is that, to secure the ritual centre of the media event and thus the sacred claim of Catholicism, the Catholic Church strove to present faith as something extraordinary that remains in some way unsearchable. To this end not only the ceremonial dramaturgy but also every position of the TV cameras was fixed in advance with media coverage (especially television) in mind and with support of media professionals from the official media partners. Beyond this, there was no room for journalists to influence the progression of the sacred ceremonies, particularly as access to the sacred ceremonies was restricted so that only a defined set of accredited journalists had a chance to take their own pictures of these events, quite often from predefined positions.

By contrast, there was a great deal more space for autonomous media coverage with regard to the people, as public space like the streets of Cologne or the Rhine's riverbanks remained uncontrollable by the Catholic Church. Consequently, the different media organizations found their own 'stories' and their own 'take' on the event beyond the official ceremonies in the public scenes. Often these were stories of jolly celebrations or explicit sexuality; that is, stories about what young Catholics do regardless of the papal doctrine.

In view of this contradictory context between the two focal points of its cultural production, one can argue that in staging the World Youth Day as a media event a hybrid symbolic space is opened up. That is a communicative space where – projected onto the pope as a religious brand symbol – the sacred claims and popular stories about lived religion intermingle in new ways that point beyond the media event itself to broader questions of religious individualization in everyday contexts. In this sense, we can see the media event as a brand space wherein the idea of what Catholicism accounts for in present-day media cultures is subjected to complex rearticulation processes. This becomes clearer if we look closer at the way the media event was represented in the German and Italia media coverage.

Representing the Media Event: The Pope as a Religious 'Brand Symbol'

In order to grasp the complexity of the media event of the World Youth Day – which in reality is the progression of a number of different events – the Catholic Church and the media used the pope as a linking 'brand symbol': just as the sacred ceremonies – at least those that were important in the media – are staged as highlights of the papal visit in Cologne and its official programme, the public spaces are integrated into the cultural production of the World Youth Day as the pope himself moves through them or at least is acclaimed by the jovial masses.

Thus, as a *hybrid* media event the World Youth Day was represented principally as a 'pope event': be it in Germany or Italy, in print or on TV, in news media, popular media products or parochial journals, the sacred arrangement was articulated as an arrangement focusing on pope-related aspects, with belief practices and traditions discussed in relation to the rather conservative position of the pope. Meanwhile, the connection between the popular and the pope came about as a result of the way in which aspects such as atmosphere, the 'pilgrims' programme' and merchandizing had been focused on the pope as well.

So, in a nutshell we can argue that the World Youth Day was a *hybrid* media event because we find both ritual celebration and popular outburst featuring prominently within it: the sacredness of media rituals and the popularity of consumer culture. That both aspects can so easily form part of the same media event is thanks to the pope, who as a 'media figure' symbolizes both the sacred and the popular dimension not only of the World Youth Day but also of present-day Catholicism in general. The following Figure 7.1, published during the World Youth Day in the largest German youth magazine BRAVO (issue 34/06) with sales of more than 600,000 copies per week in this time (first quarter 2006), is a demonstrable illustration of this.

On the one hand, this poster is obviously a religious image with definitely sacred implications: Pope Benedict XVI is in front of a deep blue sky with white clouds, waving a hand half in greeting and half in blessing. His sacred position is emphasized by the glittering signet ring and the shiny Cross on his chest. On the other hand, the poster clearly comes within the framework of popular culture, for it adopts arguably the style of representation usually associated with the promotion of popular music or TV stars. Underlined with 'Bravo, Bene!', informal nickname and ironic wordplay at the same time, the poster suggests a personal relation to Benedict XVI as a 'religious star'. Thus, as a Catholic brand symbol the pope is capable of symbolizing and – maybe even more important – visualizing both the extraordinary holy (or sacred) and the everyday popular dimension not only of the World Youth Day as a (media) event but also of present day-Catholicism.

As a media celebrity, however, the pope inevitably points to multiple tensions related to present-day religious change; that is, questions about the relationship between Catholicism and other world religions under the conditions of globalization, the significance of religious and especially Catholic values in increasingly mediatized and individualized late modern societies, and so on. This in turn means that, in a global age, the brand symbol of the pope has to be regarded against the horizon of meaning of Catholicism as a 'deterritorial religious community', that is, a religious community whose 'thickening'[32] of meaning is beyond the national.

This becomes evident as we look at the media coverage in Germany and Italy. Comparing the gathering in Cologne to the 'United Nations General Assembly' or the 'Socialist Internationale', the media event is placed within the global context of Catholicism as 'world church' or 'world religion'. Its 'nation-transgressing connections' are represented by young people from different parts of the world

---

[32]   Orvar Löfgren, 'The Nation as Home or Motel? Metaphors of Media and Belonging', *Sosiologisk Årbok*, 14/1 (2001): pp. 1–34.

Figure 7.1   Poster of Pope Benedict XVI, BRAVO, 17 August 2005

who, playing regional music, singing and waving flags, symbolize in a peaceful way the reach of Catholicism across the world.

From this perspective, the media figure of the pope provides an outstanding opportunity to communicate Catholicism transculturally. Just as he already symbolizes both the position of the Catholic Church and its global pretension and the hybrid nature of a mediatized and individualized Catholic youth culture that, again, defines itself *per se* in a transcultural deterritorial frame, the pope is known and recognized as a religious brand symbol internationally. So, as a transculturally accessible 'projection' for the sacred and popular dimension of present-day Catholicism, the pope as a *media celebrity* allows for the staging of the Catholic faith offer in the mediated centre of increasingly globalized and individualized media cultures.

Appropriating the Media Event: Individualized Religion and Religious Branding

In the face of the deterritorial extent and global claim of Catholicism, we have to ask how individual seekers position themselves within the hybrid communicative space articulated by the media event and how they relate to the pope as a symbol for Catholicism thereby. The interviews we conducted with young German and Italian Catholics who witnessed the media event at home, indicate two ways of appropriating the media event: on the one hand, the World Youth Day is primarily regarded by some as a 'pope event', intended by the Church to improve its own image; on the other hand, there are those who see the transcultural arrangement of the media event as evidence for the vitality and plurality of the Catholic community. The latter – to quote from our interview data – highlight the extraordinary 'feeling of togetherness' and of being part of 'something really big', of a 'global community'. They appropriate the special atmosphere where – as they see it – 'everybody is in a good mood, people are singing and no matter which language they speak they understand each other' as an affirmation of their personal commitment to the Catholic or Christian community respectively. By contrast, the jolly atmosphere is encountered with confusion or at least from a more distant position by the former, who face difficulties in aligning the supposed enthusiasm for the pope with their individual religiosity shaped by reflectivity, self-communion and a rather critical stance on the institutional Church.

Apart from these differences, the interesting point is that in neither case the media event is approached in terms of religious questions in the narrow sense. Neither the controversies over ecumenism and Catholic sex morals raised by the media, nor explicitly religious matters addressed in the official speeches and sermons at the World Youth Day, are important points in our interview data. Rather, the media event displays its relevance as a representation of a lively and blissful everyday 'unity in plurality' instead of dogmatic rigidity, which is contrasted with the formal religion being represented by the institutional Church. In this sense, the two perspectives on the World Youth Day point to different ways in which young people defining themselves as Catholic in the broadest sense cope with religious individualization in everyday life – that is, their challenge to find a personal pathway through an ever more complex and dynamic religious landscape.

Drawing on our interviews we can typify patterns of individualized Catholic religiosity: one we can call *me-religiosity*, the other *group-religiosity*. In the first case, the articulation of personal belief relates more to personal self-discovery and self-reflectivity about vital matters, while the group-religiosity is tied intrinsically to a mostly local group of the likeminded, often connected to the parish, and the idea of a global Catholic or Christian movement living on in the personal engagement of its members. In both cases Catholicism is approached in individualized ways – that is, as a *possible* faith offer that has to be appropriated within the context of everyday life.

This becomes clear if we look at how the pope as a 'media celebrity' is appropriated in relation to each orientation. Although in the context of me-religiosity the mediated presence of the pope does not promise a direct spiritual experience, there can be observed a certain curiosity about how Benedict XVI acts out his new role as pope and media celebrity. Consequently, the attention is directed to the mediated staging of the pope as an 'authentic person'. This means that for me-religious Catholics the pope, presented in the media as a Catholic 'brand symbol' personifying a clear moral instance, is an outstanding example in terms of integrity and lived spirituality. In this sense, we can argue, his religious significance in relation to a me-oriented set of beliefs is not that of a religious authority but that of a mediated 'moral lighthouse' in an otherwise 'secular' social and cultural environment. The branding-like *distinctiveness* of his moral position is appreciated, but not the position itself, which is more or less rejected.

From a group-oriented point of view, the pope symbolizes the centre of the World Youth Day. He is the person who attracts the masses, who 'centres' the different happenings, interests and perspectives in the sacred ceremonies and thus is constitutive for the media event in a double sense: as a religious celebrity he serves as a shared point of reference for participants, media and audiences; as head of the institutional church, this mediated presence is seen as a recognition of young people's needs and demands within the centre of the Church, and thus as legitimizing their hopes on a more open, more liberal and – especially in Italy – more democratic Church. Consequently, group-religious Catholics are attracted especially by media representations that visualize a significant closeness or 'immediacy'[33] regarding the relation between the pope and the young people on site.

To sum up, young Catholics approach the pope as a 'brand symbol' within the contradictory context of a desire for reliability and orientation on the one hand and the hope for democratization and liberalization within the Church on the other. Thus, in the context of everyday life the potentiality of 'branding religion' lies in

---

[33]   John Tomlinson, *The Culture of Speed: The Coming of Immediacy* (London: Sage, 2007).

the possibility to resolve these apparent contradictions symbolically in the staging of the pope as a media celebrity: as brand symbol the pope is accessible to readings of continuity as well as of change.

The Power of 'Branding Religion'

We started our chapter with the argument that 'branding religion' should be seen as an adequate communicative pattern of religious mediatization. Focusing on the Catholic World Youth Day as a media event, we investigated these branding processes on different levels of religious meaning-making. Reflecting upon this, two aspects are striking.

First, if we understand 'branding religion' not primarily as a form of 'promoting' religion via the media but as a complex pattern of mediatized religion, this opens up a different understanding of the rearticulation of religious meaning-making. In present media cultures, the articulation of religion happens in broader popular symbolic forms and communicative patterns. The staging of the pope as a media celebrity exemplifies this.

Second, mediatization as branding religion inevitably goes hand in hand with its hybridization; that is, it opens up hybrid symbolic spaces that are accessible transculturally – not only in the sense of 'beyond national cultures' but also in relation to very heterogeneous individualized forms of belief. As the integration of the sacred and popular dimension of present-day Catholicism into a narrative of a lively and peaceful deterritorial community in the context of the World Youth Day illustrates, this provides the opportunity to stage an inherently complex and contradictory, even controversial, faith offer such as Catholicism across different media landscapes. However, as soon as religious institutions like the Catholic Church engage with the media, this is at the price of its communicative sovereignty.

Both points demonstrate that we have to understand mediatization as 'branding religion' as being interrelated with further processes of cultural change, namely individualization, deterritorialization and intermediacy.[34] It is related to the *individualization* of religion, as only when religion becomes a 'personal decision' its staging around 'brand symbols' or 'celebrities' like the pope appears reasonable. This makes sense only if one tries to communicate a certain belief offer in a mediatized 'sense market'. It is related to *processes of deterritorialization*, as by the staging of Catholicism in high diversity but at the same time around a 'brand symbol' the deterritorial character of this belief community becomes communicable. Finally, it is related to the *becoming of intermediacy*, as the simultaneous staging of the event around the pope as a 'brand figure' results in a moment of synchronized attention – while certain meanings of such a branded event are appropriated in individualized ways.

---

[34]   Cf. Hepp, 'Differentiation'.

To sum up, we can understand the mediatization of the World Youth Day as an interrelation of 'media moulding forces' on the Catholic Church to stage itself and its faith offer in a certain way. While doing this, the institution develops knowledge of using these media possibilities for their own (power) interests, resulting in a branding of religion around the pope as a kind of Catholic 'brand symbol'.

Therefore, as regards the way religion is rearticulated in the media, branding religion is inherently ambiguous. On the one hand, in centring media representations on a religious brand symbol like the pope it may open up access to the mediated centre of society. On the other hand, it may unfold dynamics that are not only unexpected but uncontrollable, especially for religious institutions like the Catholic Church. The last point especially can also be understood in a positive way. Mediatization as branding religion does not result in a *one-dimensional* increasing power of religious institutions. In the case of the World Youth Day the Catholic Church is not able to 'use' the media to 'affect' audiences directly. Moreover, the church loses at least a part of its authority as patterns of popular media culture become the main moulding forces of staging religion. In this way religion becomes more and more a product of contestation within present media cultures.

Chapter 8
The After-Life of Born-Again Beauty Queens

Karen W. Tice

We have been made in the image of the most beautiful One ever. We are drawn to, nourished by, and stimulated by beauty. We should not dismiss it from our lives.

(Nancy Stafford, Miss Florida)[1]

Although bibles, bodies and beauty have had a volatile relationship in the US, contemporary neo-liberal and post-feminist rationalities for self-governance fusing consumerism, self-improvement, self-enterprise, body discipline and makeover technologies have helped to reconfigure evangelical Christian body and beauty prescriptions. They have revamped the historical relationship between Christianity and beauty pageantry, as well as generated an unparalleled growth of faith-based, body-centred makeover ministries by born-again beauty queens who extol beautification, body stewardship and self-discipline as strategies for fostering spiritual development – rather than being merely worldly diversions.

Although once condemned by many churches as tawdry displays of flesh peddling, sin and crass commercial agendas, beauty pageantry is increasingly freighted with religious significance as many contestants use the catwalks to praise Jesus. Concurrent with the increasing presence of evangelicals in the public sphere in the 1960s and 1970s, the Miss America pageant underwent a Christian conversion. The 1965 Miss America winner, Vonda Kay Van Dyke, proclaimed her Christian faith during pageant competition. She told emcee Bert Parks that she always carried her Bible with her since it was 'the most important book she owned'.[2] Church groups flooded the Miss America organization with requests to have Van Dyke speak to their congregations. In response to such favourable reactions, the Miss America pageant dropped its ban against public discussion of their religious convictions by contestants, paving the way for subsequent Christian beauty queens to use their thrones for public evangelization. By allowing such public affirmations of Christian faith on stage, the longstanding rupture between bibles and bathing

---

[1] Leslie McKellar, 'Beauty by the Book', *Christian Health* (September 2002): p. 17.

[2] John Kennedy, 'Miss (Christian) America', *Christianity Today International*, 41/3 (2003): p. 20.

suits was moderated and many evangelical women entered secular beauty pageants mediating the crosscurrents of glamour, glitter and godliness.

Since then many beauty pageant contestants have increasingly embraced secular beauty pageants as divine opportunities for professing faith and engaging in both religious recruitment and retail. The normalization of religion in conventional beauty pageants, the creation of Christian beauty pageants and the establishment of faith-based makeover ministries by born-again beauty queens conjoining beautification and body stewardship with worldly prosperity and spiritual salvation have fractured and reconfigured conventional binaries of body and soul, the material and spiritual, and religion and popular culture.

Using their beauty reigns as pulpits and springboards, and making use of both secular and Christian media outlets, born-again queens have hosted Christian television shows such as *The 700 Club* and *The Potter's Touch with T.D. Jakes*, published Christian beauty, fashion and weight loss books, and become gospel music singers. Numerous born-again beauty queens have launched post-pageant careers as televangelists, makeover coaches, pageant consultants and inspirational speakers. They use their beauty queen fame to market a spectrum of God-centred beauty programmes and products to help Christian women court God's favour by uplifting their sluggish spirits and sagging bust lines. Converting formerly profane pageant stages into pulpits, beauty contestants fuse the sacred and the scriptural with body-centred transformation, materiality and personal empowerment, and assertively use their tiara celebrity to embody and spread Christian evangelical convictions and new body theologies that celebrate rather than condemn and camouflage the flesh. This fusion of spiritual and secular discourses, both on the pageant stage as well as in entrepreneurial ventures that focus on the enhancement of bodies and the acquisition of earthly bounty and beauty, has proven to be a profitable synthesis – one that is giving birth to a new ministerial trajectory, that of the Christian beauty-queen entrepreneur. As beauty queen Nancy Stafford asserts, Christian women could now be interested in both 'mascara and the ministry'.[3]

Conflating idealized Christian bodies and self-presentation with spiritual and economic fulfilment, born-again queens are reshaping normative expectations for sacred femininity, evangelical bodies and Christian identities in unprecedented ways. In this chapter, I analyse how black and white evangelical beauty queens in the US have mobilized and merged religiosity, popular culture, neo-liberalism/post-feminism, beauty pageantry, embodiment and entrepreneurship. I also examine the ascension of Christian beauty pageants and the myriad of faith-based businesses and ministries established by former born-again beauty queens that peddle salvation through a contradictory amalgam of secular and spiritual discourses of body stewardship, self-improvement and lifestyle/personal transformation. Rosalind Gill has noted the affinities between post-feminism and neo-liberalism, arguing that the 'autonomous, calculating, self-regulating subject

[3]   Nancy Stafford, *Beauty by the Book: Seeing Yourself as God Sees You* (Multnomah, OR: Sisters, 2002), p. 22.

of neo-liberalism bears a strong resemblance to the active, freely choosing, self-inventing subject of postfeminism.'[4] These contemporary socio-political rationalities for governance, self-renewal and personal empowerment through self-enterprise, self-modification, corporeal/psychic upgrades and personal choice also resonate among evangelical Christian women and have helped to engender new incarnations of normative Christian femininities.

The Pageant Stage as a Pulpit

> God can even use pageant girls. He can use somebody besides a pastor or a missionary.
>
> (Tara Christensen, Miss America 1997)[5]

Increasingly, many evangelical women have embraced beauty pageantry for a myriad of reasons, including as a strategy for doing God's work and promoting themselves as public evangelists. Charles Reagan Wilson has aptly observed that 'all aspects of life can provide religious illumination when believers see them in a sacred perspective'.[6] Beauty pageantry is no exception. The Westernized beauty contest of individuated competition is itself a plastic form that has been altered to fit an array of differing historical and cultural contexts, personal and political agendas, and shifting idealizations of raced, classed, gendered and, in this case, sacred femininity.[7] Born-again beauty queens employ an array of meanings and justifications for their pageant participation, including following God's design, winning scholarships, promoting Christian politics and enhancing career skills. Indeed, the recent post-pageant political visibility afforded ex-beauty queens such as Sarah Palin, US vice-presidential candidate, and Carrie Prejean (whose recent stand on gay marriage in the Miss USA 2009 pageant has afforded her widespread fame on the Christian media circuit) attests to the power of the throne as a gateway to national prominence.

The visibility of evangelical Christianity in beauty pageants has steadily increased beginning in the 1970s. In 1973, for example, when Terry Meeuwsen

---

[4]   Rosalind Gill, 'Postfeminist Media Culture: Elements of a Sensibility', *European Journal of Cultural Studies*, 10/2 (2007): p. 164.

[5]   Rebecca Grace, 'Miss America Crowns Purity as Priceless Message', 15 February 2005, at http://www.christiansunite.com/Religion_News/religion02270.shtml, accessed 14 November 2007.

[6]   Charles Reagan Wilson, *Judgment and Grace in Dixie: Southern Faiths from Faulkner to Elvis* (Athens, GA: University of Georgia Press, 1995), p. 158.

[7]   Karen W. Tice, 'Queens of Academe: Campus Beauty Pageantry and Student Life', *Feminist Studies* 31/2 (2005): pp. 250–83, and Maxine L. Craig, *Ain't I a Beauty Queen: Black Women, Beauty, and the Politics of Race* (New York: Oxford University Press, 2002).

won the title of Miss America, the historical clash between bibles and beauty pageant spectacles was further assuaged. Meeuwsen was especially successful in navigating the tensions between commercialized displays of pulchritude and the pulpit, making effective use of her post-pageant fame to evangelize for Jesus. On the eve of her Miss America pageant, Meeuwsen acknowledged the labours that it took to discipline her flesh in her quest to win the crown, saying that she 'felt like a racehorse that had been exercised, fed, and groomed for a year. I was ready to go'.[8] Like many evangelical queens, Meeuwsen justified her pageant participation as rooted in Christian mission, claiming that Miss America was 'a great vehicle' for doing the work of the Lord.[9] After her reign, Meeuwsen became a popular televangelist and since 1993 she has co-hosted *The 700 Club*, a weekly TV evangelical Christian ministry with Pat Robertson. She also co-hosts *Living the Life* on the Christian Broadcast Network, and she has written four devotional books for women.

Cheryl Prewitt, Miss America 1980, also used her throne to testify for Jesus. In her autobiography, she recounts her miraculous recovery from a car accident. She had been told that she would never walk again since one of her legs was two inches shorter than the other. She later attended a revival meeting and after a Pentecostal minister laid his hands on her legs, Prewitt claimed to have felt like she was immersed in a hot tub. She then seemed to be whisked away to 'some faraway bright-shining place – a private place inhabited only by myself and Jesus'.[10] Subsequently, she testified that her leg grew two inches instantaneously.

According to Prewitt, this 'miracle' was a sign of God's power and love and, as a result, she had a burning desire to go out and proselytize to connect people to Christianity. She wondered if 'trying for the title of Miss America could be what God wanted me to do with my life; that is, if my purpose was to use the position as a means of witnessing for Him on a world-wide scale? The more I thought and prayed about it, the more certain I became that it was'.[11] Since her crowning, Prewitt's ministry has spanned Christian television, gospel music, book publishing (*Choose to be Happy*) and marketing beauty pageant competition products. Prewitt believes not only in miracles but in neo-liberal/post-feminist self-formation, observing that 'everyone has a choice to make, and … each person can take charge of their life and be the success they always dreamed of'.[12]

Following the crowning of Meeuwsen and Prewitt, other born-again beauties choose the pageant stage to showcase their flesh and devotion to Jesus. Since 1980, more than half of the Miss America winners have identified as evangelical

8   Shirlee Monty, *Terry* (Waco, TX: Word Books, 1982), p. 33.
9   At http://terrymeeuswsen.com, accessed 21 July 2007.
10   Cheryl Prewitt with Kathryn Slattery, *A Bright Shining Place: The Story of a Miracle* (Tulsa, OK: Praise Books, 1981), p. 127.
11   Ibid., p. 210.
12   Ibid., p. 260.

Christians.[13] In 1989, Miss America bestowed the crown on Debbye Turner, a born-again Christian. Turner received media attention not only for being black but for her willingness to publicly identify as a queen 'whose bible was her constant companion'.[14]

Christian mission and passion also drove Miss America 2003, Erika Harold, who was described by one of her fellow beauty contestants as 'just on fire for the Lord'. Harold observed that 'God has creative ways of using people to make a difference. We should never limit Him to the traditional ways we conceive of ministry'.[15] Harold vehemently defended her religious convictions on sexual abstinence throughout her beauty reign despite the fiery tempest her chastity platform unleashed within the Miss America organization. Harold's pastor, Gary Grogan, recognized the effectiveness of Harold's merger of beauty pageantry and religious zeal, boasting that although 'she has been through the wringer, the Lord has vindicated her. It's one thing to be bold in church; it's another thing in the public arena. She's reaching more lost people in a year than the average preacher will in a lifetime'.[16] Harold spoke at the 2004 Republican National Convention and has stated that she had aspirations to run for president of the US.

In addition to Harold, other Miss America winners have understood beauty pageantry to be an outlet for women's ministry and Christian politics. Miss America 1990, Tara Christensen, testified that 'God called her to do quite a strange ministry … he wanted her to do beauty pageants in the name of the Lord and to give him the glory and the praise'.[17] Like Harold, Christensen trumpeted the divine opportunities that Miss America offered evangelical women by noting that the 'winner is watched not only for a year but for a lifetime. No other program gives such a voice to women. When I was at the pageant I cared nothing about the crown, the money, the glitz, or the glamour. I realized this was my opportunity to make a difference for everything from literacy to abstinence. There is something about a crown that makes people listen to what you say'.[18] Tangra Riggle, a former Miss Indiana, likewise celebrates the virtues of secular pageants as a showcase, a powerbase and a source of authority for evangelical women. She claims that 'because of the state crown I now have a microphone. Miss Indiana is a platform to effectively minister to many'.[19]

---

[13]   Kara Briggs, 'Postcard from Miss America: Faith Becomes a Miss America Theme', *The Oregonian*, 15 August 2002: p. E01.

[14]   Lynn Norment, 'Here She Is, Miss America! Black, Beautiful, Brainy, and Born-Again', *Ebony*, December 1989, p. 132.

[15]   Kennedy, 'Miss (Christian) America', p. 6.

[16]   Ibid., p. 5.

[17]   Tara Christensen, 'Journey with Christ', at http://www.taradawn.net/, accessed 12 August 2007.

[18]   Kennedy, 'Miss (Christian) America', p. 2.

[19]   Ibid., p. 4.

Yet at the same time, evangelical queens face criticism for their participation in what some still see as merely tawdry, flesh-peddling spectacles. The recent ascension of Christian beauty pageants is intelligible in a shifting cultural economy where glamorized made-over bodies are increasingly indexed to signify Christian devotion, yet longstanding Christian fears of body exposure, loss of feminine virtue and containment of sexuality persist. For instance, the swimsuit competition is a beauty pageant staple that has spawned recurring opposition from both feminist and religious organizations, including at the 1996 Miss World pageant in India.[20] Ericka Harold, however, resolved this tension by simply asserting that Christians wear bathing suits and the ones worn in competition are more modest than those at the beach. Other born-again queens resolve the paradox of parading in a bathing suit while crusading for modesty and chastity by attributing a higher Christian purpose to their motives.

The Miss Christian International Pageant system attempted to moderate these tensions over public exhibitions of women's bodies by banishing the swimsuit competition, and by declaring that a beauty pageant is part of a higher purpose 'to spread the Gospel of Jesus by any means necessary'.[21] Virtue International Pageants, founded in 2000, also justifies beauty pageants as a pulpit for Christian beauties seeking to use tiaras to do evangelical outreach and testimony. To compete, each contestant must submit a character reference from her pastor, be a member of a Christ-centred church, and 'confess a personal relationship with Jesus Christ as Lord and Savior'.[22] Contestants are required to share their faith and assert their allegiance to Christian goals by 'getting baptized or [being] more involved in church, teaching Sunday school or becoming missionaries'.[23] Diane Washington, Ms. Black USA and president of Virtue & Valor Ministries has also 'Christianized' pageant protocols by establishing the Miss Christian America pageant system. Contestants give presentations on their outreach ministry and participate in a biblical Q&A as well as attend both virtuous woman self-development seminars and salvation and witnessing training seminars.[24]

Marketing Christian Makeovers and Bodily Renewal

Although religion has always helped to shape socio-political ideologies and personal identities, new faith-based excursions into beautification, body fitness

---

[20]   Rupal Oza, 'Showcasing India: Gender, Geography and Globalization', *Signs*, 26/4 (2001): pp. 1067–95.

[21]   At http:/misschristianinternational.org/home2.html, accessed 21 April 2006.

[22]   At   http://www.virtueinternationalpageants.com/christianworld.html,   accessed 5 September 2006.

[23]   Ibid., 'Virtue'.

[24]   At http://www.christianpageants.com/html_files/pageant_fact_sheet.html, accessed 17 September 2010.

and self-renewal are integral parts of contemporary neo-liberal rationalities. Neo-liberal narratives that weld self-enterprise, self-control, style, lifestyle and consumption with prosperity, mobility, self-confidence and, increasingly, personal salvation, are flourishing in global cultural economies. Nikolas Rose rightly notes that neo-liberalism has spawned a proliferation of 'devices for governing conduct' that 'implant in citizens the aspiration to pursue their own civility, well-being, and advancement'.[25] Individuals are encouraged to 'capitalize themselves, to invest in the management, presentation, promotion, and enhancement of their own economic capital as a capacity of their selves and as a lifelong project'.[26] Success and distinction are vested in privatized consumerist solutions and self-improvement efforts, not in equitable social relations and social supports.

As evangelical discourses of worldly self-actualization are increasingly interwoven with neo-liberal and post-feminist projects of self, the lines between religious and secular prescription become further blurred. The ascendancy of these logics, however, also helps to foster new psychic, spiritual and body anxieties by Christian women and thus has fuelled a market for faith-based programmes and products to assist Christian women in disciplining their bodies, improving their selves, and ultimately saving their souls. Former Mrs. America, Sheri Rose, evokes these worldly logics of individual responsibility and a competitive upwardly mobile subject to encourage body fitness among Christian women. She notes, 'Do you know that in a race, all the runners run, but only one gets the prize? Run in such a way as to get the prize. Everyone who competes in the games goes into strict training. They do it for a crown that will not last; but we do it to get a crown that will last forever'.[27]

Although historically religions always have issued edicts regarding embodiment, gluttony, purification and worldly prosperity, the shape, scale and impact of contemporary religious fervour and enterprise for beautification and spiritual/life/bodily conversion is unprecedented. The combination of divine decrees and neo-liberal imperatives for achieving self-renewal, heavenly 'temple bodies' and worldly fulfilment has proven to be very good business. Thousands of evangelical women primp, tone and slim for Jesus, and many born-again beauty queens effectively market Christian makeovers for the flesh and spirit. This occurrence should not be surprising in light of a cultural milieu in which desires to improve the self are prevalent. Over 150 makeover shows have flooded cable television since 2000, resulting in what Rachel Moseley has described

---

[25] Nikolas Rose, 'Governing Advanced Liberal Democracies', in P. Miller and N. Rose (eds), *Governing the Present: Administering Economic, Social, and Personal Life* (Cambridge: Polity Press, 2008), p. 202.

[26] Nikolas Rose, *Powers of Freedom: Reframing Political Thought* (Cambridge: Cambridge University Press, 1999), p. 162.

[27] Sheri Rose Shepherd, 'Fit for a King Diet Plan', at http://www.hisprincess.com/Resources/Articles/122744.aspx, accessed 9 October 2007.

as a 'makeover takeover'.[28] In such a cultural economy, new formulations of spiritualities, creation and redemption are deeply tethered to materiality, makeover, self-help and commerce. As beauty queen Nancy Stafford observed, 'We have a higher standard as Christians to be creative and celebrate God's creation. We should look for ways to express our uniqueness in what we wear, how we look – broadening the definitions of beauty and fashion'.[29]

Faith-based inner/outer beauty and life makeovers have thus become significant parts of Christian enterprise. Valorie Burton, a former Miss Black Texas USA, and author of several self-help books including *Rich Minds and Rich Rewards*, observed that 'the makeover craze has been going strong for sometime now. At first it was hair and makeup, then wardrobe makeovers. Now we have extreme makeovers complete with televised plastic surgery. Even homes are getting makeovers these days. It has occurred to me that quite a few of us could use a life makeover'.[30] A former co-host of *The Potter's Touch with T.D. Jakes*, Burton offers faith-based life makeover coaching for churches and corporations as well as operating an online ministry.

Many other Christian queens have also embarked on lucrative careers as beauteous makeover missionaries. For example, former beauty queen Cynthia Allen and her daughter Charity Allen Winters, a professional fashion model, have helped to popularize the contemporary cultural mania for body-centred life makeovers among Christians. Allen likens Jesus to a cosmetic surgeon, explaining that 'I turned my inner self over to Jesus Christ – the Great Surgeon who can make over even the hardest cases. He transformed my personality and spirit. I guess that is the appeal of the *Extreme Makeover* show. They take someone and make him or her into someone entirely different. That's what Jesus Christ does for us – He makes us new creations'.[31]

In their book, *The Beautiful Balance for Body and Soul*, Allen and Winters urge Christian women to embark on their own 'makeover miracle' and 'soul surgery'. They warn that our 'bodies are as much us as our thoughts are. This is why calls to ignore our outer appearance as spiritually irrelevant do not help us. Quite the contrary, the more we honor our bodies as us, as intertwined with our spirits, as limbs of Christ, temples of the spirit and bearers of God's image, the more we understand and manage well the power of physical appearance in our lives'.[32]

---

[28]   Rachel Moseley, 'Makeover Takeover on British Television', *Screen*, 44 (2000): pp. 299–314.

[29]   Jeanette Thomason, 'More Than a Pretty Face', *Aspire Magazine*, April 1997, p. 25.

[30]   Valorie Burton, 'Five Signs You Need a Life Makeover', 20 June 2005, at www.valorieburton.com, accessed 5 September 2006; also at http://mylife425.vox.com/library/post/do-you-need-a-life-makeover-sat-24-feb-07.html, accessed 28 September 2010.

[31]   Margaret Feinberg, 'Makeover Mania', *Christianity Today*, 42/5 (2005): p. 24.

[32]   Cynthia Allen and Charity Allen Winters, *The Beautiful Balance for Body and Soul* (Grand Rapids, MI: Fleming H. Revell, 2003), p. 18.

Allen and Winters remind Christian women that they have divine assistance in refining and enhancing their bodies since 'the Holy Spirit is our secret weapon as Christians for conquering the old nature, or fleshy will and appetites'.[33] Conjoining skin care principles, scripture and spiritual beauty, they urge women to 'Cleanse by the washing of the word ... Freshen with the fellowship of believers ... Exfoliate by submitting to God and others ... Moisturize with the oil of the Holy Spirit'.[34]

Evoking similar logics fusing spiritual and corporeal cleansing, refreshing and purification, Tara Christensen, through her *Cross & Crown* ministry, uses scripture to frame her 'Made Over in Christ' seminar. This seminar includes 'a strong foundation, both in makeup and in our lives through Jesus', as well as 'scriptural encouragement and a plan of salvation'.[35] A proper make-up foundation is trumpeted as praiseworthy, signifying Christian piety.

Sally Gallagher and Christian Smith point out that evangelicalism is an 'engaged orthodoxy'.[36] Consequently, many born-again beauty queens have effectively engaged the power of media technologies and popular culture to popularize religiously guided life makeovers. Although some evangelicals distrust the mainstream media and popular culture since they believe these to be inimical to Christian values, many contemporary evangelical women have attempted to purify and reshape media and popular culture for their own purposes. Brenda Brasher has observed that many evangelicals attempt to redefine American culture from within 'by converting its most seductive products (rock music, videos, commercial packaging) to Christian purposes'.[37] Through women-only ministries on the web, television and radio talk shows, devotional books and Jesus-themed retail, numerous faith-based business endeavours have been established to help Christian girls and women enhance their appearances. One former campus beauty queen, Monica McKinney, operates the Virtuous Crown, a faith-based beauty pageant business that was founded on a belief in 'the Holy Bible in its entirety and the Trinity'.[38]

Religious presence in politics, retail, popular culture and the media has escalated in recent years. Evangelical leaders have founded a myriad of religious institutions including universities, media networks, publishing houses and mega churches. James Dobson's Focus on the Family, for example, is an important forum for distributing gender-specific advice on beauty to Christian girls and

---

[33] Ibid., p. 90.

[34] Ibid., pp. 91–2.

[35] At http://www.taradawn.net/, accessed 14 November 2007; also at http://www.taradawnchristensen.com/25womensministryissues.html, accessed 28 September 2010.

[36] Sally Gallagher and Christian Smith, 'Symbolic Traditionalism and Pragmatic Egalitarianism: Contemporary Evangelicals, Families, and Gender', *Gender & Society*, 13/2 (April 1999): pp. 211–33.

[37] Barbara Brasher, *Godly Women: Fundamentalism and Female Power* (New Brunswick, NJ: Rutgers University Press, 1998), p. 167.

[38] Monica McKinney, Presentation given at the National Black College Queens Conference, Nashville, TN, 2004.

women, including in *Brio*, their magazine for teen girls that publishes stories of Christian teen beauty contestants.[39] Andrea Stephens, beauty editor of *Brio* and a former beauty pageant contestant, also has written Christian beauty books for girls including *Bible Babes: The Inside Dish on Divine Divas*.

A rash of television programmes also peddle and popularize new pedagogies of psycho-spiritual reformation, self-actualization, beauty, consumerism and conversion. Probably the best-known spokeswoman is the former Miss Black Tennessee and Miss Fire Prevention winner Oprah Winfrey, who has become the queen of talk shows. She introduced spiritualized guidance on her 'Change Your Life TV' programme in 1998, successfully merging 'spiritual counsel with practical encouragement, inner awakenings with capitalist pragmatism'.[40] In addition to such talk shows that pepper Christian themes such as testimony, conversion, resurrection and salvation throughout their narratives, numerous reality TV makeover shows use religion and revival as motivating principles for their makeover/conversion regimes.[41]

Former beauty queens have also established hundreds of women's ministries, conferences and online devotional communities. Many Christian beauty queens have made ample use of the Internet to establish online ministries, many of which focus on weight loss. Sheri Rose Shepherd, a former Mrs. United States of America, for example, maintains an online ministry, 'His Princess Ministries', that promotes her weight loss books including *Fit for a King*, *Life is Not a Dress Rehearsal* and *Someday My Prince will Come*. Shepherd gives lectures on her transformation from a 'fat, Jewish, drug-addicted teenager from a broken home' to a Christian-identified beauty queen.[42] She also offers 'His Little Princess Crowning Ceremonies', which crown young girls with rhinestone tiaras to help them 'seal their identity in Christ'.[43]

Christian weight loss programmes such as Rose's have become increasingly popular. An early forerunner to the recent surge of devotional diet, fitness and beauty experts marketing God-centred beauty, diet and fitness products was beauty queen Deborah Pierce, whose 1960 book, *I Prayed Myself Slim*, chronicled her battle to lose weight through prayer. As R. Marie Griffith has observed, Pierce preached

---

[39]   Jennifer Hilde, as told to Martha Krienke, 'Christ Before the Crown', *Brio*, 20 June 2005, at http://www.briomag.com/briomagazine/reallife/a0006107.html, accessed 8 May 2006.

[40]   Kathryn Lofton, 'Practicing Oprah; or, The Prescriptive Compulsion of a Spiritual Capitalism', *The Journal of Popular Culture*, 30/4 (2006): pp. 599–621.

[41]   Brenda Weber and Karen W. Tice, 'Are You Finally Comfortable in Your Own Skin? The Raced and Classed Imperatives for Somatic/Spiritual Salvation in *The Swan*', *Genders*, 49 (2009), at http://www.genders.org/g49/g49_webertice.html, accessed 4 October 2010.

[42]   Sheri Rose Shepherd, *Who Would Have Thought* (Scottsdale, AZ: Shepherd Marketing, 1995).

[43]   Sheri Rose Shepherd, 'My Introduction to the Ministry', at http://www.princess.com/AboutSheriRose/SpeakingTopics/default.aspx, accessed 9 October 2007.

a gospel of self-denial anchored in a long history of Christian asceticism that has 'reaped wondrously modern-day results, as Pierce embraced the body and beauty standards of American white middle-class culture as God's will for all, marking deviance from that model as sin'.[44] Since then, many other evangelical spiritual coaches have urged Christian women to avoid divine disapproval by embarking on a rigorous regime of sweat, spandex and sacrifice including Joan Cavanaugh's (1976) *More of Jesus, Less of Me*, Patricia Kreml's (1978) *Slim for Him* and more recently La Vita Weaver's (2004) *Fit for God: The Eight-Week Plan that Kicks the Devil Out and Invites Health and Healing In*. Fitness groups such as 'Praise Aerobics', 'Take Back Your Temple' and 'Believercise' have become commonplace, as many women seek slender born-again bodies and spiritual renewal.

Body Stewardship and Makeover

> We are royalty and we are called to honor our King with our bodies. This does not mean we have to become 'Barbies with Bibles'. Our bodies are temples of the God's Holy Spirit, and it is time for us to learn to treasure those temples. The spirit of the living God has chosen our bodies as his dwelling place. He desires that we, the King's princesses, honor him with our bodies. (Sheri Rose Shepherd)[45]

Body stewardship is a foundational component for Christian beautification and makeover efforts. Christian women are urged to care for their temple-bodies in order to honour God's dwelling place. Forsaking the plain and fat as ungodly, new body gospels urge Christian women and girls to tend to their bodies and appearance in order to make radiant testimonies to God's power as well as to achieve a deeper relational intimacy with God. Flab is not a good witness to God's glory, nor does it signify a morally disciplined Christian self. Spiritual accomplishment is understood as well-honed and maintained outer bodies that denote inner spiritual stamina, beauty and strength. Former beauty queen Cynthia Culp Allen and her fashion model daughter Charity Winters lament that too often many Christian women 'don't understand the concept of stewardship. All of us are born with so much potential – physically as well as spiritually – but Christians often think it is more spiritual to ignore their physical selves or dress themselves like the school marm on Little House on the Prairie'.[46] They state that 'a Christ-like Christian is wonderful, no matter what she looks like. But a sharp-looking Christian, with

---

44   R. Marie Griffith, *Born Again Bodies: Flesh and Spirit in American Christianity* (Berkeley, CA: University of California Press, 2004), p. 162.

45   Sheri Rose Shepherd, 'His Princess Devotionals', at http://www.hisprincess.com/ Resources/HisPrincessDevo/22003.aspx, accessed 9 October 2007.

46   Feinberg, 'Makeover Mania', p. 24.

godly character and a confident smile, is dynamite'!⁴⁷ Christian women, they say, have a responsibility to 'please God with the thoughtful stewardship of all His gifts to us including caring for one's God-given fleshy resources'.⁴⁸ Corporeal gospels such as those proclaimed by Allen and Winters help to reshape constructions of evangelical feminine worthiness as well as buttress the belief that slim and fashionable bodies serve sacred purposes.

Although this contemporary devotional body-centred culture follows in the footsteps of longstanding and variant forms of Christian body scriptures, Griffith argues that contemporary Christian edicts for shaping the body are distinguished by the willingness of adherents to 'accept and even celebrate the most extreme cultural body standards, converting them from social constructs into divine decree'.⁴⁹ They champion a normative, body-centred, secular makeover regime while claiming higher spiritual purposes.

In addition to marketing weight loss, the market for religious products such as Jesus-themed trinkets and fashion items including 'thongs of praise' that feature a picture of Madonna and Jesus is flourishing. Born-again queens have marketed an array of such products, including former beauty queen Nancy Stafford whose online store offers 'Jewelry with Purpose', a line of necklaces billed as 'more than a fashion statement – a statement of faith'.⁵⁰

Cheryl Prewitt-Salem, Miss America 1980, is an especially illustrative example of Christian beauty queen religious commerce. In addition to a ministry of gospel music and books such as *Choose to be Happy*, Salem also peddles such beauty pageant competition products as push-up breast pads, chandelier earrings, double-stick body tape (for binding breasts and buttocks) and competition swimwear as part of her ministry. She claims that the Lord revealed to her the righteousness of marketing pageant bathing suits. She reports that 'When I was a contestant I saw an uneven playing field. I also saw the need for the girls to be able to compete without compromise. It seemed like girls who had a budget had the advantage. But what about the girl next door who had talent drive, determination, and grit to dig in and do what it takes to win? I knew there was an answer out there so I sought one from the Lord. My pageant business was created out of that prayer'. Prewitt-Salem reassures skittish Christian women that it is possible to wear one of her swimsuits and retain one's moral virtue. She states that 'when I competed, I was modest, conservative but I also recognized the necessity of being competitive. I certainly always competed to win but I was never willing to sacrifice my standards for the sake of the crown. I searched for an answer and the Lord revealed to me how to

---

⁴⁷ Allen and Winters, *The Beautiful Balance*, p. 21.

⁴⁸ Ibid., p. 91.

⁴⁹ Griffith, *Born Again Bodies*, p. 204.

⁵⁰ At http://www.nancystafford.com/store_jewelry.html, accessed 28 September 2010.

find the perfect marriage of modesty, competition, affordability, and convenience without compromising yourself or the quality'.[51]

Conclusion

The affinities between ascendant neo-liberal and post-feminist rationalities for self-formation and evangelical Christianity is epitomized in the increasing prominence of born-again beauty queens who extol the virtues of privatized journeys of sacrifice, perseverance, self-improvement, body discipline and personal gain. They embrace, embody and preach emergent normative iterations of otherwise secular and gendered body technologies as the pathway to abundance, salvation and sacred femininity. On pageant catwalks and in their ministries, they effectively use contemporary media and popular culture technologies to peddle worldly desires for beautification, financial savvy, self-determination and entrepreneurialism with faith, scripture and miracles. They urge Christian women to embark on an endless quest to repair and enhance their bodies and lives on the road to heavenly redemption. Failure is a matter of flawed spirits, defeated psyches and sagging bodies. Personal empowerment, deliverance and success lie directly in the hands of enterprising individual women, secular makeover technologies and the Almighty. As emissaries of broad socio-cultural transformations, these contemporary faith healers have enlarged opportunities for evangelical women in beauty and self-help ministries, yet they do so by perpetuating deeply troubling individualistic and unrealistic body-centred standards for the achievement of spiritual renewal and worthiness.

---

[51]   At http://www.cpannie.com/aboutus.asp, accessed 25 September 2007.

Chapter 9

How Congregations are Becoming Customers

Rob Warner

A professor of theology asked me, 'Why did my Roman Catholic friends become Anglican just because they did not like their new parish priest?' My answer was simple: 'Autonomous religious consumption'. In a detraditionalized, post-denominational religious marketplace, the individual consumer is king, reserving the right to relocate their religious practices according to present personal preference. Brand loyalty is in decline and increasingly transient. Religion of choice is replacing religion of birth.[1] In the construction of individual or familial identity, long-term allegiance is being subverted by the immediate or imminent gratification of 'what I want now' or 'what's best for my children'. In short, congregations are becoming customers, and with new-found confidence are shopping around. Churchgoers are moving from an inherited and given denominational allegiance to an individualized choice that may be provisional and transient, reserving the right to sample other religious outlets.

This consumerist trend comes at the end of 150 years of declining participation in European Christianity. Funerals have been the rite of passage most resistant to change, but infant baptisms, church weddings and attendance at church services have all declined through several generations. For classical forms of European secularization theory, this signifies the close correlation between the Weberian iron cage of the rise of bureaucratic, rationalist modernity and the decline of organized religion, which has retreated from the public to the private, from the normative to the optional, and from the communal to the individual.[2] Moreover, in the UK this long-term decline intensified from the 1960s, resulting in the replacement of

---

[1]   Grace Davie, *The Sociology of Religion* (London: Sage, 2007).

[2]   Emile Durkheim, *The Elementary Forms of Religious Life* (Oxford and New York: Oxford University Press, 1912 [2001]); Max Weber, *Science as a Vocation*, in H.H. Gerth and C. Wright Mill, *From Max Weber* (London and New York: Routledge, 1948; new edn 1991); Bryan Wilson, 'The Secularization Thesis: Criticisms and Rebuttals', in Rudi Laermans, Bryan Wilson and Jaak Billiet (eds), *Secularization and Social Integration* (Leuven: Leuven University Press, 1998), pp. 45–65; Bryan R. Wilson, *Religion in Secular Society: A Sociological Comment* (London: C.A Watts, 1966).

the sacred with a secular canopy,[3] and the death, variously diagnosed, either of Christian Britain[4] or of God him-/herself.[5]

This chapter develops the argument in two sections. First, the religious economies of America and England are compared, and in both cases it is market-responsive churches that show greater resilience faced with secularizing trends. Second, case studies are presented from the city of York, England of three neo-Pentecostal churches that exemplify the move towards successful market-responsiveness, with the unintended consequence of legitimating autonomous religious consumption. In these case studies a church has clearly defined its target market, and each congregation appears increasingly to function as a peer group of consumers, with a clear sense of market focus, conceived in evangelistic terms. While naturally articulating faith in terms of commitment and service, each one appears increasingly to function as a peer group of consumers who have migrated to the niche-church that addresses their priority needs.

Towards Market-Responsive Churches

Finke and Stark demonstrated that America's relative religious vibrancy should not be perceived as universal growth or resilience.[6] Mainline denominations have been in long-term decline in the United States, with the exception of Roman Catholicism, which has been buoyed through the twentieth century by successive waves of Catholic immigration. Of course, first-generation immigrants, whether Irish Catholics in America or Polish Catholics in England, often intensify their piety in order to strengthen their communal and ethnic identity.

Three critical factors contribute to sustained American religious vibrancy, in contrast with the Old World. First, the sustainability of Christianity has not been dependent upon the enduring prominence of any particular organization: religious vitality has been sustained by the continuous evolution of contemporary forms of religious life that gradually supplant existing denominations. Marler and Hadaway reported in 2003–2004 that all American churches founded between 1810 and 1960 (with the anomalous exception of those founded in the 1920s) had declined

---

[3]   Peter L. Berger, *The Sacred Canopy: Elements of a Sociological Theory of Religion* (Garden City, NY: Doubleday, 1967).

[4]   Callum G. Brown, *Religion and Society in Twentieth-Century Britain* (Harlow: Longman, 2006); Callum G. Brown, *The Death of Christian Britain: Understanding Secularisation 1800–2000*, 2nd edn (London: Routledge, 2009; 1st edn 2001).

[5]   Steve Bruce, *Religion in the Modern World: From Cathedrals to Cults* (Oxford, Oxford University Press, 1996); Steve Bruce, *God Is Dead: Secularization in the West* (Oxford: Blackwell, 2002).

[6]   Roger Finke and Rodney Stark, *The Churching of America, 1776–1990: Winners and Losers in Our Religious Economy* (New Brunswick, NJ: Rutgers University Press, 1992).

in attendance.[7] This points to the continued emergence of culturally contingent variants of Protestantism, and suggests that the absence of an established church may have advantaged religious resilience, by removing a significant inhibitor to such innovation. While Finke and Stark observed that in the States the mainstream is always migrating to the sidelines[8] – losing market dominance as institutional respectability overtakes the urgent ambition to win new converts/recruits – the English free churches have been in long-term freefall since their heyday in the mid-nineteenth century. (The term 'free churches' signifies Protestant churches outside the established Church of England, including the Baptists, Methodists, Reformed, Pentecostals and Independents.) This invites the question why the English free churches were not able to reinvent themselves in the early- to mid-twentieth century, in parallel with successive waves of reinvented American Protestantism. The cultural normalcy of the established church doubtless inhibited such evolution, and perhaps the European secularizing forces of that era were too powerful. Notwithstanding the emergence of global Pentecostalism[9] and the late twentieth century rise of the neo-Pentecostal house church networks,[10] British free churches continued to be religiously marginal and culturally inconsequential.

Second, in the absence of an established church, most types of American Judaeo-Christian religion have wrapped themselves in the national flag.[11] Contrary to Durkheim's foundational antithesis between individualism and religious communality,[12] the pervasive acceptance of the self-evident priority of religious autonomy[13] is often seamlessly integrated in American religion with national identity and patriotic fervour. In contrast, post-colonial English and British identities are contested and problematic. Outside the Church of England there is no equivalent to the customary prominence of the Stars and Stripes in American churches, except in the context of church parades by uniformed children's organizations, which are themselves in long-term decline. In that sense, as in the much lower levels of charitable giving among the rich, contemporary British culture is more individualistic. Post-imperial Europe is more equivocal about yoking religion with national identity, let alone with assertive patriotism. Any relatively resilient or

---

7   Penny L. Marler and C. Kirk Hadaway. 'How Many Americans Attend Worship Each Week?', *Journal for the Scientific Study of Religion*, 44/3 (2005): pp. 307–23.

8   Finke and Stark, *Churching*.

9   Allan Anderson, *An Introduction to Pentecostalism: Global Charismatic Christianity* (Cambridge: Cambridge University Press, 2004); David Martin, *Pentecostalism: The World Their Parish* (Oxford: Blackwell, 2002).

10   William Kay, *Apostolic Networks in Britain: New Ways of Being Church* (Carlisle: Paternoster, 2007).

11   Will Herberg, *Protestant, Catholic, Jew: An Essay in American Religious Sociology* (Garden City, NY: Doubleday, 1955).

12   Durkheim, *Elementary*.

13   Phillip E. Hammond, *Religion and Personal Autonomy: The Third Disestablishment in America* (Columbia: University of South Carolina, 1992).

resurgent form of Christianity in the British context would be likely to emphasize the individual without enfolding personal piety in the national flag.

Third, the cultural dominance of neo-liberalism (giving confident free rein to market forces) has contributed to the rise of a religious marketplace, not merely in terms of bookstores dedicated to 'holy hardware' and televangelists touting their wares on TV as unabashedly as other self-promoting small businesses, but also in the proliferation of choice between Sunday congregations. Streets lined with recently built churches provide a religious equivalent to the many consumer options at the shopping mall. This increasing commodification of religion has been analysed by Wuthnow and Roof as a phenomenon particularly apparent among baby boomers,[14] and has been denounced by Carette and King as inevitably reductive.[15] In the second half of the twentieth century a parade of entrepreneurial evangelical luminaries visited England, to inspire churches with new hope for growth, for example Billy Graham, John Wimber, Bill Hybels and Rick Warren. These American preachers had almost invariably founded their own organization or church, but spoke in England at events either organized by Anglicans or at which Anglican clergy were prominent. The clear implication was that establishment remained the natural or unassailable condition of Christianity in England and Europe, tempering the innovations – and indeed commodifications – of North American Protestantism. However, seismic changes have begun to emerge in what remains of Christian Britain.

The last quarter of the twentieth century marked a significant shift in the patterns of English church attendance.[16] Between 1979 and 2005, Anglican attendance declined by 47.9 per cent, Roman Catholic by 55.14 per cent, and Methodist and URC by 54.54 per cent. The aggregated decline was 51.59 per cent. In this quarter century the average congregation no less than halved in size. However, the other free churches increased in this period by 17.13 per cent. This was by no means enough to make up for the decline in the major denominations, but the contrasting trend is noteworthy. Anglican market share declined from 30.71 per cent to 27.5 per cent, and Roman Catholic from 36.59 per cent to 28.21 per cent. This reflects the fact that Roman Catholic attendance had held up better in the third quarter of the twentieth century – Catholics and evangelicals have both shown signs of 'late-onset

---

[14]   Robert Wuthnow, *The Restructuring of American Religion* (Princeton, NJ: Princeton University Press, 1988); Wade Clark Roof, *Spiritual Marketplace* (Princeton, NJ: Princeton University Press, 1999).

[15]   Jeremy Carrette and Richard King, *Selling Spirituality: The Silent Takeover of Religion* (London: Routledge, 2004).

[16]   Peter W. Brierley, *The Tide Is Running Out: What the English Church Attendance Survey Reveals* (London: Christian Research, 2000); Peter W. Brierley, *Pulling out of the Nosedive: A Contemporary Picture of Churchgoing – What the 2005 English Church Census Reveals* (London: Christian Research, 2006); Peter W. Brierley, *Religious Trends 6* (London: Christian Research, 2006).

decline' compared with mainstream and liberal Protestantism.[17] However, Roman Catholic decline was faster than Anglican in the 1990s. This was subsequently offset by Eastern European immigration, but this growth depended upon these new migrants not returning home, as many have more recently as a result of the global recession. Moreover, Catholic immigration has evidently not been able to halt declining attendance within the indigenous population.

While the more institutional free churches (Methodist and URC) declined from 18.28 per cent to 14.28 per cent, those free churches that particularly emphasize personal conversion – the Pentecostals, Baptists and Independents – have increased from 14.23 per cent to 28.65 per cent. This last religious sector, which I have designated 'voluntarist dissent',[18] made history in the 2005 census. For the first time in English history they had more church attendees than either Anglicans or Roman Catholics. Moreover, the historic denominations have a congregational age profile higher than the general population, and can therefore expect mortality to accelerate their decline. In 2005 the average of the English population was 45; Anglicans averaged 49, Roman Catholics 44, and both Methodists and URC 55. However the average age in new churches was 34 and among Pentecostals just 33.[19] English church attendance has been shifting quite suddenly and decisively towards the neo-Pentecostals, and mortality rates will intensify this trend.

If present trends continue, the balance of market share will shift with increasing rapidity towards the voluntarist innovators of neo-Pentecostalism in the coming decade as some traditional congregations quite literally die out. The quantitative data therefore indicates that relative vibrancy among experiential innovators in the American religious economy has eventually found emergent equivalence in England. In the following case studies I shall examine three market-driven churches that are resisting the general trend of rapid church decline. In each case, albeit with distinct emphases, subjectified contemporaneity and the unintended corollary of legitimating autonomous religious consumption are notably prominent.

Case Studies: Market-Responsive Churches

We turn now to case studies of three innovatory churches in the English city of York. Two are neo-Pentecostal and one is a closely related form of Anglican 'Fresh Expression'. (Fresh Expressions is an Anglican–Methodist initiative designed to facilitate experiments in the reimagining and re-enculturation of the Christian

---

[17]   Rob Warner, *Reinventing English Evangelicalism 1966–2001: A Theological and Sociological Study* (Carlisle: Paternoster, 2007).

[18]   Rob Warner, *Secularization and Its Discontents* (London: Continuum, 2010).

[19]   Brierley, *Pulling Out*.

church.[20]) All three exemplify the counter-trend of churches that are growing in the face of general decline, and all three evidence autonomous religious consumption.

York is a predominantly white city, largely exempt from the waves of Afro-Caribbean, Asian and Eastern European immigration to the UK. In the last quarter of the twentieth century the dominant church was St Michael le Belfrey, an Anglican city centre church that, under the leadership of David Watson from 1973 to 1982, was a prominent centre of British and European charismatic renewal and was accused by the local newspaper of draining the middle classes from other city churches.[21] As recently as 2003, Robin Gill not only and rightly described the Methodists of York as suffering long-term decline but also deemed the other free churches to have become marginal to religious activity in the city.[22] As I have previously demonstrated,[23] this epitaph upon the free churches was premature, not because the Methodists or Baptists reversed their long-term decline, but because of an unprecedented proliferation of neo-Pentecostal church planting; my analysis revealed that by 2006 over 1,000 adults attended some 13 churches that had been founded since 1990.

This recent and rapid expansion of neo-Pentecostal churches, running contrary to the prevailing trend of relentless decline, demands explanation. The old free churches had declined so catastrophically, both in numbers and in residual cultural capital, that entrepreneurial church planters have increasingly concluded that any advantages of identification with them has diminished to near vanishing point. It would appear that post-Thatcherite neo-liberalism had so pervaded the cultural mainstream that the ethos was not only embraced by New Labour and new age spiritualities, but also by experimental formulations of the Christian Church, who discovered in the harsh winds of hegemonic secularization a new appetite for market-responsive innovations. It may even be Anglicanism had declined towards the tipping point where the privileges of establishment were losing the capacity to inhibit the emergence of alternative Protestant expressions of Christian community. There is much to be theorized, and much empirical research to be done, particularly now that religion in Britain appears to have entered an era of rapid mutation and diversification, not only beyond the Christian churches,[24] but even within them.

---

[20]   Graham Cray (ed.), *Mission-Shaped Church* (London: Church House Publishing, 2004).

[21]   *Yorkshire Evening Press*, 19 September 1978.

[22]   Robin Gill, *The 'Empty Church' Revisited* (Aldershot: Ashgate, 2003).

[23]   Rob Warner, 'York's Evangelicals and Charismatics – An Emergent Free Market in Voluntarist Religious Identities', in Sebastian Kim and Pauline Kollontai (eds), *Community and Identity: Perspectives from Theology and Religious Studies* (Aldershot: Ashgate, 2007), pp. 183–202.

[24]   Paul Heelas, *The New Age Movement* (Oxford: Blackwell, 1996); Paul Heelas, Linda Woodhead *et al.* (eds), *The Spiritual Revolution: Why Religion is Giving Way to Spirituality* (Oxford: Blackwell, 2005); Christopher H. Partridge, *The Re-Enchantment*

Two factors many new British churches have in common, including almost every new church in York, are contemporary worship songs and *Alpha*,[25] and both are indicative of the turn to autonomous religious consumption. *Worship Today* was published in 2001 as a compilation of the 500 most frequently used songs in 18,000 British churches. Eighty-one songs were from the '70s, 165 from the '80s, and 199 from the '90s. The songs from the '90s had distinctive emphases: therapeutic, ecstatic, subjectified and promising imminent success for the church triumphant. In a previous study[26] I developed a comparison with two previous evangelical hymnbooks – *Hymns of Faith* (1964) and *Hymns for Today's Church* (1982). Comparing the representation of the great hymn writers of British Protestantism, Charles Wesley declined from 47 hymns in 1964 to 26 in 1982 to 3 in 2001; Isaac Watts from 27 to 20 to 1; Frances Ridley Havergal from 17 to 6 to 0; and John Newton from 15 to 6 to 1. In short, popular evangelicalism and neo-Pentecostalism show signs of intensive detraditionalization, together with an emphatic turn to the subjective and contemporary.

Alpha has become the most popular evangelistic programme in the modern church, adopted as a franchise by thousands of churches worldwide, and attended, according to the official website in 2009, by over two million in the UK and 13 million worldwide.[27] The programme makes a distinctive contribution to detraditionalized subjectivism in its primary approach to a decisive experience of God. For Augustine and Luther, a convertive encounter with God was mediated through the revelatory Word of the Bible. For the Catholic tradition, the normative encounter with God is through the Eucharist. For the Wesleys and Whitefield, encounter with God arose through preaching and worship, mediated in the spontaneous encounter with the 'felt Christ'. Within *Alpha*, encounter with God is primarily in the context of the 'Holy Spirit weekend', where the experience is expected to be therapeutic, cathartic, ecstatic and above all confirmatory of the courses teaching about salvation through faith in Christ. Transcendent encounter is understood to be predictable: the Spirit is on tap and immediately available. This is culturally apposite for a highly subjectified culture that expects immediate results and has abandoned deferred gratification, but the emphasis is novel with the Christian tradition. The acceptability of *Alpha* is indicative of the prevailing globalized culture of detraditionalized and commodified subjectivity – what Charles Taylor termed contemporary culture's 'massive subjective turn'.[28] The relationship between authentic faith, doctrine and experience is significantly modified, but the new model correlates so closely with

---

of the West: Volume 1 (London, T & T Clark, 2004); Christopher H. Partridge, *The Re-Enchantment of the West: Volume 2* (London, T & T Clark, 2004).

[25]   Warner, *Reinventing*.

[26]   Ibid.

[27]   At http://uk.alpha.org/, accessed 7 July 2009.

[28]   Charles Taylor, *The Ethics of Authenticity* (Cambridge, MA: Harvard University Press, 1992).

prevailing cultural norms that for many participants and advocates the transposition appears to have gone unnoticed.

We now turn to three case studies of neo-Pentecostal churches in York that exemplify contemporaneity, subjectivity and resilience. All three also reflect the rise of autonomous religious consumption. G2 is a congregation planted out from St Michael le Belfrey, which has met since January 2005 in a sports club near the city's largest university campus. The intention of the founders, including a non-stipendiary ordained Anglican, was to establish a 'church for the unchurched'. Multimedia talks are central to the service, in place of a traditional evangelical sermon, with the innovation that they are interactive and participative. When I visited, the congregation sat around circular tables, and the informal talk was broken up by opportunities to reflect, discuss or explore the implications in small groups. This approach was closer to a contemporary secondary school classroom than a traditional pulpit and pews. G2 has for several years been among the fastest-growing and largest 'Fresh Expression' congregations, and claimed by 2009 to have a congregation of 200.

G2 is strikingly different from a typical Anglican Church, not only in the style of preaching, and a musical diet comprised more or less exclusively of contemporary neo-Pentecostals songs, but in the lack of any discernible set liturgy or regular Eucharist. The liturgical peculiarities are ostensibly because the sports club where G2 meets is located in another parish, whose vicar gave permission for the congregation to meet on condition they were defined as a mission initiative, not a Eucharistic church. In 2009 G2 expressed the intention to introduce communion, 'maybe once a month',[29] but this hardly makes the Eucharist central to the life of the congregation. Of course, any notion of parish identity had been entirely abandoned: the attendees aspire to recruit likeminded contemporaries from across the city. Focused target markets were defined in sub-cultural and generational, rather than geographical, terms.

A significant factor in the growth of G2 proved to have little relation to the intended target group of the unchurched. St Michael le Belfrey enjoys a large congregation but has restrictive city-centre facilities, with little or no prospect of significant additional space. With nowhere else for the children to go, every Sunday morning the church holds an all-age service. Although this style of service is considered integral to the vision of the church, and has been the practice since the incumbency of David Watson, the fact remains that there is inadequate space for significant children's activities beyond a crèche. Inevitably, while some families thoroughly enjoy the service together, those with more noisy, active or easily bored children can find it a considerable ordeal. When G2 began to provide a full range of specialized children's activities alongside part of the Sunday service, a number of nuclear families with young children soon began to migrate from St Michael's, and more have continued to join them.

---

29   At http://g2york.org/category/resources, accessed 7 July 2009.

Although the intention of the church leaders was to create a point of contact with the spiritual quest of the unchurched, in practice the new congregation connected unmistakably with the familial needs of the churched. These couples had almost invariably married before having children, in contrast with the prevailing cultural trend beyond the church, and so their presence might even reinforce the gulf from the majority culture. G2 aspired to be market driven by the felt needs of outsiders, but in practice the vision was redefined, at least in part, by familial priorities among existing churchgoers. Their migration to G2 was determined not primarily by missiological experimentation, but rather by a consumer preference for themselves and their children. Nonetheless G2 positions itself not as a church or congregation but a 'café-style event':

> If you are interested in exploring the Christian faith, or maybe just find traditional church difficult, then G2 might be for you.[30]

One member of St Michael's Parish Church Council (PCC) told me that G2 was strictly for outreach purposes. This carried two implications: first, the absence of the Eucharist was unproblematic because, she explained, 'They *should* come back to St Michael's for that'; second, she asserted, 'People should only be there for the missionary vision of reaching the unchurched. If they are there for any other reason, they should be told to return to St Michael's main congregation.' This attitude was hopelessly anachronistic. In common with the majority of church attendees in the UK, many going to G2 were no longer attending church more than once on a Sunday, which meant if they did not receive the Eucharist there, they would receive it rarely or not at all. Furthermore, this view of the authority of a PCC was naively unrealistic: gone are the days when most attendees' choice of congregation could be dictated by church officials. Most churchgoers attend a particular Sunday service strictly according to their autonomous preference.

Turning to our second case study, the Rock Church is the rebranded York Assemblies of God, belonging to one of the longstanding Pentecostal denominations. In some ways the church continues to be typical of classical Pentecostalism, emphasizing exuberant up-tempo worship songs and the visionary leadership of an archetypal Pentecostal 'mighty man of God'. However, and intriguingly, this is combined with a theatre and dance school, including training in stage make-up. Although contemporary charismatic churches have long since colonized the idiom of pop, folk-rock and even stadium rock music,[31] it is a significantly longer journey from classical Pentecostalism to the performing arts, particularly dance and greasepaint. In a striking, even astonishing, subversion of puritanical Pentecostal legalism, the church has a women's group entitled 'Rock Chicks'. Moreover, the church website describes their senior pastor, in a rather bizarre comparison with the movie *Braveheart*, as a metaphorical 'kiltlifter'.

---

[30]   At http://g2york.org/, accessed 7 July 2009.

[31]   Pete Ward, *Selling Worship* (Carlisle: Paternoster, 2005).

On display that day was something far more than male flesh; it was a spirit,
nakedly exposed, which said a loud, emphatic NO to tyranny & oppression,
which refused to bow and walk away from the challenge at hand, which
determined to fight for freedom at all costs. This is the spirit of the Rock and the
heart of its leader and is the true spirit of Christ.[32]

Sustaining its unconventional but emphatic entrepreneurialism, the church's
main weekly meeting is on Saturdays at 18:45. The ethos is emphatically
detraditionalized, even explicitly hostile to tradition:

This experience is best enjoyed if your traditions (ceremonial 'hand-me-downs'
with no relevance to current day requirements) are left at the door![33]

The explanation is expressly and unapologetically market-driven:

The Church, like all businesses, who are seeking to attract new clientele, must
keep up with the times, and quite honestly, Sunday morning at 10.30 isn't the
'time' anymore and hasn't been for some time either. Ok, if you are already a
God follower and you don't like your Sundays messing with, then we're sorry
but the church as an organization doesn't exist for those who are in it (although
those who are in it act and think as though it does!) It's actually more about
making God accessible to those who aren't. Why the church insists on putting on
its service at a time when people don't want to come, just beats me.[34]

Quite clearly this is a church that retains no regard for traditional denominational
loyalties. The congregation must like their Christian worship extrovert, loud and
emphatic; otherwise they would self-evidently be better off elsewhere.

York Elim Church had been in long-term decline until the present pastor
arrived in 1999. He soon closed the evening service, and then moved the Sunday
morning service from the centre of York to a school near the university. In 2002 he
reinvented the morning service in what he described to me as 'café style'. There was
an evident tension between coffee at the tables and discussion, and yet a continued
commitment to 30 minutes or more of expository preaching. This church has grown
rapidly and has become the second most popular student church after St Michael's.
It was unclear how much this resulted from the café-style experimentation, their
new proximity to the university, the pastor's charisma, or the fact that Elim is a
marginal brand within British Christianity that nonetheless enjoys international
recognition as a result of the exponential growth of global Pentecostalism.[35] The

---

[32]   At http://www.rockchurch.org.uk/about/kiltlifter.asp, accessed 7 July 2009.

[33]   At http://www.rockchurch.org.uk/communicatinglife/, accessed 7 July 2009.

[34]   At http://www.rockchurch.org.uk/communicatinglife/saturday.asp, accessed 7 July
2009.

[35]   Martin, *Pentecostalism: The World Their Parish.*

pastor also acknowledged in interview that, although they enjoyed recruitment and conversions among the international students, it was far more difficult to connect with the unchurched majority in the indigenous UK population.

A period of rapid church growth has brought its own tensions: by 2006 they had run out of space for the café-style approach, and had been forced to revert to a conventional Pentecostal morning service, albeit in contemporary idiom. If Elim's café style was conceived as a means of cultural correlation with the unchurched, which was also the intention at G2, it had been overtaken by events, subsumed by the numerical growth among those willing to trade down missiological experimentation. Just as G2 resembled a mildly charismatic congregation for nuclear families, the Elim experiment in reaching the unchurched had been moderated as a result of the successful recruitment of a thriving international congregation sympathetic with a contemporary variant of a fairly conventional Pentecostal Sunday service. If G2 became a natural home for nuclear families who were not comfortable with the all-age services of St Michael's, and the Rock Church suited devotees of Christian rock music and the performing arts, Elim evolved into the church of choice for many international students looking for enthusiastic and cosmopolitan inclusivity.

These three churches represent relatively successful reinterpretations of the Christian tradition, each attracting existing churchgoers and some new recruits despite operating in an era of significant church decline. What these churches have in common is very significant. Coming from different denominations, they share a pragmatic approach to cultural correlation. They are strongly detraditionalized, as is the prevailing culture. And they are consumer-focused, ostensibly upon the outsider whom they aspire to reach, even if in practice they also appear demand-led, shaping their supply of religion to the hegemonic preferences of their congregants. These reconfigurations, in some ways remote from the prevailing trends in their originating denominations, indicate that religious identity is no longer so determined by denominational context. Some in the Rock and Elim retain a default preference for a Pentecostal church, even if not many traditional Pentecostals have a penchant for stage make-up or café-style worship. And some at G2 unambiguously retain the conviction that Anglican churches are culturally *de rigeur*, even if they now attend a church without a parish, liturgy, conventional preaching or the Eucharist. Nonetheless, in all three cases the prevailing ethos is emphatically contemporary and detraditionalized. In each case, religious consumers have selected the 'service provider' that best meets their aspirations, and perceived primary needs of identity formation.

Conclusion

The nationwide rise of neo-Pentecostalism and the ethos of these newly reconfigured churches in York both indicate that the UK is entering an era of autonomous religious consumption. The changing face of the English church is no longer so dominantly determined by the givenness of the establishment, but is increasingly influenced by the pluralistic marketplace and the pre-eminent authority of consumer choice.[36] The religious market is shifting towards the pragmatic, experiential, detraditionalized, post-denominational and therapeutic.

More empirical research is required to explore the extent to which churchgoers are migrating from the authority of their denomination and received doctrine and ethics to the authority of personal experience and the private judgements of the autonomous individual. This is likely to mean that, in an era when increasing numbers of churches have been developing intentional contemporaneity of practice, the unintended consequence has been an acculturated modification of doctrine and ethics. New expressions of church may be conducive not only to cultural re-engagement, but to cognitive and ethical bargaining with the majority culture.[37]

The emerging trends of preference among religious consumers reflect, to build upon Giddens,[38] the reflexive project of the late modern *spiritual* self. Participation within a particular congregation and denomination has become provisional and contingent, sometimes even ironic. The default cultural option is to construct individual identity through autonomous consumption (however illusory or circumscribed that presumed autonomy). The orientation found in our case study among neo-Pentecostal pragmatists, but almost certainly emerging throughout the congregational domain, can appropriately be designated 'autonomous religious consumption'. Believers are increasingly shopping for a church.

The durability of individualized religion not only contradicts Durkheim's diagnosis that heightened individualism is necessarily corrosive of religion,[39] but subverts his most famous aphorism that religion is society worshipping itself. In secularized late modernity, religion has become the individual worshipping herself. And in churches that emphasize traditional households, religion is the nuclear family worshipping itself.

---

[36]   Rob Warner, 'Pluralism and Voluntarism in the English Religious Economy', *Journal of Contemporary Religion*, 21/3 (2006): pp. 389–404

[37]   James Davison Hunter, *American Evangelicalism: Conservative Religion and the Quandary of Modernity* (New Brunswick, NJ: Rutgers University Press, 1983); James Davison Hunter, *Evangelicalism: The Coming Generation* (Chicago, IL–London: University of Chicago Press, 1987); Rob Warner, 'Autonomous Conformism: The Paradox of Entrepreneurial Protestantism', in Abby Day (ed.), *Religion and the Individual* (Aldershot: Ashgate, 2008).

[38]   Anthony Giddens, *Modernity and Self-Identity: Self and Society in the Late Modern Age* (Cambridge: Polity, 1991).

[39]   Durkheim, *Elementary*.

Chapter 10

US Evangelicals and the Redefinition of Worship Music

Anna E. Nekola

'Praise and Worship' music is playing a key role in the 'worship awakening' that many American evangelicals say characterizes the beginning of the twenty-first century. This 'revival' of worship is marked by a renewed interest in the practice of worship as well as by a proliferation of products promising to enable better worship practice.[1] These 'worship' products – including not just musical CDs and DVDs but also magazines, books, concerts tours, and even Caribbean 'worship' cruises – belong to a larger popular movement within American evangelical Christianity in the twenty-first century that sought to identify one's personal life choices – including one's musical choices – as 'worship'. Within evangelical discourse worship no longer refers only to a specific act or context, such as Sunday church service, but it has become both the outward and inward expression of evangelical identity; as many termed it, worship has become a 'lifestyle.'[2]

With the variety of worship products available, including Christian popular music CDs and DVDs that claim to provide a worship experience, American evangelicals independently decide what these goods mean and how they will use them to practise their faith. This commodification of worship products raises important questions about the beliefs and practices of American evangelicalism. If worship is increasingly something that can be done alone at any time – a lifestyle, encouraged by the music industry and guided by individualistic motivations, where one's everyday choices, purchases and hobbies constitute worship – what are the implications for the ongoing tensions between institutional authority and individual autonomy? When the balance of ecclesiastical power shifts so far away

---

[1] See Robb Redman, *The Great Worship Awakening: Singing a New Song in the Postmodern Church* (San Francisco, CA: Jossey-Bass, 2002), p. xii. Robert Webber also refers to this period as a 'worship awakening.' See Robert E. Webber, *Worship is a Verb: Celebrating God's Mighty Deed of Salvation* (Peabody, MA: Hendrickson, 2004), p. v.

[2] The common understanding of a worship lifestyle is that it is a refocusing of one's personal and individual conduct as an ongoing act of reverence to God. In other words, washing the dishes or mowing the lawn could potentially be 'worship' when done with the conviction that even these mundane actions served God. See Heather Hendershot, *Shaking the World for Jesus: Media and Conservative Culture* (Chicago, IL: University of Chicago Press, 2004), p. 4.

from the collective to the personal that faith is something that can be maintained and practised with just an iPod and an Internet connection, how is worship itself being redefined, and with what consequences for American evangelicalism?

All of these worship accessories, and indeed the so-called worship awakening as a whole, could be interpreted, on the one hand, as simply a diversification and specialization of the Christian products market that tries to get more consumers to buy more stuff, and on the other perhaps as evidence, if one is already inclined to this opinion, of the further decline of Western church music. However, the marketing strategies and consumption practices surrounding these products imply changes in the understanding and practice of worship itself. As social and economic factors have contributed to the privatization of religion, and as individuals within evangelicalism have continued to gain ecclesiastical power to discern and define their faith, these individuals have sought to define and defend their own understandings of what worship means and how it is practised; they have sought to build their own churches and denominations, their own practices and theologies.

Worship in the Marketplace: Appealing to 'Seekers'

Changes to worship practice usually provoke controversy, and historical debates over the role and style of Christian worship music have long been especially fraught, so it comes as no surprise that the 'worship awakening' of the early twenty-first century was preceded by what some have dubbed 'worship wars': internecine battles over everything from church architecture to music. Opponents of Christian popular musics view the spread of charismatic Christianity in the 1960s and 1970s as being responsible for what they believe is heretical practice: the adoption of 'worldly' musics into the church. Yet many evangelicals, especially those adhering to the marketing principles recommended by the Church Growth movement, have insisted that the only way to evangelize and engage people in worship is to use popular musical styles. These evangelicals argue that these sounds both attract new believers to church and assist them in the personal experience of God's spirit. In addition, the confluence of Protestant Christianity with the democratic ideology of the United States has helped to produce a particular spiritual climate wherein religion has become increasingly individualistic. Within the 'spiritual marketplace' that characterizes contemporary religion in the US, many Americans report that they 'seek' a faith and/or a spiritual community that offers 'authenticity' and personal satisfaction.[3]

First, it is important to contextualize contemporary popular worship music within a history of pietism in Protestant Christianity in which personal emotions and experience rank above doctrine and institutional religious authority: as

---

[3]   Wade Clark Roof, *Spiritual Marketplace: Baby Boomers and the Remaking of American Religion* (Princeton, NJ: Princeton University Press, 1999), pp. 9–10.

American revivalism brought ideas of religious self-discernment and radical self-transformation to more and more Americans, it also popularized the pietistic hymnody of composers like Isaac Watts and Charles and John Wesley. Collections of nineteenth-century campmeeting hymns, usually assembled many years after the actual event, reveal how the practice of singing in these rustic and emotional events helped privilege hymns that were easy to remember and transmit orally, and the creation of choruses, added to hymns by Watts and the Wesleys, contributed to both congregational participation as well as the heightened emotional state conducive to producing conversion experiences.[4] In the post-war years in the US, prominent public evangelical events, particularly the Billy Graham Crusades and the Youth for Christ movement, succeeded in popularizing the use of popular musical genres in congregational worship.[5] The popular worship of the late twentieth and early twenty-first centuries came out of the confluence of the Jesus Movement and the growing popularity of charismatic and Pentecostal churches in the 1960s and 1970s. As such, music's role in charismatic worship was similar to that of the campmeeting: a tool for achieving a transcendental experience during worship but also, as in the Jesus Movement, a tool for evangelism.

The cultural and economic changes of the 1950s and 1960s weakened the authority of religious institutions overall and mainstream Protestant denominations in particular, while at the same time the prosperity of the post-war years enabled Americans greater freedom of choice in their personal lives.[6] As a result Americans increasingly began to interpret democracy and freedom through the lens of market capitalism: to be free in America was to have choice, and to be free in the American market economy was to have *consumer* choice. According to sociologist Robert Wuthnow, this shift has also affected how Americans understand their relationship to religion and spirituality, since they are nominally free to choose whichever religion suits their individual spiritual tastes. In this way, the balance of power between the religious institution and the individual has altered so that religious experience is seen as ultimately 'subjective'.[7] Similarly, Wade Clark Roof describes the changes to the practice and ideology of religion in the United States as being a 'shift in the center of religious energy' that privileges 'inwardness, subjectivity, the experiential, the expressive, the spiritual'. Roof suggests that these unsettling

---

[4]   Dickson D. Bruce, Jr., *And They All Sang Hallelujah: Plain-Folk Camp-Meeting Religion, 1800–1845* (Knoxville, TN: University of Tennessee Press, 1974), pp. 90–98.

[5]   Kevin Kee, 'Marketing the Gospel: Music in English Canadian Protestant Revivalism, 1884–1957', in Richard J. Mouw and Mark A. Noll (eds), *Wonderful Words of Life: American Hymns in American Protestant Theology* (Grand Rapids, MI: William B. Eerdmans, 2004), pp. 96–122; and Thomas E. Bergler, '"I Found My Thrill": The Youth for Christ Movement and American Congregational Singing, 1940–1970', also in Mouw and Noll (eds), *Wonderful Words of Life*, pp. 123–49.

[6]   Robert Wuthnow, *After Heaven: Spirituality in American since the 1950s* (Berkeley, CA: University of California Press, 1998), pp. 66–9.

[7]   Ibid., p. 83.

changes have also provided momentum for the 'spiritual quest'. Individuals are looking for 'an authentic inner life and personhood' more than they are 'doctrine, theology, community, or institutional structure'.[8]

Within evangelical Christianity, these larger shifts in the operation of religion in American culture coincide with a belief system in which the individual already plays a key role in two ways: first, in the initial conversion experience of personal transformation – the act of being born again – and second, in the ongoing maintenance of a faith in which the most important relationship is the personal one between God and an individual. In many ways, a shift in American religion away from the institution to the individual follows trends already established in American evangelical culture and simultaneously confers authority on this same evangelical belief system.

The music industry's marketing of popular worship music reflects this religious self-determination and personal spiritual quest. Indeed, much of the discourse surrounding contemporary worship assumes an individualistic ideology where individuals seek truth, authenticity, fulfilment and experience. Although the evangelical desire for these values belongs to a larger history of Protestant religious ideology that challenged the authority of religious institutions, it also belongs within an American national ideology where individuality, self-determination, self-discernment and, most recently, consumer choice have come to define the American experience.

The Worship 'Experience' and Consumer Choice

In the three decades since its beginnings, worship music companies have made popular worship music into a 'multimillion dollar industry' of recordings, videos, books, magazines and Internet web services for believers. Within the larger Christian music industry, the enormous popularity of congregational Praise and Worship music[9] among Christians has resulted in the proliferation of commercial recordings that focus on worship. According to Seay, writing in 2003, Christian music industry insiders described worship as the 'latest "trend," "genre," and "Move of the Holy Spirit"'; popularity was practically guaranteed for 'anything and everything emblazoned with the magic word: worship.'[10] During this time, a flood of worship music hit the market for evangelicals to listen to in their cars or

---

[8]   Roof, *Spiritual Marketplace*, pp. 7–8, 10.

[9]   Usually these songs are composed for voices and instruments such as piano, guitar and percussion, and characterized by a repeated chorus, a limited vocal range and uncomplicated lyrics; they are created to be easy to learn and easy to sing. The lyrical content of most Praise and Worship songs emphasizes a personal, often intimate, relationship with God, expressed using both first-person singular and plural.

[10]   Davin Seay, 'Worshipping in the Marketplace: What is Worship Worth?', *Worship Leader*, July/August 2003, p. 17.

at home, and karaoke-style music videos enabled worshippers to gather in front of their televisions and sing along with the projected texts. Some worship CDs and DVDs feature live recordings of 'worship events' or 'worship concerts', featuring worship leaders like Matt Redman leading large crowds in Praise and Worship songs.[11] Others featured Christian popular music stars, such as Michael W. Smith, singing a mix of Praise and Worship songs along with newly composed songs labelled 'worship'. Thus, so-called worship albums included: live recordings of churches and groups singing Praise and Worship, Christian songwriters in solo performances of their own Praise and Worship songs, Christian stars singing Praise and Worship songs composed by others, and Christian stars singing their own new material labelled 'worship'.

Although the Christian music industry initially marketed many of these worship music products to church musicians and worship leaders, recordings of Praise and Worship music have become popular with many Christians who listen to these recordings outside of organized church services. In the 1990s the Christian music industry began marketing worship albums to a broad evangelical market, identifying them as opportunities for individuals to engage in the practice of worship by claiming on the cover that the recording will make worship 'come alive', or by inviting listeners to 'Sing the Songs. Pray the Prayers. Bring Your Life.'[12] Integrity Media's 2002 album 'iWorship: A Total Worship Experience' states on the inside cover that it's 'not just a double CD … it's a one-of-a-kind multimedia *encounter*', signalling to listeners that this music facilitates a personal meeting with God.[13] Furthermore, according to Steve Rabey in the July 1999 issue of *Christianity Today*, 'through skillful marketing programs, recordings of Praise and Worship music found a home not only within the church, but on car stereos as believers began to listen to praise music wherever and whenever they wanted.'[14]

Just like the worship albums, videos of worship concerts are marketed as an invitation to join others in 'experiencing' these concerts or worship events, thus claiming to transform solitary acts of media consumption into corporate worship.[15] The back of Michael W. Smith's DVD *Worship* reads:

---

[11]   See for instance: *Revival Generation, Let Your Glory Fall: The Year in Worship* (Worship Together–EMI Christian, 1999), WTD 0229; *Worship Together Live: King of Love*, volume 1, (Worship Together–EMI Christian, 1999), WTD 0225R; *Winds of Worship 7: Live From Brownsville* (Vineyard Music, 1996), VMD 9210.

[12]   *iWorship: A Total Worship Experience* (Integrity Music 2002), 23362, and *Passion: The Road to OneDay* (Sparrow Records 2000), SPD 1740.

[13]   *iWorship: A Total Worship Experience* [emphasis mine].

[14]   Steve Rabey, 'The Profits of Praise: The Praise and Worship Industry has Changed the Way the Church Sings', *Christianity Today*, 12 July 1999, pp. 32–3.

[15]   These concerts and 'worship' events are not 'worship' services as such. Some of these events bear little to no discernable difference from Christian popular music concerts.

Witness the event that is sweeping the nation as Michael W. Smith's *Worship*
comes to life on Video and DVD ... Join Michael W. Smith and 15,000 other
worshipers and experience *Worship*.[16]

Similarly, Third Day's *Live in Concert: The Offerings Experience* reads:

On March 31, 2001 ... Whether you saw the tour live or you're experiencing it
for the first time, *Third Day: The Offerings Experience* allows you to be a part of
this special night over and over again ... Be ushered into God's presence.[17]

These DVDs and videos advertise themselves as allowing one to 'experience'
one's favourite Praise and Worship songs in the comfort of the home, inviting
the viewer to 'witness', 'to be a part of this special night over and over again', to
'relive' the worship event. But, even more significantly, the audience in the video
substitutes for the congregation and by extension the larger evangelical imagined
community; this allows the viewer to simulate corporate worship – without the
sermon or any of the other parts of a corporate worship service – thus beginning
the slippage between worship, worship music and worship as a lifestyle.

These artists' relocation of worship music onto albums of music intended
for consumption *outside* of the church challenges the traditional understanding
of worship as a corporate activity. This relocation suggests that worship, long
understood as the coming together of a religious community, could in fact be
individualized and commodified. Furthermore, producers of popular worship music,
who position themselves as spiritually altruistic since their products help 'people
worldwide experience the manifest presence of God', congratulate themselves on
providing the ultimate in American products: choice. By 'harvesting' the best songs
from churches around the world and reflecting back to people their own music,
the worship industry gives back to American evangelicals their favourite popular
worship music as well as the freedom to listen to it at their convenience.[18]

The popularity of worship albums by Christian music stars, as well as the many
different collections of popular worship sung by soloists, raises questions about
what defines a particular style of music as 'worship'. Many of these so-called
worship albums contain songs that, unlike corporate Praise and Worship songs,
are not musically designed for worship as a group activity but, like Christian
popular music more generally, are more musically suited for individual listening.
In other words, many of these worship songs share more sonic characteristics with
the varieties of Christian popular music that have long been primarily *outside*

---

[16]   Michael W. Smith, *Worship* (Reunion Records, 2002), 02341-0051-9, DVD
[emphasis original].

[17]   Third Day, *Live in Concert: The Offerings Experience* (Essential Records, 2002),
83061-06839-4, DVD.

[18]   Integrity senior vice president and general manager Danny McGuffey, quoted in
Rabey, 'The Profits of Praise'.

of church than they do with Praise and Worship. If one of the key problems that evangelicals find with worship music is that it no longer fosters active mental or physical engagement, this new outpouring of so-called worship music would seem likely to engender the same critique as the old: it is too commercial, too slick, and fundamentally inauthentic. Among fans of the music, as well as those in the music industry, this music's 'Christian' status is not in question, but how it operates as worship is, in many ways, mysterious. What seems to differentiate newly composed songs on many worship albums by Christian popular artists from songs on other albums by these same artists is simply the label 'worship' itself. In other words, many of these so-called worship songs often display little or no noticeable musical or lyrical difference from other kinds of Christian popular music written and performed, ostensibly, for the praise and glory of God but marketed as popular music for personal consumption.

Worship, then, would seem to be a flexible concept based not on the style of the sound but on the interpretation of that sound by its listeners guided by marketing and other discourses. As such, whether it is 'authentic' or not is also a matter of interpretation. As Allan Moore argues, 'authenticity does not inhere in any combination of musical sounds. "Authenticity" is a matter of interpretation which is made and fought for from within a cultural and, thus, historicized position. It is ascribed, not inscribed.'[19] Since both Christian popular music and this new worship music by Christian pop stars have the potential to be interpreted as authentic, the key to the musical difference between these songs is in how they can affect the practice and the ideology of worship. The sonic distinctions between different kinds of popular worship represent possibilities for multiple kinds of worship practice, which themselves suggest a larger ideological trend within American evangelicalism where worship is increasingly something defined by the participant and not by tradition or doctrine.

Some musicians argue that the message of worship is communicated in the text and not in any particular communal experience. For example, Robby Shaffer of the band MercyMe explained that 'worship is worship primarily because of what it says lyrically'.[20] Furthermore, when asked by the magazine of the 'Praise and Worship' movement, *Worship Leader*, to describe what the difference was between their worship albums and their rock albums, Mac Powell of Third Day answered, 'not much'.[21] Thus, if within Christian popular music worship is only the label of the season, then the boundaries between worship albums and Christian popular music appear to dissolve. Given the confluence of this consumer culture and charismatic Christianity's further empowerment of the individual spiritual agent, it should come

---

[19]   Allan Moore, 'Authenticity as Authentication', *Popular Music*, 21/2 (2002): p. 210.

[20]   In Seay, 'Worshipping in the Marketplace', p. 18.

[21]   In Davin Seay, 'Third Day: On the Way to Worship', *Worship Leader*, July/August 2003, p. 20.

as no surprise that many American evangelicals have adopted the discourse of the marketplace to refer to their everyday lives as enacting a 'worship lifestyle'.

Individual Spiritual Agents and the Power to Define 'Worship'

Religious commodities play a significant role in how people understand their faith, and they encourage the investigation into how individuals, in an age of increasingly privatized religion, practise their faith. Lynn Schofield Clark notes that, in the past, scholars of religion discussed popular culture primarily through the lens of whether it weakened or 'trivialized' faith.[22] Instead of dismissing religious popular culture, scholars including Colleen McDannell suggest that, through their interactions with objects and products, Christians learn how to 'practice' their religion. She argues for the need to look at how religious objects and products, including music, provide significant sites of spiritual meaning.[23]

Similarly, John Fiske's theory of popular culture suggests that we can also look at worship music as a cultural product whose meaning comes not solely from its authors and its content but also from its audience. Although the industry, the marketplace, the musicians or the worship leader have some power to define music as 'worship', the fans (or in this case, the worshippers) hold the power to define music as worshipful. Fiske says that we can look at commodities for the role they play in a cultural economy, where there are 'no consumers, only circulators of meanings, for meanings are the only elements in the process that can be neither commodified not consumed: meanings can be produced, reproduced, and circulated only in that constant process that we call culture.'[24]

Thus, if evangelicals are individual agents who have the power to craft their own spiritual identities by deciding how they will practise their faith and with which material goods or products, then the individual has become the primary site of ecclesiastical authority. Churches, Christian bookstores and, increasingly, mainstream retail outlets have become purveyors of goods and services in a spiritual market economy, whereas Christians have become spiritual consumers as well as seekers. In this way, worship products, including CDs and DVDs of popular worship music, are a key site of the maintenance of a spiritually sincere 'worship lifestyle' and can provide important insight into how individuals use music as part of practising their religious faith.

The market has recognized this trend, designing its products and its advertisements to speak to the individual Christian consumer. For instance, Chuck Fromm, president of the worship media company Maranatha! Music, stated: 'Our

---

[22]   Lynn Schofield Clark, 'Introduction to a Forum on Religion, Popular Music, and Globalization', *Journal for the Scientific Study of Religion*, 45/4 (2006): p. 477.

[23]   Colleen McDannell, *Material Christianity: Religion and Popular Culture in America* (New Haven, CT: Yale University Press, 1995), pp. 1, 259–66.

[24]   John Fiske, *Understanding Popular Culture* (New York: Routledge, 1987), p. 27.

vision at Maranatha! Music is to make every car, every home, every church, every heart a sanctuary.'[25] In other words, Maranatha! Music promised customers the personal spiritual satisfaction that one might experience in an organized worship service by bringing the worship and the church to them. In 2000, Integrity Music similarly linked the car and worship in an advertisement for popular worship music that offered its customers the opportunity to worship on the road. In an appeal to the stressed-out driver looking for peace and comfort, the ad stated: 'Basically you have two choices. You can bang on the steering wheel, curse the asphalt for the existence of cars, and cry into your latte. Or you can worship God. Slide Don Moen's "I Will Sing" into the deck and enter into the calming presence of a living God.'[26]

Advertisements for popular worship music, if they feature images of people, rarely depict them in public acts of worshiping. Instead, these ads depict worship as an internal and individual activity conducted in private. For instance, ads for Integrity Music (see Fig. 10.1) and Wal-Mart both depict young white women who are listening to worship music through headphones with their eyes closed. Both women appear comfortable and content as they tune out the world around them and tune in to worship music, demonstrating that 'worship' is indeed a 'lifestyle' where one can choose to worship anywhere, at any time.

Sociological findings support a reading of these images as representing active religious meaning-making. According to research by Robert Wuthnow, many 20- and 30-year-olds actively used music in their personal spiritual practices outside of institutionalized religion and organized, corporate worship. A significant percentage of young adults from a range of religious and spiritual perspectives in the US described themselves as actively engaged with music during what they consider personal prayer or meditation; according to this research, close to 35 per cent of Americans aged 21 through 45 'listen to music or sing' during 'prayer and meditation'.[27] In other words, listeners of Christian popular music and popular worship music are active agents who possess the power to define the practice of their faith.

Some evangelicals have worried about the commodification of evangelical culture, especially worship: whereas some of their co-religionists may have pure hearts and intentions, others may be opportunists seeking profit. For example, Davin Seay – the same writer who documented the 'worship awakening' at the

---

[25] James I. Elliot, 'Maranatha! Music', in W.K. McNeil (ed.), *Encyclopedia of American Gospel Music* (New York: Routledge, 2005), p. 241.

[26] Integrity Music advertisement, *Worship Leader*, November/December 2000, p. 33.

[27] Robert Wuthnow, *After the Baby Boomers: How Twenty- and Thirty-Somethings are Shaping the Future of American Religion* (Princeton, NJ: Princeton University Press, 2007), p. 129.

Figure 10.1   Advertisement for iWorship from Integrity Music, CCM magazine,
               September 2003

2003 Gospel Music Association convention – questioned the commercialization of worship:

> Should worship, in any form, be sold? Does the experience of corporate worship translate to radio bandwidth, video imagery or a CD listening session in rush hour traffic? … Has an ethical firewall been breached in the Christian music industry's wholesale stampede onto the worship bandwagon?[28]

For Seay, the commodification of worship mixes two seemingly incongruous elements: worship's sacred quality and 'spiritual mandate', and the fundamental profit-seeking character of the music industry. On the other hand, Jeff Deyo, formerly of the Christian band Sonicflood, is less concerned about the commodification of worship and the potential for profit-seekers who could seek to exploit the medium. He asks:

> Who knows what the actual motivations are behind some of these worship albums? I wonder if it really matters that much. You can sing a worship song from a less-than-pure heart, but does that mean the audience can't still worship God?[29]

With this answer, Deyo asserts the potential agency of worship audiences who are making their own meanings – their own worship experience – when they attend a worship concert outside of church, watch a worship music DVD, or use a Praise and Worship song on the car stereo in order to 'yield to God' in the midst of rush-hour traffic.

Tensions over the Nature and Practice of Faith in American Evangelical Christianity

Contemporary American evangelical Christianity exists in a wired and increasingly wireless service- and product-oriented, and above all, individualized culture. Worship products, including popular worship music, invite and encourage the practice of worship outside of church, empowering individuals to decide exactly what worship is and how it is done. Evangelical Christianity has long struggled with the shift of ecclesiastical power from institutional sources of authority to the individual. Yet not all American evangelicals are completely satisfied with the industrialization and commodification of religious practices and the proliferation of worship products and services in the spiritual marketplace. Nor are they content with how the privatization and individualization of evangelical Christianity has

---

28   Seay, 'Third Day: On the Way to Worship', p. 18.
29   Jeff Deyo quoted in ibid., pp. 18–19.

led to spiritual autonomy. Too much autonomy, they argue, is incompatible with the practice of evangelical Christianity.

The commodification of worship in an age of both 'lifestyle worship' and 'unchurched' spiritual seekers reveals two important tensions within evangelicalism. In the twenty-first century, as in previous eras, American evangelicals experience the tension of living in the world but not conforming to it. Yet, as R. Laurence Moore points out, American Protestants, especially those committed to evangelism and revival, have actively used the free market to fulfil their evangelical mandate of spreading the Good News, and indeed have contributed to the commercialization of religion.[30] In addition, anxiety over the continued shift of ecclesiastical power from the institution to the individual reminds us that, although humans are commanded in the Bible *not* to serve both God and Mammon, American evangelicals *are* called to be both loyal to the institutional church as well as to their personal faith.

Recently, prominent evangelicals have responded to the declining numbers of Americans who are involved with institutional religion, calling them back to the church and reminding them that Christianity is based on both an internal spirituality and also community. Eugene H. Peterson argues that 'religion' and 'spirituality', though they appeal to different qualities, could and *should* coexist.[31] Similarly, Philip Yancey argues that as a human institution the church may be fundamentally flawed, but that it serves several key functions necessary for a balanced Christian life: it provides the opportunity to worship and commune with God, and it serves to unite Christians in a diverse but forgiving kingdom on earth.[32]

American evangelicals are thus caught in a 'double bind' between the individual religious authority they have been taught to maintain through their personal commitments to an evangelical Christian faith and the authority of American conservative evangelical culture. Tim Stafford, noting that '[t]he Bible does not know of the existence of an individual, isolated Christian', has sounded the alarm that evangelical Christians need the institution of the church to complete their spiritual life.[33] He says that Christians need to preach to their unchurched brothers and sisters to return to the church. What Stafford does not offer, however, is a solution concerning how to belong to both a faith and a national culture that simultaneously require independence from and loyalty to larger institutions.

The discourse surrounding worship products and services, especially audio and video recordings of worship music, reveals how individuals are empowered to actively construct their own ideas about what worship means and how it is done, even

---

[30]   R. Laurence Moore, *Selling God: American Religion in the Marketplace of Culture* (New York: Oxford University Press, 1994), p. 250.

[31]   Eugene H. Peterson, 'Preface', in Philip Yancey, *Church: Why Bother? My Personal Pilgrimage* (Grand Rapids, MI: William B. Eerdmans, 1998), p. 11.

[32]   Yancey, *Church: Why Bother?*, pp. 24–30, 99–100.

[33]   Tim Stafford, 'The Church: Why Bother?', *Christianity Today*, January 2005, pp. 42–9.

if that construction clashes with institutional definitions of worship. These products enable individual spiritual agents within the constraints of the religious consumer marketplace to define, structure and understand their own religious experiences, and to take worship out of the church and away from religious institutions. Both the term and concept of 'worship' are newly up for contestation with a range of industrial and religious forces vying with individual believers for control over what worship means and how it should be practised. Yet the worship practices engendered by new worship products further exacerbate struggles over ecclesiastical authority between individuals and institutions.

In conclusion, within the realm of popular worship music and worship commodities, the marketplace of goods and services has legitimated and encouraged individualistic tendencies in order to profit, through money and/or converts, from the intersections of religion and consumption. A result has been an intensification of the struggle for religious authority and the power to determine what kinds of Christianity will be practised and how. This is not a two-way competition between church leaders and individual Christians, but a struggle among multiple sites of power and authority, including denominations, the market, influential Christian rock stars, and the power of tradition itself. The point for this study is that when individuals, within the context of the choices, constraints and discourses of the market, decide for themselves what kind of music to listen to, where and how to listen to it, and what it means for them, they are subtly but certainly asserting their authority to determine the practices, meanings and culture of their faith. Other institutions may resist this authority, question it, seek to contain or co-opt it, or accede to it, but in the contemporary US context it is very difficult to deny it entirely. In that sense, the 'worship awakening' reveals more than just a market trend in Christian popular culture; instead it highlights a struggle for power over evangelical Christianity itself, what it means, and how one believes and practises the faith.

PART III
Youth

Chapter 11

The Making of Muslim Youth Cultures in Europe

Thijl Sunier

Introduction

Around 5.00 p.m. one of the central halls of the town hall of Amsterdam gradually fills with invited people. It is a very diverse audience. There are young Muslim men and women dressed as young executives, some wearing headscarves in fashionable colours. We see well-known central figures of 'Islamic Netherlands', such as representatives of organizations, 'opinion leaders', politicians. In addition there are numerous invited non-Muslims. There are official and non-official representatives of other religions; there are some local and some national politicians. There are people who are in one way or another connected to the 'Dutch Islamic scene', like myself. And there is, last but not least, the mayor of Amsterdam.

At the entrance we are welcomed by ladies who issue name tags. Many of the invited people look around to see who else is there, shake hands, exchange business cards, meet acquaintances, work at their personal network. The whole scene bears a striking resemblance to the average New Year's reception. This is actually how it has been organized. But this is the 'National Iftar', the reception at the end of the month of Ramadan. It is organized as part of the yearly 'Ramadan festival' in the Netherlands. It is one of the last events of four weeks during which there has been a variety of activities that revolve around the Islamic fasting period. There are cooking competitions, public lectures, music, Islamic fashion events, film, all very much designed to provide this Islamic obligation with a flavour of modern spirituality that perfectly fits the social environment in which young Muslims in Europe function.[1]

In 2006 Dutch television showed a so-called 'video-testimony'. The maker, Samir A., is one of the protagonists of the Hofstad group, a network of alleged Muslim terrorists in the Netherlands who had been arrested by the police in late 2004, following the murder of filmmaker Theo van Gogh that November. The message was the first one of this kind turning up in the Netherlands. The news programme *NOVA* dedicated a special item to the case in September 2006, in

---

[1]   See http://www.ramadanfestival.nl/index.php?s=&kdatum=01-2009, accessed 23 September 2010.

which experts on Islam were asked about the religious meaning of such practices and about the religious convictions of the suicide killer.

The video-testimony has become a well-known means by which Palestinian suicide bombers publicly announce their intended attacks on Israeli targets. In the short performance, generally some ten minutes, the bomber explains his/her planned attack, and motivations based on quotes from the Quran and other sources. He or she explains the political goal of the attack, and salutes his or her family, rejoicing about their reunion in Heaven. The practice was soon to be taken over by Al Qaeda bombers. The perpetrators of the bombings on the London Underground in July 2005 issued a similar statement. Most of the video-messages of this sort have an ominous, sometimes sinister outlook. The more professionally made videos have background music, images of previous attacks, a well-thought-out camera direction and a well-prepared statement. The performer looks straight at the camera, addressing the spectator directly. We should keep in mind that these kinds of video-message have also become standard communicative devices of many radical Islamist organizations. For quite some years Al Qaeda leader Osama Bin Laden has been sending out his messages through videos that are distributed and submitted to broadcasting companies. His facial expression, his gestures, his well-chosen words, his phrasing and timing should be considered as a particular communicative style that has been mimicked by many other radicals.

On the video at stake here we see Samir A. dressed in a white suit and a black waistcoat, a scarf around his head and an automatic gun against the wall behind him. In perfect classical Arabic he first addresses his parents, warning them to obey God and to follow the Quran. He addresses his fellow members of the Hofstad group to encourage them in their struggle. He then gives a warning to the Dutch audience.

By mimicking the gestures of Bin Laden, Samir A. replicates meticulously his style and performance. According to some of the experts in the news item, this is a means to invoke respect from among young fellow Muslims. His public is principally Dutch society and his message is designed for a primarily non-Islamic audience. Samir A. knew that his performance would have an impact on the Dutch public. Certainly since Al Qaeda applied and elaborated this strategic device, the communication with the 'West' and with the 'enemy' has become much more important in determining and developing the particular format and language used. The careful composition of the video-testimony and the specific narrational build-up reveals a thorough understanding and application of particular figures of performative style and figures of speech that make sense in the 'West'.

The common-sense explanation of these two seemingly contrasting cases would be that they exhibit the two sides of integration. Samir A. represents the world of a small number of young Muslims who are said to have almost completely disengaged themselves from mainstream society. The organizers and participants of the National Iftar and the other activities during the Ramadan festival, on the other hand, are well on the way to turning their 'problematic' religion into a cultural relic comparable to Christmas or Easter. The argument I want to put forward, however, is that the two cases have much in common: they are both contemporary examples of the making of religious selves among Muslim youth in Western Europe.

The cases and the data presented below are part of a research project I am piloting that deals with the reproduction and reconstruction of religious practices and outlooks among young people of Muslim background in Europe and the role of modern mass media in this process. In this chapter I shall map out some theoretical lines along which the project is set up.

Religion and Individualization

The mass immigration of people with an Islamic background to Europe in the second half of the twentieth century has often been explained as the beginning of a series of fundamental transformations in the make-up of Islam. Not only has it caused a change in the social structure of indigenous Islamic communities; it has led to a fragmentation of religious normative thinking. In the past few years we have witnessed a sharp increase of studies that deal with the question of how Islam has been transformed in the new European context and what this means for religiosity. A considerable number of authors on Islam argue that with the spread of modern mass media and the continuous process of globalization, normative religious frameworks have been critically undermined and there is a gradual retreat of religion from the public realm.[2] This process, it is argued, has been instrumental in the spread of individualized 'copy-past Islam', especially among young Muslims. This so-called 'individualization thesis' also assumes the de-legitimation of religious authority: by using all kinds of modern (re)sources young Muslim create their own Islamic self-understanding for which there is no need for religious authority.[3] One of the consequent effects, it is argued, is that many young Muslims are turning into unpredictable – even dangerous – subjects. Some have argued that the migration process itself is instrumental in this transformation because it has unsettled the social texture from which Muslims migrated. This has led to a critical attitude among second-generation Muslims in Europe towards the 'Islam of the parents'.[4] That is to say, young Muslims break away from the 'Islamic culture' of their parents in search of a pure Islam. Thus Nederveen Pieterse has argued that

---

[2]   See, for example, J. Cesari, *L'islam à l'épreuve de l'Occident* (Paris: La Découverte, 2004).

[3]   S. Amir-Moazami and A. Salvatore, 'Gender, Generation, and the Reform of Tradition: from Muslim Majority Societies to Western Europe', in S. Allievi and J.S. Nielsen.(eds), *Muslim Networks and Transnational Communities in and across Europe* (Leiden: Brill, 2003), pp. 52–77; F. Peter, 'Individualization and Religious Authority in Western European Islam', *Islam and Christian–Muslim Relations*, 17/1 (2006): pp. 105–18.

[4]   See, for example, P. Mandaville, *Transnational Muslim Politics* (London: Routledge, 2001); P. Mandaville, 'Towards a Critical Islam: European Muslims and the

it is not the manifold religious practices that travel; only the Quran is portable.[5] Others have argued that it is the engagement, or should we say confrontation, of Islam with democracy and 'Western values' that has caused these transformations.[6] Transformations are thus understood in the context of a more general process of modernization in which religion retreats into the private sphere.

A considerable part of both qualitative as well as quantitative studies takes up the individualization thesis and assumes that young Muslims will increasingly neglect religious obligations and will eventually lose their religious convictions altogether.[7] On the other hand, there is a growing number of studies that deal with the opposite, namely why a number of young people opt for radical versions of Islamic thinking.[8]

Since the attacks on the Twin Towers in New York in 2001 and subsequent events in several cities in Europe, there is enormous interest in why and under what circumstances young people radicalize. This interest has of course to do with security, which is a prime political goal in Europe at the moment. More crucially, when it turned out that perpetrators of the bomb attacks in London were not foreign agents but British citizens, the prevention of radicalism became a prime goal in integration policies, both within the UK and Europe more generally. Indeed, research on radicalization has become the dominant field in the study on Islam among young people.[9]

Changing Boundaries of Transnational Religious Discourse', in Allievi and Nielsen (eds), *Muslim Networks*, pp. 127–45.

[5]   J. Nederveen Pieterse, 'Traveling Islam: Mosques without Minarets', in A. Öncü and P. Weyland (eds), *Space, Culture and Power* (London: Zed Books, 1997), pp. 177–200.

[6]   Cesari, *L'islam*.

[7]   For example, K. Phalet, C. van Lotringen and H. Entzinger, *Islam in de multiculturele samenleving: opvattingen van jongeren in Rotterdam* [Islam in the Multicultural Society: Views of Youths in Rotterdam] (Utrecht: European Research Centre on Migration and Ethnic Relations, 2002); M. Crul and L. Heering, *The Position of Turkish and Moroccan Second Generation in Amsterdam and Rotterdam* (Amsterdam: Amsterdam University Press, 2008); W. Jacobi and H. Yavuz 'Modernization, Identity and Integration: An Introduction to the Special Issue on Islam in Europe', *Journal of Muslim Minority Affairs*, 28/1 (2008): pp. 1–6; R. Pauly, *Islam in Europe: Integration or Marginalization?* (Burlington, VA: Ashgate 2004).

[8]   F. Buijs, F. Demant and A. Hamdy, *Strijders van eigen bodem* (Amsterdam: Amsterdam University Press, 2006); R. Eyerman, *The Assassination of Theo van Gogh* (Durham, NC: Duke University Press, 2008); A. Gielen, *Radicalisering en Identiteit* (Amsterdam: Aksant, 2008); B. Lewis, *What Went Wrong? The Clash between Islam and Modernity in the Middle East* (New York: Harper, 2002); B. Tibi, *Islam's Predicament with Modernity* (London: Routledge, 2009).

[9]   G. Kepel, *The War for Muslim Minds* (Boston, MA: Harvard University Press, 2006); Tibi, *Islam's Predicament*; J. Cesari,*When Islam and Democracy Meet: Muslims in Europe and in the United States* (New York: Palgrave Macmillan, 2006).

But is not just security that accounts for this interest in radicalization. The underlying assumption in most studies is that migration to Europe has caused a normative 'culture clash' between traditional sources of Islamic reasoning on the one hand, and the privatized understanding of religion in a secular public realm in the West on the other. This clash has brought many Muslims into disarray.[10] But where the first generation can rely on their traditional networks, for young people it has brought chaos, existential uncertainty and an identity crisis. They live betwixt and between two irreconcilable cultural environments. And whilst most young Muslims are able to reconcile the opposing requirements, some cannot, which may result in feelings of resentment and envy. It is in relation to such cases that some scholars have identified the influence of radical Islamist ideologies that promise a better future.

At this point we can observe a strange contradiction. The radicalization thesis sketched here rests on the assumption of a process of individual creativity, yet at the same time radicalization is seen as the result of extreme ideological pressure 'from outside'. This contradiction has to do with the particular understanding of 'identity'. In most studies dealing with radicalization, culture and identity are key analytical concepts.[11] The crucial question that implicitly – and often explicitly – underscores this kind of research is whether young Muslims are able to cope with the 'cultural schizophrenia' that is brought about by migration. They fall in between 'two cultures' and develop behavioural problems. The assumption that lies behind this line of reasoning is that cultures are stable, identifiable and distinguishable categories.[12] 'Culture', 'religion' and 'identity' are supposed to be basic features with explanatory power. Identity denotes something stable that individuals possess in a world that is in constant flux. When identity is not as stable as it should be, this may lead to an 'identity crisis'. The assumption of an identity crisis has been re-introduced into the study of youth from migrant backgrounds by linking it to cultural change.[13]

Acts of political violence are then easily perceived as the result of 'cultural pathology' and 'hybrid misfit'. Despite their thorough socialization in Western Europe, with its long-term democratic traditions, radical Muslims totally reject modern society and are ready to fight that society with violent means out of sheer frustration. They suffer psychological distress as the result of cultural clashes. Young people who do not resort to radical, violent or criminal behaviour are said to live 'between two cultures', which can easily lead to 'identity problems' and thus constitute a potential category of 'cultural drop-outs'. The sensationalists

---

[10]   This argument has been elaborated most explicitly by Lewis in *What Went Wrong?*

[11]   Gielen, *Radicalisering.*

[12]   R. Brubaker and F. Cooper, 'Beyond "Identity"', *Theory and Society*, 29/1 (2000): pp. 1–47.

[13]   For example, H. Abdel-Samad, 'Alienation and Radicalization: Young Muslims in Germany', in G. Jonker and V. Amiraux (eds), *Politics of Visibility. Young Muslims in European Public Spaces* (London: Transcript Publishers, 2006), pp. 191–213.

gaze at radical practices, and styles in television programmes and in popular academic writings portray radicalization as a giant step into another universe, incomprehensible to ordinary people.

The 'between two cultures' image not only assumes inbuilt cultural tensions in the trajectory towards modernity framed in an evolutionist discourse; it also shapes perceptions on processes of cultural change. A girl of Muslim background donning the veil, wearing jeans, attending university, and shaking hands with male co-eds is perceived as a 'transitionary hybrid'[14], combining 'traditional' and 'modern' cultural elements as two clearly separable fields. It is clear that this line of reasoning fits well within the domestication paradigm. The very concept of radicalization, the common-sense notions of its characteristics, and its relation with integration, assumes the secular nation-state as the 'normal' frame of reference.

Islam, Subjectivation and Agency

One of the consequences of this simplified view of religious identity, and the skewed emphasis on a relatively small proportion of young people who are allegedly attracted to violence and radical ideologies, is that there is hardly any interest among researchers in agency, let alone in new forms of religious appropriation, signification and practice that are to be found among young Muslims.[15] One of the few thorough studies on Muslim youth that does not follow the identity crisis approach, and that does not consider the attractiveness of *salafist* ideologies as the result of cultural pathology, is Martijn de Koning's *The Quest for a Pure Islam*, published in 2008. De Koning demonstrates that *salafism* is a practice of self-making, a 'normal' quest for authenticity and truth. It is a process of subjectivation in the Foucauldian sense in that the religious self develops in the context of regimes of truth and power.[16] Young Muslims do not just construct their own Islam out of nothing; they relate to Islam and other Muslims discursively.

Saba Mahmood, in her study of a pious group of female Muslims in Cairo, elaborates on the aspect of training and argues that through the disciplinary training of the *salat* (ritual prayer) these women articulate conventional formal acts of the ritual with intentions and spontaneous emotions. In other words, they identify the act of prayer as a key practice for purposely moulding their intentions,

---

[14]   J. Ferguson, *Expectations of Modernity. Myths and Meanings of Urban Life on the Zambian Copperbelt* (Berkeley, CA: University of California Press, 1999).

[15]   In the pilot interviews we have so far carried out, it turns out that the common-sense notions of religiosity hardly apply to the ways in which young people construct their religious environment.

[16]   M. Foucault, 'Afterword: The Subject and Power', in Hubert Dreyfus and Paul Rabinow (eds), *Michel Foucault: Beyond Structuralism and Hermeneutics* (Chicago, IL: University of Chicago Press, 1983), pp. 208–26.

emotions and desires.[17] Far from being a formal and externalized act of religious duty, the *salat* becomes an embodied practice that shapes the self. Mahmood understands the body not just as a signifying medium but as a tool for arriving at a certain kind of moral disposition. The body is thus trained to acquire moral capacities and sensitivities one does not have beforehand, even if one is convinced believer. Furthermore, this is a deliberative process that social actors may or may not embark upon and it should always be looked at within a particular context.

The great advantage of this approach is that we are able to overcome the paralysing contradiction between a kind of free-floating individuality on the one hand ('the ideal individual religious subject') and a suppressive and normative understanding of religious doctrines that leaves no room for reflection, interpretation and self-making. Indeed, when one explores the production of religiosity among young people, one is struck by the endless creativity of this process and the multifarious articulations between politics, religion, commodification and popular culture. There is thus no single field that can be called religious. What is more, religion is a set of mediatory practices between the self and a meta-empirical sphere that may be glossed as supernatural, sacred, divine or transcendental.[18]

Of course, the spread of new media in the past decades has had a tremendous effect on the articulation of religiosity in general. As Meyer puts it:

> The transcendental is not a self revealing entity, but, on the contrary, always 'affected' or 'formed' by mediation processes, in that media and practices of mediation invoke the transcendental via particular sensational forms ... Not only do modern media such as print, photography, TV, film, or internet shape sensational forms, the latter themselves are media that mediate, and thus produce the transcendental and make it sens-able.[19]

This is certainly observable among young Muslims in Europe, and it should be taken on board in the study of Islam in Europe. The interplay between Islam, mass media, popular culture and the commodification of religious experience is instrumental in producing new forms of community and authority.[20] A quick glance

---

[17]   S. Mahmood, *Politics of Piety: the Islamic Revival and the Feminist Subject* (Princeton, NJ: Princeton University Press, 2005); S. Mahmood, 'Feminist Theory, Embodiment and the Docile Agent: Some Reflections on the Egyptian Islamic Revival', *Cultural Anthropology*, 16/2 (2001): pp. 202–35.

[18]   B. Meyer, *Religious Sensations. Why Media, Aesthetics and Power Matter in the Study of Contemporary Religion* (Amsterdam: VU University, 2006); see also H. De Vries (ed.), *Religion beyond a Concept* (New York: Fordham University Press, 2008).

[19]   Meyer, *Religious Sensations*, p. 13.

[20]   D. Schulz, 'Promises of (Im)mediate Salvation: Islam, Broadcast Media, and the Remaking of Religious Experience in Mali', *American Ethnologist*, 33/2 (2006): pp. 210–29; D. Eickelman and J. Anderson (eds), *New Media in the Muslim World. The Emerging Public Sphere* (Bloomington, IN: Indiana University Press, 2003).

at the numerous websites set up by young people of Muslim background – and not just radical Muslims – reveals an ever-increasing diversity of forms in which Islam is imagined, mediated and performed. Simple dichotomies like radical/non-radical, democratic/non-democratic, but also religious/non-religious do not capture the wide range of expressive, performative and sensational forms of religiosity that we witness today. Rather, there are numerous practices and activities, performative and aesthetic articulations that fall outside established definitions of 'mainstream' religiosity. For example, an Islamic fashion show, a religious entertainment evening, a 'halal reception', a public speech, a religious hip-hop group, an Islamic stand-up comedian, a media training session for Muslims, a training session for Muslim women to learn how to act in public, an Islamic healing session aimed at strengthening self-confidence, the public appearance of women in *niqaab* or *chadori*, the production of video-testimonies, all pertain to the religious realm. For the people involved in these kinds of activities they are utterly relevant in the making of the religious self and the constitution of a religious community, but they are still largely neglected in mainstream studies on Islam in Europe.

There is a enormous increase in semi-religious activities and practices that do not fit the picture of 'normal' religiosity. Commodification and mass mediatization of Islam have a tremendous impact on the production and expression of religiosity. Contemporary notions of religiosity and religious belonging are rooted in current experiences of believers rather than in conventional exegesis of religious texts. Traditional forms of religious knowledge and conveyance no longer match young people's lifeworlds. Today young Muslims in Europe feel, more than ever, the need to reflect on the origins of their religion and reconcile them with their experiences. The complexities of modern urban life in which the majority of young Muslims live require specific competences. Modern media have not only caused a 'globalization of Muslim affairs', but have also created *new* publics that could not be reached by traditional leaders and traditional means. These new publics ask new questions and challenge the traditional production of knowledge by *ulama*.

Reaching a public today requires much more than knowing traditional texts and commentaries. Spokespersons among Muslims must be sensitive about what goes on in the minds of believers, what takes place on a local, but also on a national and transnational, level and form an opinion about it. It thus requires knowledge about what goes on in the world and at home, and the intellectual ability to 'translate' that into a religious discourse that makes sense and appeals to people. This has resulted in a fragmentation and multiplication of publics that often have to be addressed at once, and, not least, in an unsettling of religious authority altogether.[21] Next to the imams and the spokespersons of Muslims organizations, there are new types and new forms and styles of religious leadership that do not fit the traditional picture of an Islamic leader. Their number is increasing rapidly. In all countries of Europe with a considerable Muslim population we see the emergence of persons who are important players in the Islamic field, yet they can no longer be linked to particular

---

21   See Schulz, 'Promises'.

organizations or movements. They are preachers and at the same time they are opinion leaders, public figures who act on certain situations and events. Sometimes they emerge from within the ranks of organizations and, while becoming publicly known, they tend to detach from their original organizational bedrock and become free-floating public figures. Some are known only in a relatively limited public realm, or they emerge and disappear after a short while. They deliver speeches, appear in the media to comment on events and in some cases they have become the centre of new devotional practices and beliefs. Sometimes they act from a great distance and count more as a source of inspiration than as a tangible figure *in situ*. Sometimes these figures are genuine celebrities who owe their public role and popularity to modern mass media. They have supporters, fans, who attend their lectures and public performances, and they have persuasive qualities.

The best-known and controversial celebrity at this moment is undoubtedly the Swiss Muslim philosopher Tariq Ramadan, who worked for the Rotterdam municipality and the Rotterdam University, but was sacked recently because of his alleged links with the Iranian government. Ramadan is at once immensely popular among well-educated young Muslims in Europe and highly suspected by European governments. They do not know how to deal with him. Domestication of Islam requires a leadership that fits within the integration regime. Religious leadership is probably the most sensitive issue in the contemporary debate on Islam in Europe. The styles of leadership just sketched are elusive and therefore perceived as a threat to the public order. Tariq Ramadan, but also Tariq Ali, Fethullah Gülen, Amina Wadud, Yusuf al-Qaradawi are but a few names among the many Muslim intellectuals who are extremely popular among young Muslims today. But there are many more, less well known figures that play an important role in the lives of young people, not least women. Their writings have sometimes been analysed by scholars on Islamic theology, but there are no thorough analyses of the basis of their popularity and how authority is produced and how community building revolves around these leaders.

Styles of Religiosity

A way to overcome the omissions and fallacies in much of the present day research on young Muslims is by elaborating on recent insights in the study of youth cultures and bringing back the agency of young Muslims into the analysis, by approaching them not as victims of a cultural clash and trapped in an identity crisis, but as active agents of their own cultural environment. Instead of treating Muslims' cultural practices as transitory and dependent phenomenon, they should be assessed as (youth) cultural traits in their own right.[22]

---

[22]   See V. Amit-Talai and H. Wulff (eds), *Youth Cultures: A Cross-Cultural Perspective* (London: Routledge, 1995).

'Ritual', 'style', 'performance' and 'commodification' are in my view central concepts in the understanding of the reproduction of Islam among young people in Europe and they need further elaboration. The concept of style denotes the specific forms in which religious belonging and religious practices among young Muslims take shape. Not only does style fit better with the mediatized, public and sensational forms of religion we encounter today; together with ritual it covers more adequately the wide range of practices that we wish to include. Style, loosely defined as a 'signifying practice', has been coined as a central analytical tool by the CCCS of the University of Birmingham in the 1970s in their studies on youth culture. The 'Birmingham School' shifted the attention from culture and cultural change as a source of coercion, stress and conflict to the active role youths play in the creation of youth cultures, and to the visible and performative aspects of culture.[23] Style is continually reproduced. It is not the expressive outcome of a preconceived identity, but rather a practice that generates identity. Style is an prerequisite of modern religious subjectivation.

James Ferguson has reconsidered the concept of style by elaborating some essential aspects. One important issue concerns the role of discipline and power.[24] Ferguson contends that style as it was conceptualized by the CCCS might easily slip into a sort of voluntarism. Youths adopt any style they like and drop it as they wish. But style is not simply 'having ideas', but an embodied practice that is durable and assumes cultivation and disciplining. In short, it assumes an achieved competence in performing a certain style and this resonates well with Mahmood's insights into embodiment and discipline discussed above. There is thus no principal distinction between the ways in which religious styles on the one hand and subcultural youth styles on the other are adopted and embodied. Ferguson also pointed to the 'interactionist fallacies' that are often attached to style. If we consider style as the externalized (superficial) form of human interaction, if we assume that style is just externalized expression of internalized convictions, we tend to overlook the power relations in which the microsociological logic of styling takes place. Styles develop in a situation of duress and this is also the case with religious styles. Donning the headscarf, for example, is a stylistic device, but we cannot fully understand its implications if we ignore the symbolic significance of the veil, its normative underpinnings and not least the embodied moral disposition that comes with it. Donning the veil is as much a 'body technique' invested with passion and emotion as a religious symbolic act that enacts a certain relation towards a discursive tradition.

Religious styling, denoting an integrated set of signifying practices, has several advantages over the much more widespread term religious identity. Like ritual, it shifts the emphasis to practice and performance and the economy of discipline that it implies, but includes a somewhat wider variety of forms, acts and attributes.

---

[23]   See S. Hall and T. Jefferson, *Resistance through Rituals* (London: Routledge, 1976).

[24]   Ferguson, *Expectations of Modernity*.

The concept of style connects the notion of religion to the insights from the study of youth cultures. Styling frees religion from its normative constraints and brings back agency, without ignoring the relations of power. Style also allows for an approach of religion and religious belonging among young Muslims in Europe as alternative lifestyle and not as a cultural residue from a previous stage.

Conclusion

It is quite clear that research on the production of religiosity among young Muslims in Europe is only in its initial phase. One of the biggest challenges for research on Islam in Europe in the coming years is how to explore the unmistakable process of fragmentation, and indeed individualization, without slipping into voluntarism and neglecting disciplining practices and the discursive tradition within which young Muslims make religious selves. Religious subjectivation among Muslims is a process that requires thorough investigation. I have shown that we need to focus on the complex interplay between (1) performance and self-styling, (2) discipline, embodiment and techniques of the self, (3) authenticity, truth and authority, (4) identity politics and the public sphere. Although these conceptual clusters are not new in themselves, modern mass media have had a tremendous impact not only on how they are interrelated, but also how they come about. Research into the production of religiosity among young people starts from the actual fact that Muslims constitute an integral part of European society, but at the same time as modern mass media and modern means of communication enable Muslims to build networks and communities across borders. This is very much in evidence. Religious practices and religious modes of expression reflect multiple attachments and multiple orientations. Instead of evaluating these practices as integration issues, as researchers we must develop new ways and new approaches that do justice to new realities. It is not their position on an integration trajectory as such that accounts for their engagement with Islam. Their position in receiving societies is but one aspect of the complex process of religious identity formation.

Chapter 12

Religious Experience of a Young Megachurch Congregation in Singapore

Joy Kooi-Chin Tong

Introduction

It has been argued that, under the influence of postmodernity and globalization, the primary challenge to religious faith is not cognitive but rather the commodification of everyday life.[1] This argument aptly applies to religious phenomena in the modern and industrialized Singapore. Indeed the principal issue facing religious leaders here is how to retain the loyalty of the next generation amidst fierce competition from 'Madonna, Microsoft and McDonalds'. Nevertheless, the obvious turning of thousands of young people towards megachurches over the last decades has posed the questions: how do megachurches construct a modern and authentic religious experience that excels in the religious marketplace? What constitutes their spirituality?

The intriguing relationship between the now very popular megachurches – defined as non-Catholic churches with at least 2,000 members – and the global market culture with all its promises has become more apparent recently. Studies have attributed the growth of megachurches to their proactive engagement with consumer culture and media, and therefore to their commodified aspects.[2] Yet studies have also shown that both megachurches and religious commodification are not new issues. America has had its large churches with more than 2,000 members at the beginning of the twentieth century.[3] Also, as Moore points out, one of the significant features of American churches is their application of commercial

---

[1]   Bryan S. Turner, *Orientalism, Postmodernism, and Globalism* (London: Routledge, 1994); David Lyon, *Jesus in Disneyland* (Cambridge: Polity Press, 2000).

[2]   See, for example, Robert McClory's article 'Superchurch' in *Chicago Reader*, 6 August 1992, at http://www.chicagoreader.com/chicago/superchurch/Content?oid=880201, accessed 4 October 2010; Charles Trueheart's 'Welcome to the Next Church' in *The Atlantic Monthly*, August 1996, pp. 37–52; George Ritzer, *The McDonaldization of Society* (Thousand Oaks, CA: Pine Forge Press, 1993); Wade C. Roof, *Spiritual Marketplace: Baby Boomers and the Remaking of American Religion* (Princeton, NJ: Princeton University Press, 1999).

[3]   John N. Vaughan, *Megachurches & America's Cities: How Churches Grow* (Grand Rapids, MI: Baker Books, 1993).

techniques.[4] Therefore we might argue that what distinguishes the current crop of megachurches from its predecessors as well as non-megachurches is not so much religious commodification *per se* but rather the extent of commodification and its innovative combination of emotional expressivity with technology and a consumer ethic. Indeed, the emergence of a global technological culture has made the intimate combination of religion with consumer culture more feasible and convenient. These combinations and related underpinning values are significant as they not only create unique organizational and leadership dynamics, but also construct a distinctive religious experience and identity that contributes to the progression of megachurches. To illustrate my argument, this chapter will focus on the formation of religious experience and identity of a young congregation through a case study of City Harvest Church, one of the largest and fastest-growing megachurches in Singapore and Asia.

Religious Identity, Experience, and Young People in Modern Culture

One of the most surprising moves in recent sociology has been the centring of issues of identity into its discussions. Previous research has mainly associated identity with ethnicity, nationality or role, and seldom given it any theoretical significance. Yet work on reflexive modernity[5] and postmodernity[6] has given rise to debate about identity change in late modern societies – it argues that identity formation has undergone critical transformation due to the decline of class identities, the emergence of consumerism in which traditional forms of community and authority have been undermined by the new communitarianism and cult of the self;[7] and de-traditionalization, which causes traditional identities such as gender and nationality to become less significant.

Nevertheless, given the facts of religious revivals in many societies, especially among the young people,[8] it seems that conventional religions like Christianity have been one of the means to help people to negotiate their personal identity.

---

    [4] R. Laurence Moore, *Selling God: American Religion in the Marketplace of Culture* (New York: Oxford University Press, 1994).

    [5] Anthony *Giddens, The Consequences of Modernity* (Cambridge: Polity Press, 1990); Ulrich Beck, *Risk Society: Towards a New Modernity* (London: Sage, 1992).

    [6] Scott Lash and John Urry, *The End of Organized Capitalism* (Madison, WI: University of Wisconsin Press, 1988); Zygmunt Bauman, *Legislators and Interpreters: On Modernity, Postmodernity and Intellectuals* (Cambridge: Polity Press, 1987).

    [7] Daniel Bell, *The Cultural Contradictions of Capitalism* (London: Heinemann Educational, 1979).

    [8] See, for example, Donald Miller, *Reinventing American Protestantism: Christianity in the New Millennium* (Berkeley, CA: University of California Press, 1997); Fenggang Yang, 'Lost in the Market, Saved at McDonald's: Conversion to Christianity in Urban China', *Journal for the Scientific Study of Religion* 44 (2005): pp. 423–41.

This phenomenon appears to contradict the expectation that religion, like other traditional institutions, has decreased in importance in identity formation. It is therefore significant to ask, for modern people who are part of the consumer culture of hedonism and narcissism, what are the particular practices and experiences that religious institutions, in this case megachurches, have successfully established to help them to negotiate a modern self. This chapter seeks to show that it is mainly through 'authentic' expressive experience, a sense of belonging and the modern identities that are created in the process, that megachurches are able to keep their young members. Here authenticity refers to a sense of autonomy over one's life or a sense of individual self-expression that is created through forms of symbolic identification and performativity. Yet this identification can be achieved not merely through individualized forms of activities, but also through communication and grouping, including forming a religious community. In fact the collective expressive, in the form of shared emotion, solidarity, loyalty, belonging and ritual processes of identity transformation, is of central importance to the formation of a new identity. Such group identifications, which are also based on shared values, help built a common outlook on the world and assist individuals to deal with its uncertainties. The choice to join like-minded others as a source of self-expression and identity should not be underestimated.

The City Harvest Church has about 27,000 weekly attenders with average age 26 years. The case study shows how the church's construction of a whole lifestyle identity and values, mainly through emotional expressivity and adaptations to consumer culture, has effectively appealed to young, educated, working middle classes. This chapter focuses on young people as they are frequently the platform on which religious identities are negotiated and religious worldviews reinforced. They are often portrayed in religious discourses as the 'spiritual leaders of the future', a formulation that highlights the significance of youth formation for the development of religion as a whole. Also, because they are often assumed to be marketing-savvy and culturally innovative, they arguably play a vanguard role in socio-cultural change. Of course thousands of young people choose to involve themselves in megachurches for many reasons. Yet above all, as we shall see later, many come to experience a new identity and a life-transforming journey. The data were collected through participant observation since June 2005 in a wide variety of the church's activities and in-depth interviews sampled through the snowballing method. Various sources, including the church's website, television broadcasts, its online magazine *Harvest Times*, distributed literature and its members' blogs were analysed to broaden the representation of this portrayal.

Christianity and the Megachurch Movement in Singapore

Singapore society is religiously pluralistic. The *Singapore Census of Population, 2000* indicates that the main religions practised in Singapore were Buddhism (42 per cent), Islam (14.9 per cent), Christianity (14.6 per cent), Taoism

(8.5 per cent), Hinduism (4 per cent), and others. While the number of Christians may be comparatively small, Christianity is significant for the following reasons:[9] (1) the substantial growth in adherents compared to 10.1 per cent in 1980 and 12.7 per cent in 1990; (2) many of the Christian population tend to be of relatively higher social economic status in education, occupation and income; and (3) its attractiveness to the emerging young population. Christians form the largest religious group among university graduates, with one-third of graduates professing Christianity in 2000.

The growing influence of Christianity is partly indicated by the emergence of megachurches in the 1990s. Starting from tens of worshippers, these churches are growing by leaps and bounds and instil intense dynamics into the local religious scenario. There are at least three megachurches in Singapore that have more than 10,000 sustained weekly worshippers. These independent churches are notably great in number (altogether they have about 55,000 attenders for their weekly services), strong in their full-time staff, operate with multimillion-dollar budgets,[10] boast of spiritual power, diverse services, contemporary worship, and appear to have an upwardly mobile spirit.[11] The City Harvest Church (henceforth CHC) is the youngest and yet claims to be the largest in Singapore and one of Asia's fastest-growing churches.[12] Starting from a group of 20 young members in 1989, the church has attracted approximately 27,000 members within 20 years, with about 15 per cent growth each year.

Such growth is remarkable if we take into account the multi-ethnic and multi-faith secular conditions of Singapore society. Yet this development should not be seen as too abrupt if we consider how the milieu of Singapore society has prepared for the sprouting of rationalized settings such as megachurches. As a recently founded nation with scare natural resources,[13] Singapore needs to do 'everything that is necessary to achieve capitalist growth',[14] which notably includes enforcing a centralized rational management system that takes full responsibility for almost all aspects of the everyday life of its citizens. Thus there are clear expectations of well-ordered and standardized services, rules and decision-making processes in both private and public settings. In this sense, clearly, the megachurches, which

[9]   C.K. Tong, 'The Rationalization of Religion in Singapore', in J.H. Ong *et al.* (eds), *Understanding Singapore Society* (Singapore: Times Academic Press, 1997), pp. 198–215.

[10]   In the case of City Harvest Church, its budget for the year 2002 was $24 million: Edwin Koo, 'Singapore's Pop Pastor Combines Gospel and Glitz', Reuters, 4 July 2002, at http://wwrn.org/articles/11716/?&place=singapore&section=other-groups, accessed 4 October 2010 .

[11]   FCBC, 'Rise of New Churches', at http://www.fcbc.org.sg/fcbc_mediacenter_009.asp, accessed 4 October 2010.

[12]   At http://www.chc.org.sg, accessed 23 September 2010.

[13]   Singapore became independent from Malaysia in 1965.

[14]   B.H. Chua, 'Singaporeans Ingesting McDonald's', in B.H. Chua (ed.), *Consumption in Asia* (London: Routledge, 2000), p. 184.

have displayed a pattern of rationalization of production and consumption,[15] have a definite appeal to the Singaporean disposition.

City Harvest Church: A Case Study

The church was founded by Kong Hee, then a 25-year-old graduate from the National University of Singapore, with a handful of teenagers, and settled initially in a single-storey terrace house with old wooden tables. When the congregation outgrew the place, the church moved to places like Duke Hotel, Bible House, World Trade Center and Hollywood Theater before it finally acquired its spanking new building in 2001. The church now runs eight services with different languages each weekend, including services for the intellectually disabled. It has also about 45 affiliated churches across the region, a bible training centre that enrols hundreds of students yearly, community services, an education centre, a bookstore, a webcast, a television broadcast programme and a magazine.

The church has the first titanium-clad building in Asia and is modelled after the Guggenheim Museum in Bilbao, Spain. It prides itself on a '$583,000 Broquard fountain, Europe imported limestone, stylistic bathrooms designed by [a] French designer, a reflecting pool, a putting green for golf enthusiasts, a 18,300-sq ft underground auditorium and the world largest stainless steel rotating cross'.[16] In its theatre-style auditorium, which is the largest column-free sanctuary in the Southeast Asian Peninsula, there is a centre stage designed by a top New York stage designer, an LED video-screen, the largest and of the highest resolution in Singapore, and a world-leading 60-channel sound console. This postmodern and pastiche architecture contributes to form a sort of world-class theatre experience for its audience. More significantly, this building is a steadfast exhibition of the church's promoted value, namely excellence. This can be seen from Kong Hee's comments about the church building project,

> … all the finer details of the entire construction were extremely vital to the church leadership. The cleanliness and hygiene, the greenery and landscaping, the positioning of our furniture, the comfort of our chairs, the color scheme and lightings of our halls, the quality of air in the building, the paint job, the cleaning of unsightly scratch marks, fingerprints and sawdust in the facility were all important details that reflected excellence.[17]

---

[15]   J.K. Tong, 'McDonaldization and the Mega-Church: A Case Study of City Harvest Church in Singapore', in Pattana Kitiarsa (ed.), *Religious Commodications in Asia* (London: Routledge, 2008), pp. 186–204.

[16]   At http://www.chc.org.sg.

[17]   Hee Kong, 'Understanding Excellence', at http://www.chc.org.sg/harvesttimes/ht_17/ht_17_01a.asp, accessed 4 October 2010, .

Values visibly make a difference. This difference is revealed not merely through the church building, but also through the extra and professional facilities provided by the church. The church has a bookstore that sells CDs, books and knick-knacks (located at the main entrance so that purchases can be made both on entering and leaving), coffee carts along the driveway, an open-air rooftop garden and a spacious cafeteria with free wireless broadband, the first Singapore church that offers such a service. The church provides hundreds of shuttles to transport people to the church from every train station every weekend and offers more than 30 types of ministries for people to volunteer in. Arguably the well-resourced building and its comprehensive facilities have created a less churchy and more a one-stop-mall impression of the church.

Nevertheless, what is outstanding about this church is not its architecture or facilities, but the unique religious experience that presents its postmodern consumers with intimate attachments and effervescent services. Meetings held in the gorgeous building are bound up with expectations and entertainment – with spotlights beaming onto the stage, enthusiastic music bouncing through the hall, cameras, giant screen, lines of people streaming in – the atmosphere is infectious. The meetings 'use contemporary music and settings for praise and worship, with a choir in an environment similar to a rock concert with the related musical instruments'.[18] Thousands of young people in the audience rise to their feet, clapping and singing with vigour and excitement; at times they shout and jump, at times weep and kneel, under the leadership of the worship leader. The scenario holds people in awe and the engrossing atmosphere turns into a perfect channel for them to release their feelings. Preaching, too, is restyled to fit its young audiences: sermons such as 'Marketplace evangelism' or 'Cultural mandate' are claimed to be 'very relevant and contemporary';[19] the preaching styles are highly interactive; and the main preacher Kong Hee, who is 'young, hip, energetic' and has 'rock-star appeal',[20] moves around with passionate voice, gestures, personal stories and sometimes dramatic action to engage the audience. On some occasions, he launches the service into a healing and blessing session. Hundreds of people stream to the stage, praying, receiving miraculous healings and prophetic utterances; opening up their emotional and physical needs to be ministered in a unique and yet collective way. This is aptly illustrated by the following quotation from a blog: 'Going to City Harvest is like attending a concert and that's what young people like', said business development manager Eric Ko, 27, of the church's slick worship sessions, which he sometimes attends.[21]

Such emotional experiences are certainly not limited to Sunday services. They can be found in the cell-group meetings, prayer meetings and conferences.

---

[18]   At http://www.last.fm/music/City+Harvest+Church, accessed 23 September 2010.

[19]   At http://www.chc.org.sg

[20]   At http://rix177holyspirit.blogspot.com/2008/10/ps-kong-hee-founder-of-city-harvest. html, accessed 23 September 2010.

[21]   Ibid.

Cell-group meetings happen on a weekly basis. they typically start with a prayer for the Spirit of the living God to be present in the meeting. Then the participants enter into a time of intense worship, although a group might have only about 20 people. It is normal to see people clapping their hands, moving to the music and shouting. After half an hour of singing and praying, they begin to give thanks for God's bountiful provision in their lives. The leader of the group that I attended started this energetic storytelling time with something like 'Do you feel encouraged, compelled, and invited by God to share?' And members of the group responded, 'Amen!' The room was filled with joyous sounds and laughter as people raised their voices and took turns to share their stories. The message shared by the group leader was equally stimulating – it was centrally designed by Kong with stories and applications. After the participants had shared prayer requests and prayed for one another, the meeting ended in celebration and thankfulness for what God had done. Generally the church services intend to offer, as mentioned by Kong, 'inspiration, celebration and transformation … [t]hat apparently is striking a chord with many church-goers today'.[22]

Obviously many other churches besides the CHC, especially those of Pentecostalism, emphasize emotional experience and bring joy and hope to people's lives.[23] Religion has become an expressive experience that people produce and consume collectively.[24] Yet, unlike the case with most commodities, its producers' and consumers' lives and identities are readily transformed while they participate in the process. Identity change, which might be both the reason and outcome of life change, is particularly prominent among the CHC's membership because its overwhelmingly young members are in a critical stage of their lives in forming their sense of self. Young people who are seeking for a set of convincing values, a relevant identity, and a new understanding of life can easily find their answers through participation in the church. It is typical to hear young members sharing their testimonies of a 'new understanding of self'. One smartly dressed 20-something commented:

> I am a sales executive but I was timid and lacked of confidence. I wanted to change and it happened only after I joined this church. I experienced tremendous spiritual things like healing and prophesying and tongue speaking that changed my whole life. I found my gifts and I see myself from a new perspective. Now I lead a big group of young people, I speak in public and I dare to pray for people. People like me do things that others will never try throughout their lives!

---

[22] Ibid.

[23] Paul Alexander, *Signs & Wonders: Why Pentecostalism is the World's Fastest Growing Faith* (San Francisco, CA: Jossey-Bass, 2009).

[24] Laurence Iannaccone, 'Why Strict Churches are Strong', in N.J. Demerath *et al.* (eds), *Sacred Companies* (New York: Oxford University Press, 1998), p. 271.

This quotation reveals the new sense of self and the pride that people feel in being members of one of the fastest-growing churches in this region. Indeed, this is one of the important reasons that people join the church – they are proud to be a member of this big and global family. According to the church's survey in 2007, membership was made up of 24 different nationalities. Also, in view of the church's worldwide branches, it is common to see church leaders and members travelling from one country to another to minister, and overseas speakers flying in to preach. These links give the congregation a feeling of global brotherhood, and that they are part of a progressive community. Being a Christian at CHC and the idea of 'modern and contemporary' thus seem to intertwine. Furthermore, as the resources of the church grew and the cultural space for activity expanded, the church has created an increasing array of services and activities to enrich the life of its members, which results in stronger religious identity. For example, besides the routine small group fellowships, the church prepares well-designed daily devotion materials, organizes workshops dealing with issues from romance, parenting, financial education to corporate leadership as well as marketplace insights. These networks, resources and emotional supports are equally crucial in shaping the making of the religious self.

The church has endeavoured, in building an ultra-modern, energetic and upwardly mobile image, to reach its targeted person – one who is 'confident … because of education, increasing wealth and exposure to the world; he speaks English on formal occasions; his kids are hot over America's Britney Spears as Japan's Uttada Hikaru; he knows about Hollywood and MTV; he wants to get rich, drive snazzy cars, wear the latest fashion and use the latest mobile phone models; he wants to excel in his career; he doesn't like "organized" religion', and so forth.[25] In order to construct this identity effectively, a brand – a lifestyle, a set of values, tastes and symbols – has to be built concurrently to distinguish the church's members from others, which inevitably involve various kinds of consumption. On the corporate level, the church spent a huge amount of money in constructing a 'ultra-modern' church – even the toilets 'exemplify the very meaning of style'[26] – as does a stately 'bright and futurist'[27] corporate office located at the heart of Singapore's central business district, Suntec City Tower. At the individual level, people are encouraged to spend money on appearance and lifestyle in order to form their new subjective identification, which is 'colorful, artistic, fashionable, ultra-current and sophisticated'.[28] For instance, the church has recently organized 'Better Life' workshops to provide lessons to young people on improving their self-image and fashion outlook. Also, at one of the services in September 2005, a leader and preacher related how he brought his mother-in-law to Hong Kong

[25] *Church Introductory Class*, published by the City Harvest Church.
[26] Way of Life, 'High on Praise Music', 8 July 2010, at http://www.wayoflife.org/files/0ebb40475fe887c2fc42e3d254e68a5a-603.html, accessed 4 October 2010.
[27] At http://www.chc.org.sg
[28] Ibid.

Disneyland, persuaded her to try on stylish dresses, gave her a ticket to attend a concert in the Esplanade, and concluded his story by asking the audience, 'Am I not changing her life?' He even continued by indicating his 'mission' to transform the senior congregation through changing their dress. It is not surprising that this idea received thunderous applause from the young audience. Another example is exhibited through the church's Bible Training Center. In its *Student Handbook*, item no. 6.1, the general attire for students, states:

> Men: formal business shirt, tie, business trousers, socks and formal shoes.
> Ladies: office best with full cosmetic make-up.
> Hairdo: coloring and having funky hairdos are acceptable for male students, but strictly no long hair.

Obviously some people are attracted to the church because they already have a lifestyle that fits what the church offers. Yet for others, by literally buying into this corporate image – inevitably involving the acquisition of certain goods that are always functional and simultaneously a symbolic agent in the display of style or taste[29] – they can fulfil the promise of the new life given by the church. They become different people from what they were before, and their sense of what is possible for them changes. One informant mentioned that two of her friends changed their jobs, from secretarial posts to insurance agents, after joining this church, as they 'are more courageous to try on new things after seeing many examples'. Another informant commented that on her usual journey to the church on Sunday morning, she could roughly estimate which of the train commuters were probably also going to the CHC by looking at 'their age, their outfits, their Bibles at hand, even the men's hairstyles …'. Implicit in these comments is an understanding that the changed outfit and lifestyle suggest particular personalities that match the church's identities and values.

Nevertheless, image alone is inadequate in constructing a person's identity. What is also needed is the underpinning of a set of values, often presented as biblical virtues in themselves. Above all, success and freedom stand out. Many members of this church are successful in terms of educational and career achievements; as Kong once mentioned, most of his church's members are 'middle-class, a few millionaires and some poor people'.[30] Generally they are success- and goal-oriented people who highly value their achievements. The church, which claims to be a place where 'dreams are realized, success is celebrated',[31] has obviously contributed to such a mentality by teaching that salvation is not only about soul but includes material blessings. Success has a religious and biblical motivation – it is 'to glorify God', 'to bear witness to Jesus', 'to prove that obedience to God's

---

[29]   Pierre Bourdieu, *Distinction: A Social Critique of the Judgment of Taste* (London: Routledge, 1989).

[30]   Koo, 'Singapore's Pop Pastor'.

[31]   At http://www.chc.org.sg/eng/index.php, accessed 23 September 2010.

principles brings blessings' and so forth. In short, success, especially financial blessings, is seen as good and desirable as it is the manifestation of God's goodness. Yet it comes with a cost. To be successful, individuals need to work extra hard. Also, they should receive divine blessings by finding out God's principle and obeying it, so that they will reap the fruits of their investments in higher returns. For example, paying tithes is a very common and necessary commitment for church members. Many of them have in fact committed to set aside more than a tenth of their personal profit, as prescribed by the Bible, to the church and its mission works. They see giving money to God as the first biblical principle that needs to be followed if one desires prosperity and success.[32] Plenty of messages have been carefully built on this concept, and testimonies of recent business, relationship and academic successes, continuously shared by its members at Sunday services or at other times, have helped to validate this principle. For example, an article that appeared in *Harvest Time*, 'Giving that pleases God',[33] mentioned that 'those who obediently heed the voice of God will continually experience blessing and increase in their lives'. Also, on one of its members' blogs, it was written that 'the friend that brought me say they always shared about money during the testimony, which proves to be right'.[34]

Indeed, their gospel is expressed in the language of triumph and confidence – this partly explains why young, middle-class and newly converted members are drawn to this church, as an informant said:

> I attended another church occasionally before I joined [CHC]. I was not baptized then because I felt the church didn't like businesspeople like me. They saw earning money as worldly and unspiritual. So whenever I faced problems in business I would think oh, it must be a punishment or a reminder from God. But what this church teaches is totally different. Wouldn't that be a refreshing relief to know that hey, there is nothing wrong about making money and pursuing success in business! In fact we should ask God to bless us financially and to claim his promises in whatever we do!

We might argue that such teaching, which tends to equate this-worldly gains with God's blessings, appears to validate the values of most middle-class men and women, who have well-defined life expectations and are keen to accumulate material and cultural assets in forming their identity.[35]

As well as success, the concept of 'free to be yourself' or 'being authentic', as mentioned at the beginning of this chapter, is highlighted. One of the easiest ways to express the idea of being 'true to yourself' is through individual lifestyle

---

[32]   FCBC, 'Rise of New Churches'.

[33]   'Giving that Pleases God', *Harvest Time*, 18, July–December 2002.

[34]   At http://wui_ping.tripod.com, accessed 23 September 2010.

[35]   B.H. Chua, 'Consuming Asians: Ideas and Issues', in B.H. Chua (ed.), *Consumption in Asia* (London: Routledge, 2000), pp. 1–34.

and appearance, a widespread message that seeks to make Christianity culturally relevant and thus more accessible to young people. Kong emphasizes that this is a 'holy worldliness' church that 'allow[s] for the freedom of personal convictions and give[s] space to the Holy Spirit to lead every Christian individually'.[36] His wife, the ex-pastor and now singer Sun Ho, once said in a report, 'I am just like any other contemporary girl living in the 21st century. I love many kinds of music … I'm also very much into fashion, and I like to look trendy and hip. I just believe that my whole "package" as an artist – which includes my music, dancing, dressing and performances – should be relevant to the modern, sophisticated and cosmopolitan society we live in.'[37] This message is undoubtedly a liberating and comforting one for young people in a consumer society, in which 'individuals are encouraged to choose and display goods – whether furnishings, house, car, clothing, the body or leisure pursuits' to make their personal statement.[38]

Indeed, the pop-star preacher Sun Ho, who has often made news headlines, is the most powerful testimony of this 'liberating gospel'. She has launched herself into the Chinese, and later Hollywood, popular music industry with her first album in 2001, which sold more than 100,000 copies, and two sold-out concerts at the Singapore Indoor Stadium in June 2002. On board with commercial music label Decca, she has also appeared on cosmetics and fashion advertisements and TV shows. Her boldness in trying new things – merely 'being true to herself'[39] – has naturally received polemic reactions within and without the church community. One particular controversy raged over her seemingly contradictory 'pastor–singer' roles: a forum letter written in to a local daily mentioned that 'religion and entertainment do not mix, period',[40] yet others, especially her husband Kong, think that, as mentioned by my informant, 'this is an effective way to use her talents … [her success is also due] to the remarkable support of Christians, who probably constitute a significant portion of the entertainment market'.[41]

By challenging taken-for-granted sacred–profane boundaries through assimilating into popular culture, Sun categorically refused to be 'preachy' or 'Christian' and has thus become a critic of the stereotyped 'Victorian and straitlaced' image of a Christian.[42] As one of her reports on the church's online magazine says,

---

[36] Hee Kong, 'What City Harvest Church Is All About' at http://konghee.blogspot.com/2009/08/what-city-harvest-church-is-all-about.html, accessed 4 October 2010.

[37] Sun Ho, 'About China Wine Part 2', at http://www.wretch.cc/blog/helloSUN/8726429, accessed 4 October 2010.

[38] Lyon, *Jesus in Disneyland*, p. 82.

[39] Kong, 'Understanding Excellence'.

[40] Quoted in CY Sun, 'Ambiguity of the Sacred: Religion in a Pop Age', 2004, at https://scholarbank.nus.edu.sg/bitstream/handle/10635/14438/Thesis.pdf?sequence=3, accessed 27 September 2010.

[41] Field note on 22 August 2005.

[42] Kong, 'Understanding Excellence'.

... with striking blonde streaks highlighting her tender-brown tresses ... and with her very J-Lo but not as revealing dressings ... have defied all prior definitions one may have had of what a pastor 'should' be like.[43]

No doubt Sun's pop music efforts are market-oriented and youth-oriented. Her songs have been described as 'positive' with a thematic focus on love, self-acceptance and hope, but clearly no mention of 'God' or 'Jesus'. She collaborated with Chinese pop artistes such as Taiwanese singer Jacky Wu and was nominated in 2002 for the MTV Asia 'Favorite Music Artiste Singapore' award. She was also awarded the Top Outstanding Young Person of the World in 2003. Regardless of the differences of opinion among people regarding her musical venture (not to mention boutiques that she has opened in Singapore that bring in an American streetwear label known for its loud designs), this phenomenon has further manifested the church's ability to integrate religion and consumer culture in constructing a unique religious experience and identity, especially for young people.

Conclusion

This chapter has examined one instance of how a megachurch constructs an 'authentic and modern' experience and manages collective and individual identities. In particular, it has shown how a church has effectively integrated emotional expressivity, a sense of belonging and a consumer ethic in its youth identity constructions. If the greatest challenge of religious faith or religious commitment in a postmodern society is that everyday life has become part of a global mechanism of exchange of commodities,[44] this church has apparently turned this challenge into a great advantage: its music, sermons, prosperity theology and life examples, and its expectations of entertainment, classy design and the emphasis on personal freedom, are all endeavours to accommodate to the consumer culture, which seems to fit the profiles of its young professional congregation well. In short, the church has managed to provide an attractive choice for its young attenders, who are either coming to church for the first time or have been turned off by traditional religious settings, an opportunity to construct their modern and yet religious identity and lifestyle. In doing so, the church has set an example testifying to how some religious mechanisms not only survive the global culture of consumerism, but excel in it – CHC has become a brand that is exported and its products copied locally and regionally. Its 45 affiliated churches covering Taiwan, Australia, Indonesia, Malaysia, India and Japan, its bible school that has trained hundreds of international pastors who will extend its ministries actively, its webcast, television broadcast programme and online magazine that together reach millions of viewers worldwide, let alone the church-produced Hollywood

---

[43]   Ibid.
[44]   Turner, *Orientalism, Postmodernism, and Globalism*.

singer, have proven the market efficiency of the church in expanding its culture and value globally. Together with other megachurches, it can, to some extent, act as a 'globalizer' itself, conditioning future trends of religious organizations and, more importantly, reshaping identities and meaningful forms of beliefs to postmodern life.

PART IV
Politics and Community

Chapter 13

Recent Literary Representations of British Muslims

Claire Chambers

I

This chapter examines representations of the ethical issues surrounding representations of Islam and specific Muslim communities in recent British fiction. It is part of a broader research project to examine recent artistic representations of British Muslims in poetry, novels, short stories, autobiographies and film.[1] My research so far indicates that there was a growth of artistic interest in Islam, as it is practised in Britain, following the Honeyford and Rushdie affairs of the mid- to late 1980s, which were early examples of the British Muslim community participating in political protest, and the repercussions of the first Gulf War of 1991. In terms of literary representations, from the mid-1990s to the 2000s, such writers as Hanif Kureishi (*The Black Album*), Zadie Smith (*White Teeth*), Martin Amis (*The Second Plane*), Ian McEwan (*Saturday*), Sebastian Faulks (*A Week in December*) and John Updike (*Terrorist*), have used Islam rather reductively, typically as a marker of fundamentalism, Islamism or the stereotypical figure of the terrorist. Other, less high-profile novelists, such as Farhana Sheikh (*The Red Box*) and M.Y. Alam (*Annie Potts is Dead*), have portrayed groups of young Muslims grappling with issues surrounding identity in late twentieth-century Britain, often showing characters choosing to move away from their Muslim cultural and religious heritage towards a secular, individualized existence. For these writers, while Islam was an important concern, it remained subservient to other issues, such as gender, class, sexuality and regional identities.[2]

[1] I would like to thank HEFCE, the British Academy and the Arts and Humanities Research Council for their generous financial support of this project at various stages of its development.

[2] Of course, individual writers explored issues relating to Muslim filiations and connections in the British context before the 1990s. In his groundbreaking Arabic-language novel, *Season of Migration to the North* (1966), Tayeb Salih depicts the cultural dilemmas experienced by two rural Sudanese Muslims during sojourns in Britain, and on their respective returns to Africa. Tariq Mehmood, on the other hand, focuses on the problems faced by Pakistanis who migrate permanently to Bradford in *Hand on the Sun* (1983).

Notwithstanding these early reductive tendencies, creative interest has accelerated in the years following race riots involving clashes between British South Asian and white youths in the northern English cities of Burnley, Oldham and Bradford in 2001, the attacks on America later that year, and the onset of the so-called 'war on terror'. Since the events in 2001, which mark a watershed for a specific generation, British writers have begun to examine Islam with greater complexity. However, few critics have attempted to chart the development of such art, and religious identity has tended to be subsumed in discussions of migrant writing under such categories as ethnicity, national origins, postcoloniality and hybridity.[3] This chapter is a preliminary attempt to fill the critical gap. In fiction at least, it appears that the strategies for representing Muslim communities are beginning to undergo noteworthy alteration – to resistantly adapt Tony Blair's provocative phrase, 'the rules of the game are changing'.[4] By adopting Blair's terminology I do not wish to suggest any degree of sympathy for the coercive tactics employed by New Labour governments against people of Muslim heritage in recent years. Rather, I use the phrase ironically to suggest that British literature has become increasingly preoccupied by Islam, and that the 'rules of the game' for its representation have significantly altered.

II

This century's climate of Islamophobia, the questionable legality of the Second Gulf War and oppressive counter-terror legislation may have contributed towards

---

However, while Muslimness is taken for granted as a key component of identity by these early writers, arguably the media's portrayal of a climate of religious Manichaeism from the mid-1980s onwards leads to moments of greater self-awareness about religious identity in the more recent writers (see Sheikh, *The Red Box*, p. 19; Alam, *Annie Potts is Dead*, p. 90). Yet, with notable exceptions including Ahdaf Soueif, Abdulrazak Gurnah, Aamer Hussein and Leila Aboulela, few fiction writers explored the competing claims of Britishness and Islam in any sustained way until after 2001.

[3]   The most significant exception of a critic who draws attention to Muslim literature as a category is Amin Malak. In his timely and incisive monograph, *Muslim Narratives and the Discourse of English* (Albany, NY: State University of New York Press, 2005), Malak suggests that the relative neglect that postcolonial theory has shown to religion as a crucial 'identity-shaping valence' may be due in part to its unwitting valorization of 'a secular, Euro-American stance' (pp. 3 and 17). To redress this imbalance, he traces the development of a body of 'Muslim narratives' emerging from the Indian subcontinent in the early twentieth century and spreading over the globe.

[4]   In the aftermath of the London bombings of 7 and 21 July 2005, Blair famously used this phrase in justifying suspension of civil liberties for terror suspects; see Tony Blair, 'The Prime Minister's Statement on Anti-Terror Measures', *Guardian*, 5 August 2005, at http://www.guardian.co.uk/attackonlondon/story/0,1543386,00.html, accessed 23 September 2010.

the growing numbers of writers choosing to probe the cultural dilemmas faced by Muslims in Britain, and to represent particular Islamic communities in a more nuanced way than has previously been attempted. As Gerrit-Jan Berendse and Mark Williams indicate, cultural representations are of crucial ethical significance in the changing political order:

> If a new Cold War has indeed appeared, interpreting this revised world order will require not only repoliticised modes of understanding but also a new grammar of response. Literature and the arts, rather than media discussion or ideologically driven debate, will in time provide a place in which appropriate and adequate humane responses will be articulated, and new modes of conceiving an altered reality will take shape.[5]

In other words, cultural representations play a central role in the process of 'conceiving an altered reality' in our changing post-cold-war political order. Anyone who doubts the legitimacy of literary research in this field need only look to *The Satanic Verses* affair, which lasted from 1989 to the late 1990s, the controversies over attempts to film Monica Ali's eponymous novel in Brick Lane in 2006, and the publication of Sherry Jones's *The Jewel of Medina* two years later to see the significance.[6] Ever since Ayatollah Khomeini issued a *fatwa* or legal opinion sentencing Salman Rushdie to death for alleged blasphemy in his 1988 novel *The Satanic Verses*, it has been evident that even such an apparently elitist form as the postmodernist novel has the potential to polarize opinion about the position and status of British-based members of the Muslim transnational faith group.

Against this context, it is hardly surprising that there has been a shift in the ways in which British writers think about Islam. As Mike Phillips argues in a recent article, there is a concern to explore 'the fault lines between various Islamic cultures and the way of life flourishing in the US and western Europe'.[7] Yet, as Phillips's careful use of the plural indicates, it would be erroneous to suggest that Islam is a monolithic entity. Not only are there vast differences in the religious practices of Islam's two main branches, Sunni and Shia, as well as other groups such as the devotional Sufis and esoteric Ismailis, but there are also great variations between the worldviews and customs held by people originally from different nations and regions. Even within a particular ethnic group, there are distinctions between 'rural and urban, rich and poor, educated and illiterate'.[8]

---

[5]   Gerrit-Jan Berendse and Mark Williams (eds), *Terror and Text: Representing Political Violence in Literature and the Visual Arts* (Bielefeld: Aisthesis Verlag, 2002), p. 10.

[6]   See Kenan Malik, *From Fatwa to Jihad: The Rushdie Affair and its Legacy* (London: Atlantic, 2009), pp. 167–72 and 192–7.

[7]   Mike Phillips, 'Faith Healing: Leila Aboulela's *Minaret*', *Guardian*, 11 June 2005, p. 26.

[8]   Humayan Ansari, *'The Infidel Within': Muslims in Britain since 1800* (London: Hurst, 2004), pp. 2–3.

Identity itself is of course a protean thing that is constantly being refashioned, and one's religious affiliations as a Muslim intersect with other signifiers – such as gender, socio-economic status, age and national origins – that assume various degrees of importance in different situations. That said, there is nonetheless a need to examine religious identity constituents, especially because, as Amin Malak observes, 'many Muslims regard religion as a key component of their identity that could rival, if not supersede, their class, race, gender, or ethnic affiliation'.[9] Young people in particular are increasingly willing to describe themselves as Muslims, rather than by their parents' or grandparents' nationalities, but in using this term they tend not to be talking about Islam's tenets or religious practices. Instead, many see the term 'Muslim' as a marker that differentiates them from both mainstream society and their parents' perceived folk beliefs or misinterpretations of Islam.[10]

Furthermore, in my discussion of identity I am influenced by Tariq Modood's recent book, *Multiculturalism*, in which he argues that Wittgenstein's concept of 'family resemblance' allows us to recognize distinct ethnic and religious groups, although these groups alter in different times and space, and are internally heterogeneous.[11] His contention that we can identify Muslims as a group despite all their myriad differences, as we can detect members of the same family despite great variations in their eye colour, physique, posture, personality and so on, is helpful when thinking about writers as British Muslims. While contemporary Muslim writers in a broad sense, and the two individuals whose work I analyse here, exhibit very different features, styles and affiliations, I would argue that we can usefully speak of them as part of a loosely connected and often discordant family. Finally, it would be equally wrong to assume that 'Britain' itself is homogeneous. The recent move towards devolution has highlighted the fact that Britain is made up of discordant communities. Even within the national unit of England there are tensions between the regions, particularly the once-industrial North and the wealthy, technologized South.[12]

As such, it is perhaps inevitable that the two novels that I take to be exemplars of the closer literary attention now being paid to British Muslims – *Maps for Lost Lovers* by Nadeem Aslam (2004) and Leila Aboulela's novel of the following year, *Minaret* – have as many divergences as commonalities. While these two writers portray Muslims of different nationalities living in Britain and evince vastly contrasting attitudes towards the predicaments that their communities

---

[9]   Malak, *Muslim Narratives*, p. 3.

[10]   See Philip Lewis, *Islamic Britain: Religion, Politics and Identity Among British Muslims* (London: I.B. Tauris, 1994), pp. 8 and 176–89; Anshuman Mondal, *Young British Muslim Voices* (Oxford: Greenwood World, 2008), pp. 3–6; Hanif Kureishi, 'My Son the Fanatic', in *The Word and the Bomb* (London: Faber, 2005), pp. 63–74.

[11]   Tariq Modood, *Multicultural Politics: Racism, Ethnicity and Muslims in Britain* (Edinburgh: Edinburgh University Press, 2005), pp. 87–119.

[12]   James Procter, *Dwelling Places: Postwar Black British Writing* (Manchester: Manchester University Press, 2003), pp. 2–3.

face, both are concerned to re-map the British landscape from a broadly Muslim perspective. Through dense and often poetic descriptions of the domestic lives of their characters, Aboulela and Aslam draw attention to a Britain in which routes are navigated in relation to the minaret of a mosque, and in which Northern cities are renamed 'Dasht-e-Tanhaii', or 'The Wilderness of Solitude'.

III

To take Nadeem Aslam's *Maps for Lost Lovers* first of all: as its title suggests, this is a novel that is concerned with migrants' 'cognitive mapping' of a new landscape.[13] Aslam himself was born in Pakistan, but moved to Huddersfield at the age of 14. He wrote *Maps for Lost Lovers* over 11 impoverished years, sleeping in friends' flats in Huddersfield, Edinburgh, Leicester and Reading.[14] His mythical Dasht-e-Tanhaii bears close surface resemblance to the Yorkshire cities of Huddersfield and Bradford, with their large populations of South Asian migrants, particularly from rural areas in Azad Jammu & Kashmir and the Pakistani Punjab. Aslam details the migration process undergone by Dasht-e-Tanhaii's predominantly Muslim community, a process characterized by chain migration, in which a group of 'pioneer' migrants came to Britain and subsequently brought relatives and friends, but retained village-kin networks (*biraderi*) and strong links to Pakistan.[15] Early settlers saw themselves as transients and were motivated by the 'myth of return'[16] but, especially as families began to be reunited in Britain, increasing interest was generated in building self-sufficient communities. Since the publication of an influential article by Raymond Breton in 1964,[17] anthropologists have termed the process 'institutional completeness', by which such businesses as *halal* butchers, and South Asian restaurants and video stores come to serve migrants' needs in the new country, while at the same time operating 'to defend and perpetuate [the migrants'] traditional social forms, values, beliefs and ethnic identity'.[18] Aslam painstakingly describes the ways in which racism, social exclusion and self-

---

[13]　Fredric Jameson, 'Postmodernism, or, The Cultural Logic of Late Capitalism', *New Left Review*, 146 (July–August 1984): pp. 89–90.

[14]　Marianne Brace, 'Nadeem Aslam: A Question of Honour', *Independent*, 11 June 2004, at http://enjoyment.independent.co.uk/books/features/article42260.ece, accessed 23 September 2010.

[15]　Badr Dahya, 'The Notion of Pakistani Ethnicity', in Abner Cohen (ed.), *Urban Ethnicity* (London: Tavistock, 1974), pp. 77–118, and 82–6.

[16]　Muhammad Anwar, *The Myth of Return: Pakistanis in Britain.* (London: Heinemann Educational, 1979); Dahya, 'Pakistani Ethnicity', p. 83.

[17]　Raymond Breton, 'Institutional Completeness of Ethnic Communities and the Personal Relations of Immigrants', *American Journal of Sociology*, 70/2 (1964): pp. 193–205.

[18]　Dahya, 'Pakistani Ethnicity', pp. 94–5.

segregation have all contributed towards Dasht-e-Tanhaii's Muslim population existing within a ghetto, to the extent that white people are seen as the Other by many members of the community. This is particularly true of the older generation, few of whom speak fluent English, who rarely have contact with indigenous Northerners, and who discipline recalcitrant children with the threat of giving them away to a white person.

Although this is by now a fairly recognizable account of migration, stylistically Aslam is innovative, deliberately defamiliarizing the industrial, inner-city landscape inhabited by his characters. He transmutes this cityscape into a pastoral scene, in which the prevalence of exotic flora and fauna – tamarind trees, fireflies, parakeets and sugar-cane – make Aslam's world seem far removed from the more usual '[b]asements and bedsits, streets and cafes, ... suburbs and the city' that have featured as the cardinal locations of post-war British diasporic writing.[19] In one sense, Aslam is simply documenting the ways in which Pakistani migrants are transforming their localities by the establishment of South Asian foodstores, cultural events, clothing and customs. Yet what is also immediately notable about his writing is the loading up of similes and metaphors, many of them extraordinarily beautiful, and deriving predominantly from the natural and domestic spheres of Pakistan. Here, for example, is a moment from early in the novel when the central character, Shamas, surveys a wintry scene near his house in Dasht-e-Tanhaii:

> ... the deep snow has at its base a thin sheet of packed ice through which the dry leaves of the field maples can be seen as though sealed behind glass. They are as intricate as the gold jewellery from the Subcontinent – treasures buried under the snow till a rainy day. ... The chilled air is as keen as a needle on the skin and the incline is forcing him to take a hummingbird's 300 breaths per minute. A frozen buried clump of grass breaks under his weight and the cracking sound is the sound that Kaukab produces when she halves and quarters cinnamon sticks in the kitchen.[20]

The first glimpse of snow is of course a recurring trope of migrant writing, as is evident in diverse texts by such writers as V.S. Naipaul, Jamaica Kincaid and Syed Manzurul Islam.[21] In this passage, although snow is familiar to Shamas after many years in England, he nonetheless makes the landscape strange, even exotic, by viewing it 'as through behind glass'. He achieves this through an abundance of imagery drawn from the subcontinent: its gold jewellery, hummingbirds and spices heat up the freezing terrain. Interestingly, we are given a sense here of ice acting as a palimpsest, half-obscuring the 'maples' of the Western tradition with

---

[19]   Procter, *Dwelling Places*, p. 1.

[20]   Nadeem Aslam, *Maps for Lost Lovers* (London: Faber, 2004), p. 8.

[21]   V.S. Naipaul, *The Mimic Men* (London: Deutsch, 1967); Jamaica Kincaid, *Lucy* (London: Jonathan Cape, 1991 [1990]); Syed Manzurul Islam, 'Meeting at the Crossroads', in *The Mapmakers of Spitalfields* (Leeds: Peepal Tree, 2003 [1997]), pp. 110–39.

warmer images deriving from Urdu literature. This figures forth Aslam's literary strategy more broadly: he layers up European and Urdu references (both to Joyce and Flaubert, and to Tansen and Chughtai) one on top of another, to open out our sense of what tradition can mean. Specifically in relation to imagery, Aslam argues that his extravagant use of metaphor is a technique in order to represent the worldviews of his characters, who, he argues, are 'constantly comparing their England with Pakistan'. He has stated 'I wanted the reader to feel [...] frustration [that they don't see their own life in England]. I wanted England to shout, as it were, "Look at me!"'[22]

He also uses subcontinental myths, art forms and religious imagery in order to translate the England in which his characters live. For instance, the novel is peppered with rich images drawn from Urdu poetry, particularly *ghazals*: tropes include the moth and the flame; stars and diamonds; wine and peacocks. The novel's evocation of the nineteenth-century *ghazal* poet Ghalib is suggestive in relation to Aslam's strategy. Ghalib used the stock images of Urdu poetry in order to create something new, and to make veiled points about the turbulent time in which he lived, the era of the Indian Rebellion of 1857 and the demise of the Mughal Empire.[23] Aslam embarks on a similar enterprise, showing that tropes from South Asian poetry have various connotations (relating to such issues as politics, love and religion) to different people in the British context. In doing so, he also refutes attempts to constrict Islam into an exclusive, singular identity as distortions of the religion's pluralist history. By evoking the opulence associated with Urdu poetry, he reminds us that Islam is a heterogeneous religion and culture, and that in the *ghazal* tradition, for instance, wine and the Beloved featured as spiritual metaphors. Given this multiplicity, it should come as no surprise that when the Qawwali singer Nusrat Fateh Ali Khan (who has great imaginative purchase on the text) dies towards the end of the novel, three of its main characters react to the information in very different ways:

> The news is genuinely devastating. 'Who will sing about the poor, now?' [Shamas] whispers in shock.

> 'And about the women,' says Suraya – his whispers are audible to her.

> 'And in praise of Allah and Muhammad, peace be upon him?' adds Kaukab.[24]

---

[22]   Brace, 'Nadeem Aslam', n.p.

[23]   Shirley Chew, 'A Question of Form: Phyllis Webb's *Water and Light: Ghazals and Anti Ghazals', in* Marc Delrez and Benedite Ledent (eds), *The Contact and the Culmination: Essays in Honour of Hena Maes-Jelinek (*Liège: Liège Language and Literature, 1996), pp. 31–43, esp. 41.

[24]   Aslam, *Maps*, p. 238.

The singer from the mystical Sufi tradition is interpreted variously as a champion of Marxist, feminist and spiritual values, according to the perspective of each listener.

As the quotation suggests, Aslam is concerned to probe the ethics of Muslim religious 'tradition', levelling particularly pointed criticisms in relation to gender. Indeed, Aslam could be criticized for overloading his discussion of religious abuses, even pathologizing some of his Pakistani characters. The novel revolves around the honour-killing of a couple who lived together out of wedlock, but it also details child molestation by a religious cleric; violent exorcism of *djinns*; damaging effects of gender segregation; women's lack of rights under Islamic divorce; and the pressures of 'shame' in the community. However, Shamas's wife, Kaukab, who in many ways functions as the text's archetypically intolerant proponent of a narrow Islamism, is to some extent also imbued with sympathetic traits. She sees the maintenance of tradition and refusal of assimilation as connecting her to her ancestors, 'her mothers and grandmothers ... those now dead and absent but still living in her mind, unsung elsewhere and otherwise'.[25] Thus, although the narrative ultimately rejects her hide-bound clinging to conventions, we are nonetheless given an insight into the sense of continuity she gets from following prescribed practices. As in the previous quotation, in which three different interpretations of the musical tradition are simultaneously held in view, Kaukab, and Islamist thinking more broadly, are examined in *Maps for Lost Lovers* from more than one interpretive standpoint.

IV

Whereas Aslam focuses almost entirely on a South Asian community in the North of England, Leila Aboulela's *Minaret* gives a greater sense of a transnational faith group, the Islamic *ummah*. It could be argued that Aboulela's belief in a transcendental *ummah* is somewhat naïve, and downplays the very real tensions between different Muslim groups within an in any case divided Britain.[26] However, what marks *Minaret* out and makes it an interesting novel of Muslim experience is that it centres on a character's journey towards, rather than away from, religion. As suggested in the early part of this chapter, most of the novels in this area to date, particularly those from the 1990s, are about young Muslims discovering 'freedom', in the shape of a secular life, and independence from familial or kinship ties. This may even be said of *Maps for Lost Lovers*, inasmuch as its couples, Chanda and Jugnu, and Shamas and Suraya, defy cultural constraints to pursue love matches, even if both relationships end in tragedy. In contrast, Aboulela's novel traces the Westernized protagonist, Najwa's, downwardly mobile journey from her privileged position as a Sudanese minister's daughter to exile in London

---

[25] Ibid., p. 116.

[26] For this broad point about the illusion of the *ummah*, see Kamila Shamsie, *Offence: The Muslim Case* (Kolkata: Seagull Books, 2009), pp. 15 and 41.

when a coup dislodges her father from power, and eventually to the life of a domestic servant to a wealthy Arab family in the former imperial capital. During this descent, an unfurling religious understanding sustains Najwa and consoles her for her losses.

Unlike in Aslam's novel, where racism is solely depicted as colour prejudice, Aboulela portrays overt Islamophobia in post-9/11 London (although interestingly the events of September 2001 are never explicitly mentioned). Najwa is referred to as 'Muslim scum' and has a soft drink thrown over her veiled head on a London bus in 2003. Furthermore, when she spends time with the devout son of her employer, Tamer, she notices the unease with which Londoners regard his beard and Arab features, which they stereotypically associate with terrorists. Yet ironically, Najwa, Tamer and their South Asian, Arab and white convert friends from the mosque, are not interested in politics. Educated as most of them were in English-medium schools, they are equally opposed to anti-American feeling as to the West's neo-colonial activities in the Middle East. For them, Islam is far less an ideology than a code of ethical behaviour and a central marker of identity in the fragmentary world of migration, asylum and family disintegration. A conversation between Najwa and Tamer illustrates this well:

'Do you feel you're Sudanese?' I ask [Tamer].

He shrugs. 'My mother is Egyptian. I've lived everywhere except Sudan: in Oman, Cairo, here. My education is Western and that makes me feel that I am Western. My English is stronger than my Arabic. So I guess, no, I don't feel very Sudanese though I would like to be. I guess being a Muslim is my identity. What about you?'

I talk slowly. 'I feel that I am Sudanese but things changed for me when I left Khartoum. Then even while living here in London, I've changed. And now, like you, I just think of myself as a Muslim.'[27]

Here the Western secular concept of the nation is shown to have little resonance for the wealthy cosmopolitan sojourner, Tamer, and the political refugee, Najwa. This tacitly reinforces Humayan Ansari's suggestion that, in response to their exclusion from normative versions of British nationhood, 'many British Muslims, especially the youth, found a valuable resource and alternative forms of identification in "religion." There was a conscious effort to move away from ethnic and national identifications towards being defined first and foremost as Muslims.'[28]

In contrast to Aslam, who is highly critical of Dasht-e-Tanhaii's religious infrastructure, Aboulela portrays the mosque – in this case, the Central Mosque

---

[27] Leila Aboulela, *Minaret* (London: Bloomsbury, 2005), p. 110.

[28] Humayan Ansari, *'The Infidel Within': Muslims in Britain Since 1800* (London: Hurst, 2004), p. 9.

in Regent's Park, which has been described as 'the most prestigious' mosque in Britain[29] – as a nurturing microcosmic community. The mosque provides shelter (Najwa and Tamer both sleep there at different times[30]); it is where Najwa finds her job as a nanny-cum-servant; it provides education, both in the form of religious classes and one-off lectures that stimulate much debate;[31] and it is also a source of friendship and female communion.[32] Several times Najwa compares her new-found religious faith with the sense of well-being she felt as a sick child being cared for in her parents' bed.[33] Religion is positioned as a substitute for parental care and, surprisingly, Aboulela to some extent conforms here to the notion of religion's infantilizing tendencies advocated by some secular fundamentalists. The mosque, even seen from a distance as a fragmented minaret, provides a sense of security, well-being and locatedness.[34] Perhaps most importantly, there is a levelling out of class and other differences in the mosque. As Hafsah Zamir points out, the mosque establishes feelings of equality among its congregation, as is attested by the fact that the Senegalese ambassador's wife prays with and gives lifts to the lowly Najwa during Ramadan.[35]

Prayer and Ramadan fasting are depicted as structuring the Muslim day and year, giving a sense of a strong imagined community. Hajj promises even more 'spiritual pleasure',[36] and at the end of the novel Najwa chooses to be funded to go to Mecca by the family she has worked for, rather than pursue a prohibited relationship with Tamer. The novel, which until its conclusion seems to broadly fit into the genre of romance fiction, with the friendship growing between Najwa and Tamer despite their age gap and the inequality of their social positions, suddenly tilts towards a different interpretation. Over romantic love, Najwa chooses religious pilgrimage, which she imagines as being made up of 'genuine joy and adventures ..., [t]he crowds, the hardship of sleeping in tents, long bus rides, the [sense of being] squeezed and wrung'.[37] *Minaret* opens as a typical novel of migration, but ends by leading into another journey, one that is bound up with notions of belonging and coherence (as opposed to the incoherent, fractured journeying of the political refugee).[38]

[29]   Lewis, *Islamic Britain*, p. 13.
[30]   Aboulela, *Minaret*, pp. 74–5 and 189.
[31]   Ibid., pp. 79 and 107–8.
[32]   Ibid., pp. 104 and 183.
[33]   Ibid., pp. 75, 132, 188–9 and 276.
[34]   Ibid., pp. 1, 107 and 208.
[35]   Hafsah Zamir, 'Carrying Islam to the West: Women in Exile in the Fiction of Leila Aboulela', unpublished MA thesis (Royal Holloway, London, 2007), p. 35.
[36]   Aboulela, *Minaret*, p. 188.
[37]   Ibid., p. 209.
[38]   I am grateful to Dr David Farrier for suggesting this point. For more information on Hajj as 'the most emblematic expression of a universal Muslim community ... [and] one of the five pillars of Islam', see Seán McLoughlin, 'Holy Places, Contested Spaces:

V

The supportive ties that Najwa discovers in the mosque are starkly contrasted with the supposed 'freedoms' of the non-religious world, which Aboulela portrays as being constrictive rather than liberatory. The notion of liberty in Western thought, since the time of Hobbes's *Leviathan*, has meant a freedom from external constraints and the right of individual self-determination. In Muslim thought, on the other hand, freedom, or *hurriyya*, has typically been regarded as an inner state of liberty from the tyranny of the senses, or as something that is experienced only as part of the collective group of the faithful.[39] It would be wrong to suggest that Muslims have not hotly debated the concept of freedom over the centuries.[40] However, in the Sufi tradition, freedom has been compared to 'perfect slavery', which indicates not only that slavery in the Arab world was, in Amitav Ghosh's words, a relatively 'flexible set of hierarchies',[41] but also that the institution was often used as a metaphor for understanding 'the relationship between Allah the "master" and his human "slaves"'.[42] Aboulela provocatively challenges Western perceptions of what freedom entails when her protagonist desires a position as her employer's family slave, or concubine:

> I don't [explain] … my fantasies. My involvement in his [Tamer's] wedding to a young suitable girl who knows him less than I do. She will mother children who spend more time with me … I would like to be his family's concubine, like something out of *The Arabian Nights*, with life-long security and a sense of belonging. But I must settle for freedom in this modern time.[43]

The issue of clashing cultural understandings of liberty highlighted by this passage is particularly pertinent in the light of the rhetoric of 'freedom' used to justify the war on terror. With its evocation of a non-Western literary text, the quotation

---

British Pakistani Accounts of Pilgrimage to Makkah and Madinah', in Peter Hopkins and Richard Gale (eds), *Muslims in Britain: Race, Place and Identities* (Edinburgh: Edinburgh University Press, 2009), pp. 132–49.

[39]   At least, this was true until the advent of colonialism and then neo-imperialism: for more recent usages of the word, see Saleh Omar, 'Philosophical Origins of the Arab Ba'th Party: The work of Zaki Al-Arsuzi', *Arab Studies Quarterly*, 18 (1996): pp. 1–13.

[40]   For an example of this kind of debate, see Mohamed Charfi's fierce refutation of Islamists' attempts to besmirch democracy as Western innovation in *Islam and Liberty: The Historical Misunderstanding* (London: Zed, 2005).

[41]   Amitav Ghosh, *In an Antique Land* (London: Granta, 1992), p. 260; see also Peter Clark, *Marmaduke Pickthall: British Muslim* (London: Quartet, 1986), p. 48.

[42]   Andrew G. Bostom, 'Is Freedom "Perfect Slavery?"', *Front Page Magazine*, 3 March 2006, at http://www.frontpagemag.com/Articles/ReadArticle.asp?ID=21473, accessed 23 September 2010.

[43]   Aboulela, *Minaret*, p. 215.

suggests uncomfortable questions in relation to feminism's unwittingly Eurocentric assumptions about what constitutes 'female emancipation'. Yet Najwa's wish has ambivalent standing within the text, particularly in the light of her later decision to perform Hajj rather than marry Tamer, and this internal monologue smacks of lugubrious, even masochistic, propensities.

Najwa has been brought up in a broadly Western tradition: she comes from an elite family that pays only lip service to Islam, and her early life, while affluent and sheltered, is nonetheless depicted as lacking some essential component. Within conventional limits, Najwa has considerable freedom in her dress, education and sexual relations, but she feels uneasy when strange men appraise her body in its revealing clothes,[44] and her only sexual relationship with a Marxist exile in London is sordid and guilt-ridden.[45] After the Leftist coup in Sudan leads to her father's imprisonment and eventual execution, her family is described as 'falling' through space,[46] an image that pithily evokes the horrors inherent in too much liberty, while of course also suggesting the fall common to both Judaeo-Christian and Qur'anic mythology, whereby Adam and Eve/Hawwa were banished from the Garden of Paradise to live on earth. Najwa's fall is complete once her brother Omar, having become involved in London's drugs scene, is imprisoned for stabbing a policeman, and her mother dies following a protracted illness. After being released from her nursing duties by her mother's death, and with her brother behind bars and unable to comment on her lifestyle, Najwa supposes that she should feel a sense of emancipation, but instead comments that '[t]his empty space was called freedom'.[47]

Paradoxically, Najwa finds an alternative to the unfulfilling Hobbesian brand of freedom in Islam's rules and precepts. It is worth noting that Aboulela herself has been approvingly described as a 'halal novelist' (in other words, a writer who is religiously permissible) by the *Muslim News*, a catchphrase that is repeated on the dustjacket for her most recent novel, *Minaret*. We can locate the *oeuvre*'s 'propriety' in the figure of its author, who wears the veil and whose book designs prominently feature this head-garb; in the quest and dilemmas of its protagonists; and in the texts' resolutions, which tend to feature Muslim solutions to contemporary dilemmas. Yet despite this 'halal novelist' tag, the portrayal of Islam in *Minaret* is seldom simplistically idealist; nor does the writer deny a vivacity associated with Western modes of living. To take just one example, considerable ambivalence surrounds the issue of veiling in this novel.[48] Najwa

---

44   Ibid., pp. 41 and 130.
45   Ibid., p. 176.
46   Ibid., pp. 61 and 239–40.
47   Ibid., p. 175.
48   For discussion of representations of the *hijab* in Aboulela's previous novel, *The Translator*, see Geoffrey Nash, 'Re-siting Religion and Creating Feminised Space in the Fiction of Ahdaf Soueif and Leila Aboulela', *Wasafiri*, 35 (2002): pp. 28–31. For more general discussion of literary depictions of the veil, see Daphne Grace, *The Woman in the Muslin Mask: Veiling and Identity in Postcolonial Literature* (London: Pluto Press, 2004).

celebrates the *hijab*'s cloak of invisibilty, which spares her the sexual harassment she experienced when she wore Western clothes and she also recognizes the subtle allure of concealment.[49] However, when she sees her mosque friends without their *hijabs* for the first time at an all-female Eid party, there is a sense of their true personalities being revealed from behind the drab disguise of the veil.[50] At one point, Najwa describes the *hijab* as a 'uniform',[51] and this word neatly indicates the positive and negative attributes that the novel suggests attach to the veil. While the veil's homogenizing tendencies are not denied, its democratic levelling out of differences and powerful symbolism as a badge of faith are also emphasized. In my interview with Aboulela, she confirmed this ambivalence, describing the sense of freedom she felt when first choosing to wear the headscarf in London in 1987, but also remarking, 'I don't really know [a Muslim woman] properly unless I see her without the *hijab*, that's how I feel. So it is a kind of uniform, it does put a distance between you and other people.'[52]

VI

To conclude, I hope that this chapter has suggested that some young writers of Muslim heritage are beginning to challenge the dominance that the concept of ethnicity has had over perceptions of migrant or diasporic writing. Writers such as Nadeem Aslam and Leila Aboulela demonstrate the urgent need, within a political landscape riven by inter-religious hatred, to explore and come to a greater understanding of worldviews shaped by religion. Although they take very different stances on the ethical questions posed by Islam, nonetheless these writers in their different ways cognitively re-map Britain from the perspective of those Muslims to whom this world is less material than the next, while remaining alert to the many people of Muslim heritage who do not subscribe to all or any of the religion's tenets.

Drawing on artistic works by Muslims and non-Muslims, the authors reflect the many influences that bear upon British Muslim identity. At stake in the frequent return to figures or texts of Muslim literature, such as Ghalib and *The Arabian Nights*, is a desire to think through Muslim subjectivity formation. The writers seek to highlight the centrality of Muslim art to global canons, and to situate

---

For an anthropological perspective, see the excellent work of Emma Tarlo in 'Hijab in London: Metamorphosis, Resonance and Effects', *Journal of Material Culture,* 12/2 (2007): pp. 131–56, and *Clothing Matters: Dress and Identity in India* (London: Hurst, 1996).

[49]   Ibid., pp. 246–8.

[50]   Ibid., pp. 184–6.

[51]   Ibid., p. 186.

[52]   Claire Chambers, 'An Interview with Leila Aboulela', *Contemporary Women's Writing*, 3/1 (2009): pp. 86–102, at 93.

their own fictions about Britain within a long history of Muslim artistic identity. The novels celebrate the Islamic religion and the civilizations it has inspired as forming a rich cultural repository from which their writing has much to gain. The intertextual referencing of a long history of Muslim artistic work refigures the category 'Muslim' as an enabling resource, and the writers' attempts to redraw British cityscapes from a Muslim standpoint are intimately connected to the artistic cartographies that are also charted in the novels.

Chapter 14

Destiny, the Exclusive Brethren and Mediated Politics in New Zealand

Ann Hardy

Introduction

The British colony, later nation, of New Zealand was established at a time when the desirability of legal separation between church and state had come to seem self-evident, when there was in fact discussion of the possible disestablishment of the Church of England.[1] While the underlying values of the emergent state were Christian, it was widely assumed that its public operations would be secular.[2] A century later, however, the consensus that religion should be a private matter and that government should be secular has come under challenge from small, but determinedly active, sections of the national community. What happens when citizens, who identify primarily in terms of a religious identity, prefer to live in a state run as a theocracy and take steps to bring about change? In particular, in what relationships to mediated communication do such activists find themselves when they try to influence the decision-making of their fellow citizens?

This chapter explores these questions by examining two case studies in political activism by conservative Christian groups around the 2005 New Zealand parliamentary elections: the apostolic, indigenous Destiny Church, and the internationally linked Exclusive Brethren. The groups are relatively small, with around 10,000 and 5,000 members respectively, and in one sense the answer to the first question above is 'not a great deal': the social order of New Zealand has not subsequently become significantly less secular. Nevertheless, there are both short- and medium-term changes that can be linked to the events this chapter outlines. In the short term, the Leader of the Opposition lost electoral credibility when he was revealed to have concealed his party's association with the Exclusive Brethren, while the then-government used the scandal as impetus to reform electoral financing legislation. Arguably, in the mid-term the events also facilitated a shift

---

[1]   Rex Ahdar, 'New Zealand and the Idea of a Christian State', in Rex Ahdar and John Stenhouse (eds), *God and Government: The New Zealand Experience* (Dunedin: University of Otago, 2000), p. 63.

[2]   Ibid., p. 61.

to the right in national politics since a change of government took place at the next elections in 2008.[3]

The primary significance of these case studies, however, is in the light they shed on the complex relationships between contemporary religious groups and processes of mediation, including different conceptions and uses of media power. While the Destiny church was already an enthusiastic user of a range of media technologies, the Exclusive Brethren were doctrinally averse to any but basic print media. Nevertheless, in attempting to engage in public persuasion – one overtly, the other covertly – both groups found themselves drawn, to their cost, into the ideological sandstorm that is contemporary multimedia news coverage. Both organizations wished to exert power in pursuit of social change, but did not wish to become the subjects of power themselves. Rather, they hoped to become alternative sources of social influence, religious variants of what Curran labels activist groups from the 'civic media sector'.[4] Instead, they found themselves engulfed in hostile situations characterized by the media's power to name and exclude.

Destiny and its Mediation

On August 2004 a group of several thousand protestors from an alliance of evangelical churches marched through New Zealand's capital city, Wellington, shouting 'Enough is enough'. Two hundred men dressed in black, many of them Maori, performed a *haka*, or challenge-dance, outside the parliament building before their leader, Pastor Brian Tamaki from the Destiny church, gave a passionate speech complaining about the 'godless liberalism' of public culture. The spiritual laxness of the country's leaders, he asserted, manifested in contempt for the institutions of marriage and the family, with a corresponding 'demonic' support for anti-family practices of prostitution, homosexuality and civil unions. While the country's politicians tried to ignore the protest, information about Destiny's condemnation of homosexuality in particular had been circulating on the Internet, and members of the city's gay and lesbian groups were present to counter-protest. Otherwise, the general public experienced the protest as surprising. That a marginalized group such as evangelical Christians could put so many people onto the streets was unexpected, as was the fervour of the march. Emotional verbal confrontations between protestors and counter-protestors also contributed to the sense that something extraordinary was happening. The march rapidly became the main topic of news coverage for that day and the next, and the fulcrum of numerous current affairs and workplace debates for days after.

---

[3]   Marion Maddox, *God under Howard: The Rise of the Religious Right in Australian Politics* (Sydney: Allen & Unwin, 2005).

[4]   James Curran, 'Mediations of Democracy', in James Curran and Michael Gurevitch (eds), *Mass Society and Mass Media* (Oxford: Oxford University Press, 2005), pp. 122–49.

The fact that the march attracted media attention was intentional, and because the organizers had some experience in shaping materials for mediation they had expected that the publicity would draw support for the issues they were highlighting. An outgrowth of the Apostolic Church movement, the Destiny church was created in 1998 by the husband-and-wife team of Brian and Hannah Tamaki, and by 2004 had church organizations in 20 locations around New Zealand.[5] Destiny operates according to a patriarchal, theocratic model of governance in which Brian Tamaki claims to have a direct relationship with God, and his authority on this basis filters down through the pastors who run the regional churches.[6] The influence of American evangelical religiosity on Destiny is evident in the style of its self-presentation as well as in its moral platform that is in the tradition of the Moral Majority and Family First movements of the United States and, to a lesser extent, of Australia.[7] As a measure of its ambition to effect social change the church had registered a political party, the Destiny Party in 2003.

Destiny already had its own television production facility and in 2000 had begun broadcasting the country's first local televangelism programme, Destiny Television.[8] Tamaki's sermons were also available in downloadable audio-formats, complemented by the distribution of videos, books and DVDs through physical and online sales networks. The church also hosts a website that eschews traditional religious iconography: its tagline, 'Destiny: Breakthrough Generation', is an indication of the branding ethos the organization embraces. That mediation strategies were essential to the church's growth is evident in the account of their development given in Tamaki's autobiography, *More Than Meets the Eye*. The colour-coded clothing of the protesters, the mass *haka*, the elevated staging of Tamaki's speech: these performative aspects were therefore the work of organizers with a certain understanding of codes of media spectacle, who wished to raise the political presence of their organization by staging an event the mainstream media would be enticed to cover.

The planners were successful to the degree that they riveted public attention. An online newspaper archive contains only 28 articles mentioning the Destiny church from 1998 through to June 2004,[9] while in the year after there were more than 400 items about the church, spread across the range of formats including features, editorials and opinion columns. Despite compelling attention, however, Destiny had insufficient knowledge of the workings of media power to forestall

---

[5]   See http://www.destinychurch.org.nz, accessed 22 September 2010.

[6]   Brian Tamaki, *More Than Meets the Eye* (Auckland: Tamaki Publications, 2006).

[7]   Maddox, *God under Howard*; see also Dolores Janiewski and Paul Morris, *New Rights, New Zealand: Myths, Moralities and Markets* (Auckland: Auckland University Press, 2005).

[8]   Tamaki, *More Than Meets the Eye*, p. 191.

[9]   The *Newztext* database stores content from the Fairfax group of newspapers and contains a representative sample from the period. See http://www.knowledge-basket.co.nz, accessed 22 September 2010.

the oppositional decodings made in, and by means of, the coverage of their protest. Or, as Tamaki later reflected, 'despite the thorough planning and preparation, we hadn't given a single thought to a post-event communication strategy which took into account potential angles and media-fuelled perceptions. My assumption had been that reporting would have focused primarily on the issues'.[10]

News-making Practices and Marginalized Religious Institutions

In considering why interest groups such as new religious movements are often disappointed by the media coverage they receive, Sean McCloud[11] proposes four theses concerning the influence of journalistic agency on the framing of news stories. First, he claims that journalists act as 'heresiographers', identifying false or inauthentic religion, thus establishing boundaries between a mainstream religious centre and a suspect periphery.[12] Secondly, he proposes that depictions of new religions tend to produce a spiritual apologetics for the dominant social order.[13] Thirdly, McCloud asserts that changing portrayals of new religions are related to changes in the broader culture. For instance, ownership of various media companies is increasingly concentrated and staffing numbers kept low to contain costs, which leads to convergence of content across media products. A fourth point is that, as heresiographers, journalists use new, sectarian religions as 'negative reference groups' in a process of identity construction defining how they perceive themselves, their readers, and culture as a whole.[14] Nonetheless, the media realm is not a monolithic unity; rather, it is a contested area of symbolic production where 'mainstream', 'fringe', 'cult' and 'religion' are constructed, contested categories.[15] In coverage of the August 2004 march, daily journalists sought to protect the dominant social order by being vigilant for 'false' religion and therefore offering a prophylactic construction of the protestors as a 'negative reference group'. The mechanisms by which this negative attribution was achieved can be glimpsed by focusing on two elements: the coverage of the *haka* and the entrenchment of a 'Nazi' decoding of the march.

A large proportion of Destiny's membership consists of working-class Maori, a demographic grouping that suffered particular hardship due to the market liberalization policies of the 1980s and 1990s. An advantage of this cultural positioning is that Destiny can mobilize symbols from Maori sub-cultures if desired: for instance, the *haka* is a traditional practice for expressing solidarity

---

[10]   Tamaki, *More Than Meets the Eye*, p. 186.

[11]   Sean McCloud, 'From Exotics to Brainwashers: Portraying New Religions in Mass Media', *Religion Compass*, 1/1 (2006): pp. 214–28.

[12]   Ibid., p. 223.

[13]   Ibid., p. 224.

[14]   Ibid., p. 225.

[15]   Ibid., p. 225.

and, as a Destiny spokesperson explained, was felt to be an appropriate instrument on this occasion:

> On a spiritual level the haka is a way of our proclaiming to the spirit realm. It needs to be aggressive because it is a challenge to the moral decay of our society. The challenge is against what is coming at us. It is a battle against Satan.[16]

Performed before an All Black rugby game, the *haka* is the apogee of national popular culture, representing the harnessing of 'warrior' energy for elite competition. Yet employed in this context it was predominantly interpreted as unsanctioned aggression, mobilizing connotations associated with race and class that typically lurk only as subtext in New Zealand public discourse, but that are occasionally brought to light in other representations such as the controversial depiction of violence in a Maori underclass in the filmic adaptation of *Once Were Warriors*.[17] This negative evaluation was then intensified by comparing the march to a social movement with a very different ethnic basis: Nazism. This specific encoding then spread rapidly as a result of the effort-saving economies of news syndication.

Initially, a reporter for the Wellington-based *The Dominion Post* produced a report entitled 'Black shirts take to the Streets', citing the pejorative evaluations of three witnesses: two of whom belonged to the gay community. An identical article, 'March arouses Nazi fears', also ran in Fairfax Media's South Island paper *The Christchurch Press*, and several other linked publications ran similar articles and editorials elaborating on the theme. For many uncritical consumers of news, especially those already unsympathetic to the concerns of evangelical churches, a negative interpretation of Destiny's motives (what the editor of *The New Zealand Herald* described as 'the fear and loathing it aroused in liberal discussion'[18]) became the enduring interpretive framework for the march.

After this initial period of reactive reporting, sections of the media did later craft more thoughtful articles. For example, two weeks later the current affairs magazine *New Zealand Listener* published a feature by religious historian Peter Lineham suggesting that Destiny and its leader be understood as a contemporary extension of the religio-political phenomenon of Maori 'prophets' reacting to the ideological and physical intrusions of colonization.[19] Balanced considerations such as this had scant opportunity to gain purchase, however, because the earlier simplistic, coverage had been so widespread. Overlaid with a fascist stain, the Destiny-led protest was evaluated as inimical to the interests of democracy rather

---

[16]   Cited in Chris Barton, 'Destiny's Children on a Mission', *The New Zealand Herald*, 12 February 2005, p. 7.

[17]   This film, directed by Lee Tamahori from Alan Duff's novel of the same name, had extensive international distribution from 1994 onwards.

[18]   Editorial, *The New Zealand Herald*, 25 August 2004.

[19]   Peter Lineham, 'Wanna be in my Gang?', *New Zealand Listener*, 11–17 September 2004, p. 24.

than as an instance of democratic action, even if its values and policies were unlikely ever to be subscribed to by a majority of New Zealanders. As events transpired, however, there was little cause for the populace to be concerned. At the next year's election the Destiny Party obtained less than 1 per cent of the party vote and had disbanded by the 2008 election.

The Exclusive Brethren and their Social Positioning

While the impudence of the Destiny threat occupied the foreground in mid-2004, there was in fact another set of mediated activities underway that would come closer to success and was more seriously contemptuous of the democratic process.

The Brethren movement originated in Ireland in the late 1820s, but later split into several branches, of which the Exclusive Brethren has been the most reclusive. Nowadays, the sect claims to have around 40,000 members worldwide and around 5,000 in New Zealand.[20] The manner in which the Exclusive Brethren envisage the ideal relationship of Christians to the world may be described as either 'rejectionist', if Christ is understood as rejecting society, politics and culture,[21] or 'perfectionist'[22] in the religio-ethical sense of seeking to live by a perfect Christian ethics. According to their literature:

> The Brethren believe that separation is a vital part of our loyalty to Christ and we derive this belief from the scriptures. Separation principally occurs in matters of fellowship and includes social activities such as eating and drinking, membership of societies and entertainment.[23]

As an aspect of separation the Brethren community observes severe restraints on media use. While members are permitted to read newspapers, they do not own radios or televisions, do not use the Internet, do not use cell phones for other than business purposes, go to the movies or attend public theatre.[24] Observation of these restraints is intensified by gender and age according to a Brethren male, as women and children are considered more susceptible to the corrupting effects of media:

> We have no TV and movies, we do have newspapers but view it [media] on merits. I might get *Time* but not *Women's Weekly* [...] especially our young ones,

---

[20]   At http://www.theexclusivebrethren.com, accessed 20 June 2009.

[21]   Colm McKeogh, personal email, 28 June 2007,

[22]   Marion Maddox, *God and New Zealand Public Life*, the Ferguson Lecture, given at St David's Presbyterian Church, Auckland, New Zealand, June 2006.

[23]   Barry Pinker and Tim Lough, *The Truth about the Exclusive Brethren*, published by the Exclusive Brethren in New Zealand (2007), p. 3.

[24]   Ibid. p. 4.

we try and keep them clear of influences that will lead them away, degrading influences.[25]

The media culture of the Exclusive Brethren is therefore more restrictive and typographically based than that of Destiny, with minimal orientation towards public relations activities.

Also forbidden in the period under consideration was direct involvement in politics by the act of voting. The Brethren were consequently in a difficult position in relation to democracy since the nature of governance in nations in which they reside is a matter of concern to them. They will not live in a country unless its government is built on Christian values, but within that context they will support whatever party is in power and they will meet the obligations of both central and local government law.[26] It appears, however, that after the appointment of a new leader, the Australian Bruce Hales, in 2002, the Exclusive Brethren intensified a move from passive acceptance to active political influence.[27] As businessmen running small- to medium-sized enterprises, many Brethren have amassed considerable financial resources; and there is evidence, uncovered by Australian investigative journalists David Marr and Peter and Bronte Trainor, that these funds have been used to provide covert support to conservative politicians in Canada, Sweden, the United States, Australia and, most recently, New Zealand.[28] In the United States they were supporters of the Thanksgiving 2004 committee, which campaigned to re-elect George Bush Jr. and also commissioned advertisements for a Senate candidate opposed to gay marriage in Florida.[29]

The Exclusive Brethren and New Zealand Politics

In New Zealand the Exclusive Brethren wanted Labour out of power because they, like the Destiny-led coalition, saw the enacting of socially liberal legislation as corrosive of Christian values. They preferred the National Party's support for the lowering of taxes and some redirection of public funding towards privatized forms of education: a policy that suited their interests as separationists running private schools. In addition there was ethnic and class compatibility between the European males dominating both political group and church that favoured a relationship between them.

In the National Party, therefore, the Exclusive Brethren found a partner willing to accept their support, yet eager, like themselves, to keep that relationship

---

[25]   Tim Lough, personal conversation, 19 February 2007.

[26]   Pinker and Lough, *The Truth about the Exclusive Brethren*, p. 5.

[27]   David Marr, 'Hidden Prophets', *The Sydney Morning Herald*, 1 July 2006, at http://www.smh.com.au/articles/2006/01/11511744019.htm, accessed 22 June 2007.

[28]   Ibid.

[29]   Ibid.

covert. National's goal was to appear sufficiently centrist to be electable in a constituency still disapproving of the free-market reforms of 20 years earlier. Beyond the immediate goal of gaining power, however, there is evidence, provided by investigative journalist Nicky Hager, assisted in this case by the 'leaking' of internal National Party emails,[30] that the party planned to return to a programme of privatization of state assets. In light of the need for delicate positioning, the National Party's communications were carefully managed by a team including the consultants Crosby and Textor, who had helped the Liberals in Australia and the Conservative Party in Britain with recent election campaigns.[31] A witty, 'attack' advertising campaign, the honing of messages after focus group feedback, and the fostering of perceptions that the government was overly sympathetic to minorities, advanced National's poll ratings to the point where the election seemed to be winnable.

In comparison with the National Party's sophisticated media management strategies, the Exclusive Brethren's skills in this area were limited to the production of basic written propaganda. Nevertheless their contribution was useful because it could extend campaign activities beyond the legal cap of one million dollars that National was itself allowed to spend.[32]

Hager's account demonstrates that the Brethren began meeting with party representatives in mid-2004.[33] In April 2005 a group of New Zealand Brethren spent around $350,000[34] on newspaper advertisements and pamphlets urging New Zealanders to 'wake up' and improve national security by strengthening the country's relationship with the United States. The materials had a clumsy, type-heavy appearance, their provenance attributed only to 'A Smith'. Then, five months later, two weeks prior to the 14 September election, a larger series of pamphlets was distributed nationwide, bringing the Brethren's outlay to around $1 million.[35] These pamphlets, authorized by 'Stephen Win', with no organizational affiliation provided, did not deal with religious or moral issues; they promised greater prosperity by means of individuals taking increased responsibility for their own health and education – tax cuts would give citizens more disposable income, the text promised. The Labour Party and its coalition partner, the Greens, were denounced for damaging

---

[30]   Nicky Hager, *The Hollow Men: Study in the Politics of Deception* (Nelson NZ: Craig Potton Publishing, 2006). This account was crafted from documents forwarded to Hager by members of the National Party ashamed, he says, of the 'unprincipled' nature of what had taken place.

[31]   Ibid., and others.

[32]   Electoral Act 1993, Section 214b.

[33]   Alister Barry's documentary *The Hollow Men* (Community Media Trust, 2008) builds on Hager's research and employs documentary footage taken pre-election to demonstrate that senior National members and the Brethren had met on several occasions.

[34]   Radio New Zealand National, 'Exclusive Brethren Interview', broadcast on *Nine to Noon*, 18 April 2007.

[35]   Ibid.

both the business climate and the international reputation of New Zealand. While not mentioning National explicitly, it was time to change the government, these publications asserted, using the blue colour associated with that party's brand.

The Green Party in particular began demanding to know the propaganda's origins; National representatives said repeatedly that they did not know. However, on 4 September former, disaffected, members of the Brethren told the media that the pamphlets were Brethren publications. During the ensuing controversy the claims of the Leader of the Opposition, Don Brash, that he was unaware of the Brethren's activities became unsustainable, especially once senior Brethren gave an unprecedented press conference and spoke of their joint planning with National. Brash's credibility was damaged and National narrowly failed to win the election. A few months later Brash resigned the leadership over this and other issues related to his integrity.

The Exclusive Brethren underwent sustained public ridicule for what was seen as a hypocritical attempt to influence an election in which they were not prepared to vote. The re-elected government lambasted them in parliament, with a Brethren spokesman later asserting that 'more than 330 demeaning comments' had been made about them including comparisons to the Taliban: accusations, he alleged, amounting to systematic persecution.[36] The government further capitalized on the scandal to introduce the Electoral Finance Act 2007, circumscribing third-party contributions to electoral campaigns, insisting both on the transparency of donations and limiting them to a cap of $130,000 from each third party.[37]

For the Exclusive Brethren in this period there was even less thoughtful coverage than there had been for Destiny, with expert commentary concentrated in academic locations such as Marion Maddox's reflections on the influence the Brethren's premillennial dispensationalist theology likely had on their actions.[38] Otherwise, discourse around the Brethren's role characterized them as markers of duplicity in the political system. For instance, Nicky Hager's book about the election campaign, *The Hollow Men*, was followed by a play and drama documentary of the same name.[39] From being loathe to engage with the media, the Brethren now circulated in popular culture as venial fools within a secular morality play, power over their own representation arrogated almost entirely by others.

After-effects

An instructive aspect of both these cases, considering earlier observations about the inescapability of media engagement for contemporary religious groups, is

---

[36]   Barry Pinker, Speech given at National Interfaith Forum, Waikato University, 19 February 2007.

[37]   Electoral Finance Act 2007, Section 2, Subparts 1–6.

[38]   Maddox, *God under Howard*.

[39]   Barry, *The Hollow Men*.

the degree to which the Exclusive Brethren and Destiny have been further drawn into contact with mainstream media in pursuit of remedy for damage to their reputations. For both there was a period of retreat and remonstration, but also a growing alignment with the assumption that the media are identified with the 'centre' of public life.[40] In the Brethren case there was the untypical reaction of calling a press conference in September 2005. When that only provided material for further controversy, they retreated. Seventeen months later a group of four male Brethren re-emerged into a limited public setting at a national InterFaith meeting. Armed with an analysis of media power, which they characterized as linked to governmental power, they requested the support of other religious groups, describing themselves as victims of prejudicial misreporting that left them unable to operate in the public sphere. 'We are political poison', one of their number said. 'We can no longer approach our elected representatives'.[41] Like Tamaki, they were also angry that the issues they had intended to use the media to advance had never been debated.

Destiny too went through a period of realizing the strength of the power that the media as a body exercises in its own right, making this evident in a DVD – *New Zealand: A Nation under Siege* – distributed at 2005 Destiny Party campaign meetings. Produced in the style of a current affairs programme with Tamaki as presenter, the DVD denounces the media as a form of 'modern-day witchcraft', carriers of the ideologies of the secular government.[42] Continuing the irony of seeking redress from oppression in the medium of oppression, Destiny sought legitimizing media opportunities: co-operating on a feature for *The Listener* magazine, and having Tamaki photographed both during a ceremony where he gained the title of Bishop and among important guests at New Zealand's national day ceremonies.[43] Recent coverage of Destiny indicates that it is building a broader powerbase by registering as an Urban Maori Authority, a secular entity that receives government funding to look after the health and education needs of city-dwelling Maori.

In the aftermath of the New Zealand scandal the Exclusive Brethren leadership in Australia appointed its first media spokesperson, the personable Tony McCorkill. McCorkill arrived in New Zealand in April 2007 to argue, during radio, television and newspaper interviews, that the situation had been misunderstood and that the New Zealand Brethren had acted as a collection of private individuals. Their actions therefore should not reflect on the whole religious organization.[44] This

---

[40]   This is an assumption explored across both Nick Couldry's and James Curran's work, for instance *Contesting Media Power: Alternative Media in a Networked World* (Lanham, MD: Rowman & Littlefield, 2003)

[41]   Lough, 19 February 2007.

[42]   Brian Tamaki, *New Zealand: A Nation under Seige*, DVD (Destiny TV, 2005)

[43]   Sarah Stuart, 'Choice Turnout for The Chosen', *Sunday Star–Times*, 19 June 2005, p. A6.

[44]   On RNZ, *Nine to Noon*, 18 April 2007.

argument was viewed by some as disingenuous, since Australian investigations had confirmed the extent of leader Bruce Hales's authority over members of the sect.[45] What experienced observers took McCorkill's claim to mean was that Hales had not given approval for the specific tactics, rather than that he had not tacitly authorized the goals of the campaign.[46] In early 2008 it was announced that Brethren members were now free to vote if they wished and that some media restrictions had been relaxed.[47]

Australian sociologist Gary Bouma therefore views the bruising encounter with mediated politics as motivation for positive change among the Exclusive Brethren. The fact that the Brethren are now, in some situations, trying to work on a private citizen versus religious membership basis is unfamiliar territory for them:

> I think what we are looking at is a group beginning to engage in a public spirit, which is a step in the right direction, because in fact it was done in a crude and brutal way in the first instance. I would not sanction that in a minute ... but they have learned from that how better to engage with a wider society. That is a step toward involvement, which has to be a healthy step in the first place.[48]

Conclusions

At one level these case studies are very legible. For a notional 'average' New Zealander they reconfirm the foolishness of marginal religious groups attempting to generate influence in a secular society and reassure us that the media are still patrolling the boundaries of social consensus. They are also emblematic of similar conflicts in Western nations around processes of mediation; indeed, in the Brethren case they are literally representative of covert campaigns undertaken in other countries, although these ended without such ignominious exposure. However, the legibility of the examples, the extent to which they have become shorthand for forms of anti-democratic threat, belies the fact that they arise from, and negotiate, a complex of forces around relationships between the media and religiously inflected politics that few fully understand.

The cases of the Destiny-led protest and the Exclusive Brethren pamphlet campaign are certainly evidence that religions today and their public reception are shaped by the media as much as religions are able to utilize the media for particular purposes. A reflexive understanding of the complexities of this double articulation is therefore an aspect of contemporary cultural competence. As Curran and Gurevitch write,

---

[45]   Ibid.

[46]   Ibid.

[47]   Patrick Gower, 'Brethren Members Free to Vote in Election', *New Zealand Herald*, 26 January 2008.

[48]   On RNZ, *Nine to Noon*, 18 April 2007.

It has become an increasingly demanding task to operate effectively in this [mediated] space, one for which expert assistance is now regarded as indispensable ... Consequently, almost all would-be political advocates – not only political parties and candidates but also the leading cause and interest groups that compose 'civil society' – must *professionalize* their approaches to media publicity and hire the services of personnel skilled in such activities as planning campaigns, conducting and interpreting opinion research, adapting to the schedules and formats of diverse media outlets, and addressing the news values and working practices of journalism.[49]

The purpose of this article is not, however, to exhort expansionist religious organizations to hire public relations representatives, although it can be seen that the dynamics of both situations did lead to the adoption of secular public relations techniques. The purpose is, rather, to indicate briefly that the exertion of media power does not come from a simple, unified source. In both cases examined it took different kinds of mediated commentary, functioning over an extended timescale, to produce a picture robust enough to demonstrate that these organizations, isolated and marginal as they were depicted to be, were in fact tied into other networks of power operating in New Zealand society. In relation to Destiny, the most evidently relevant networks were those related to class and ethnicity, where a group that suffers from collective social disadvantage expressed itself in terms of religious discourses of morality, using methods incorporating idiosyncratic re-workings of mainstream media protocols. Yet the attempt at creating a public space in which they could exercise power was efficiently constrained and discounted by the mainstream media themselves. The overarching neo-liberal economic framework, which, by contrast, privileges endeavours to achieve commercial advantage through the complex, less visible, paths of political lobbying, also emboldened the Exclusive Brethren, in their case leading them to downplay their moral and religious motivations. For a while, their access to potential power was satisfyingly direct, since what they could offer suited a political group that itself saw contemporary governance as achieved through the expert manipulation of media power. In that moment, however, that joint strategy did not succeed, due in part to another smaller division of mediated power: the investigative branch of journalism.

Finally, while the extent to which Destiny and the Exclusive Brethren exposed themselves to disciplinary ridicule from the majority of New Zealanders has been emphasized, there were other constituencies in which an opposing tendency was in fact exacerbated. The conservative Christian constituency is still only a small portion of the electorate, but, as Maddox has pointed out, 'moderate right parties can actually benefit from more extreme expressions enjoying publicity. As ... extreme positions emerge on the far right, those only slightly closer to the centre

---

[49]   In Curran and Gurevitch (eds), *Mass Society and Mass Media*, p. 115 (original emphasis).

can portray themselves as moderate by comparison'.[50] The National Party may have suffered electoral defeat in 2005, but in 2008, with a new leader, and having publicly repudiated the Brethren, it became the governing party as the result of a decisive swing away from Labour.

---

[50]   Maddox, 2006, p. 12.

Chapter 15

Social Security with a Christian Twist in John Howard's Australia[1]

Holly Randell-Moon

We are a society that respects all religions, but we should respect our own history and our own traditions.[2]

It remains the fact that the Christian religion is the greatest force for good, progress and dignity of the individual in this nation.[3]

The free enterprise parable – the parable [of the Talents] … tells us that we have a responsibility, if we are given assets, to add to those assets in a fair manner and that if we don't do anything to add to them that is not necessarily the right behaviour.[4]

Introduction

This chapter takes as its focus the retraction of public welfare services under the Australian Howard government (1996–2007) and the government's claim that Christian charities could provide both a morally sound and inexpensive welfare system. Central to this shift from governmental to religious welfare was the discursive representation of Christianity as strengthening Australian culture and the Australian state by fostering individual freedom. The excerpts above are taken from speeches made by the former Australian prime minister John Howard. They reveal how a discursive relationship between Christianity and neo-liberalism is created. This is achieved, firstly, by linking Christianity to the founding traditions

---

[1]   My gratitude to Anthony Lambert and Arthur Randell for helping me to clarify and explain the issues outlined in this contribution. Thanks also to the editors for their comments, which have helped to improve the theoretical focus of the chapter.
[2]   John Howard, 'House of Representatives', *Parliamentary Debates (Hansard)*, 3 (9 December 2004): p. 119.
[3]   Ibid., p. 118.
[4]   John Howard, 'Prime Minister John Howard's Speech at the Australian Christian Lobby "Make it Count 2007" including questions and answers from the audience – transcript', *Media Monitors*, 9 August 2007, p. 7, at http://www.acl.org.au/national/browse. stw?article_id=16870, accessed 24 September 2010.

and history of Australian culture, where Christianity is seen to contribute to the 'good' of Australian society. Secondly, Christianity is represented as 'good' because it fosters the importance of the individual and the responsibility of individuals to increase their assets, an emphasis also shared by neo-liberal economic principles.[5] Neo-liberal theory promotes the idea that individual freedom of choice and wellbeing are best secured through market forces and 'quality by competition'.[6] I shall argue that the Howard government's discursive equivalences between Christianity and goodness, goodness and individual freedom, made Christianity compatible with the government's neo-liberal policies of welfare reform.

The Howard government's welfare reforms, initiated in the late 1990s, involved privatizing welfare services and contracting them to employment agencies through a competitive tendering system. Christian church welfare and charity agencies were awarded a large number of contracts under this system.[7] The privatization of unemployment services was seen to provide a more flexible and cost-efficient delivery of welfare compared to the bureaucratic, and impersonal, government-run agencies. Privatization was also viewed as giving welfare recipients greater individual autonomy and freedom by allowing them to choose the job agency that best suited their needs.[8] The application of neo-liberal principles to welfare policy approximates the governance from a distance model of state power referred to by Michel Foucault as governmentality.[9] Foucault defines governmentality as the strategies and tactics employed by the government 'to develop those elements constitutive of individual's lives in such a way that their development also' fosters 'the strength of the state'.[10] In granting welfare recipients the autonomy to choose their own job agency and take responsibility for their unemployment status, the government is ostensibly letting welfare recipients govern themselves. At the same time, welfare recipients face sanctions (such as the removal of benefits)

---

[5]   Based on a different set of political ideals, an anti-wealth reading of Christianity is also possible. See for example Matthew 19:24, 21:12; Luke 12:15.

[6]   Robert Hogg, 'Myths and Markets: Australian Culture and Economic Doctrine', *Journal of Australian Studies*, 11 (2002): p. 239.

[7]   John Warhurst, 'Religion and Politics in the Howard Decade', *Australian Journal of Political Science*, 42/1 (2007): p. 26; see also Patricia Karvelas, 'Church Lobby to Get Way on Dole', *The Australian*, 5 September 2005, p. 2.

[8]   Neal Ryan, 'Reconstructing Citizens as Consumers: Implications for New Modes of Governance', *Australia Journal of Public Administration*, 60/3 (2001): pp. 104–9.

[9]   Michel Foucault, 'Governmentality', in Graham Burchell, Colin Gordon and Peter Miller (eds), *The Foucault Effect: Studies in Governmentality* (Chicago, IL: University of Chicago Press, 1991), pp. 87–104.

[10]   Michel Foucault, 'Pastoral Power and Political Reason', in Jeremy R. Carrette (ed.), *Religion and Culture by Michel Foucault* (Manchester: Manchester University Press, 1999), p. 151.

for insufficient progress in finding employment.[11] Thus individuals must govern themselves, but only according to the welfare regulations established by the government so that the maximum benefit from these services can be obtained.

I shall argue that the Howard government's integration of church agencies into privatized welfare was used to privilege 'Christian values' as the 'correct' way for welfare subjects to govern themselves. The government was able to promote its version of 'Christian values' but located these values in the private sphere and as something individuals could freely 'choose' as part of their welfare services. Coupled with the government's discursive promotion of a Christian nationalism as consistent with neo-liberal ideals of individual freedom and wealth creation, the government privatized its political and economic agenda through a neo-liberal governmentality. The relationship between Christian values and neo-liberal policy under the Howard government also reveals a broader set of political implications and problems with neo-liberal discourse. Neo-liberal policy relies on the construction of a market system that runs, ostensibly, as an independent entity outside of governmental or political bias.[12] For this reason, the strategies of governance deployed in areas such as welfare reform, and their connection to the political and religious ideals of the government, are removed from view when neo-liberalism is represented as simply encouraging individual choice and limited government.

The following sections will make visible the governmentality involved in neo-liberal welfare reform by charting the ways a discourse of 'Christian values' became an important part of the Howard government's political and economic agenda, subsequently attending to neo-liberalism's connections to Christianity, Christian nationalism and to welfare reform in Australia during that time.

The Howard Government and 'Christian Values'

The Coalition government, led by former prime minister John Howard, comprised a majority Liberal Party with a minority National Party, both of which are on the 'conservative' side of Australian politics. A significant part of the government's federal election successes (they won office four times) was the framing of their policies in terms of 'mainstream' Australian values. These values were positioned as having been ignored by the previous Paul Keating-led Labor government (1991–96). Labor was viewed as having privileged multiculturalism, women's rights and Indigenous issues to the detriment of 'ordinary' Australians. As a result, the Howard government fought a series of 'history wars' and 'culture wars' during its time in office to re-establish the virtue of Australia's British and European heritage. This heritage was seen to be tarnished by left-wing accounts of Australian

---

[11]   Janet Newman, *Modernising Governance: New Labour, Policy and Society* (London: Sage, 2002), p. 150.

[12]   David Harvey, *A Brief History of Neoliberalism* (Oxford: Oxford University Press, 2005), p. 68.

history that focused too readily on colonialism.[13] The culture wars and the history wars were localized responses to broader international debates about whether the 'gains made in an earlier period by the Left through the social movements of women and gays, and through campaigns against racism' were alienating to middle-class, white constituencies.[14]

It is within the context of Australia's mainstream values and heritage needing to be re-established and prioritized in government policy that Christianity became more visible in Australian politics.[15] Australian political and legal institutions have a historical relationship to Christianity due to the importation of a predominantly British–Protestant culture during colonialism in the late 1700s and early 1800s.[16] In this sense, a residual Christianity underpins political institutions even as secular neutrality has defined modern Australian government operations.[17] The more overt politicization of Christianity under the Howard government was used to bolster their claims to govern for mainstream Australians and their values. The government variously defined mainstream Australian values as: 'values of fairness, of mateship, of equality between men and women, of Parliamentary democracy, of the rule of law'.[18] 'Judaeo-Christian ethics', 'British political culture' and 'distinct Irish and non-conformist traditions' also made up Australia's cultural heritage according to Howard.[19] The association of Judaeo-Christianity with a British and Irish heritage privileges an Anglo-Celtic view of Australian culture (and Judaeo-Christianity). Representing Australian culture in this way makes invisible and unimportant the presence of Indigenous cultures and sovereignties existing prior

---

[13]   See Tony Birch, '"Black Armbands and White Veils": John Howard's Moral Amnesia', *Melbourne Historical Journal*, 25 (1997): pp. 8–16; Stuart Macintyre and Anna Clark, *The History Wars* (Carlton: Melbourne University Press, 2004).

[14]   David McKnight, *Beyond Right and Left: New Politics and the Culture Wars* (Crows Nest: Allen & Unwin, 2005), pp. 152–3.

[15]   See Marion Maddox, *God under Howard: The Rise of the Religious Right in Australian Politics* (Crows Nest: Allen & Unwin, 2005).

[16]   Aileen Moreton-Robinson, 'Indigenous History Wars and the Virtue of the White Nation', in David Carter (ed.), *The Ideas Market: An Alternative Take on Australia's Intellectual Life* (Carlton: Melbourne University Press, 2004), pp. 219–35; Anne Pattel-Gray, 'The Hard Truth: White Secrets, Black Realities', *Australian Feminist Studies*, 14/30 (1999): pp. 259–66.

[17]   See Holly Randell-Moon, 'Section 116: The Politics of Secularism in Australian Legal and Political Discourse', in Basia Spalek and Alia Imtoual (eds), *Religion, Spirituality and the Social Sciences: Challenging Marginalisation* (Bristol: Policy Press, 2008), pp. 51–62.

[18]   John Howard, 'Transcript of the Prime Minster the Hon John Howard MP Address to 10th Anniversary Dinner, Great Hall, Parliament House', 1 March 2006, at http://www.pm.gov.au/news/speeches/speech1798.html, accessed 24 September 2010.

[19]   John Howard, 'Transcript of the Prime Minster the Hon John Howard MP Address to the National Press Club, Great Hall, Parliament House', 25 January 2006, at http://www.pm.gov.au/news/speeches/speech1754.html, accessed 24 September 2010.

to and continuing after colonization.[20] The framing of Judaeo-Christianity through a specifically Anglo-Celtic heritage also downplays the role of both non-Christian and non-Anglo migrants within Australian history and culture.[21]

Christianity was central to the Howard government's representations of Australian culture because it was viewed as promoting 'good' values such as individualism and freedom. In his 2004 valedictory speech, Howard argued that 'we are a society that respects all religions, but we should respect our own history and our own traditions', naming specifically 'our' Judaeo-Christian foundations.[22] The importance of this Christian tradition stems from 'the fact that the Christian religion is the greatest force for good, progress and dignity of the individual in this nation'.[23] Christianity is universalized here as a 'force' transcendental to politics even as it is linked to specific political markers such as individualism.[24] This universalization involves downplaying the specific histories and contexts, such as colonialism, that might account for how Christianity came to be associated with Australian nationalism in favour of a Christianity that has somehow always been here.[25]

The discursive construction of Christianity as a 'force' for goodness, which seemingly exists outside of and yet underpins an Anglo-Celtic history, serves both an individualizing and collectivizing purpose in the Howard government's neo-liberal policies. Christianity is represented as a moral 'force' that binds Australian citizens together for the good of the nation but allows and promotes individual freedom. During the Australian Christian Lobby's 'Make it Count 2007' forum, Howard related his government's policies to the parables of the Good Samaritan and the Talents. The parable of the Good Samaritan 'teaches us … that every individual has an intrinsic worth of his or her own'.[26] Howard appears to read the

---

[20]　See Aileen Moreton-Robinson, 'The House that Jack Built: Britishness and White Possession', *Australian Critical Race and Whiteness Studies eJournal*, 1 (2005): pp. 21–9, at http://www.acrawsa.org.au/ejournalFiles/Volume%201,%20Number%201,%202005/AileenMoretonRobinson.pdf, accessed 1 October 2010

[21]　See Holly Randell-Moon, '"Common values": Whiteness, Christianity, Asylum Seekers and the Howard Government', *Australian Critical Race and Whiteness Studies e–Journal*, 2/1 (2006): pp. 1–14, at http://www.acrawsa.org.au/ejournalFiles/Volume%202,%20Number%201,%202006/HollyRandell-Moon.pdf, accessed 24 September 2010.

[22]　Howard, 'House of Representatives', p. 119.

[23]　Ibid., p. 118.

[24]　See Holly Randell-Moon, 'Creating Pope John Paul II: Religion, the "War on Terror" and the Politics of Discourses of Howardage', *borderlands e–journal*, 5/3 (2006), at http://www.borderlands.net.au/vol5no3_2006/randellmoon_pope.htm, accessed 24 September 2010.

[25]　Toula Nicolacopoulos and George Vassilacopoulos, 'Racism, Foreigner Communities and the Onto-Pathology of White Australian Subjectivity', in Aileen Moreton-Robinson (ed.), *Whitening Race: Essays in Social and Cultural Criticism* (Canberra: Aboriginal Studies Press, 2004), p. 45.

[26]　Howard, 'Prime Minister John Howard's Speech', pp. 6–7.

significance of the individual as the most important aspect of this parable.[27] The significance of the individual is supported by his reading of the parable of the Talents, which for Howard is:

> ... the free enterprise parable – the parable that tells us that we have a responsibility, if we are given assets, to add to those assets in a fair manner and that if we don't do anything to add to them that is not necessarily the right behaviour.[28]

The notion that it is morally beneficial for an individual to increase their wealth has resonances with neo-liberal theories that promote 'human well-being ... by liberating individual entrepreneurial freedoms and skills within an institutional framework characterized by strong private property rights, free markets, and free trade'.[29] Howard's focus on Christianity as containing 'basic tenets' supportive of 'individual choice and free will'[30] suggests a compatibility with neo-liberal economic ideals that also stress the importance of individual freedom of choice.

Christian Nationalism and Neo-liberal Governmentality

The Howard government created an association between Christianity and neo-liberal economic discourse because both were seen to support individual freedom and wealth creation. But why associate Christianity with neo-liberal ideas if, according to neo-liberalism, individual freedoms are best secured through market forces alone? The links between neo-liberal economics and a socially conservative Christianity can be explained by what David Harvey sees as the tensions between an 'alienating, possessive individualism on the one hand' and 'the desire for a meaningful collective on the other'.[31] Even as neo-liberal theory promotes individual action and choice above else, it nevertheless influences the development of nationalisms or overarching moral orders as ways 'to counteract the dissolving effect of the chaos of individual interests that neoliberalism typically produces'.[32] Harvey points to former British prime minister Margaret Thatcher's use of populist nationalism to gain electoral success in order to further her government's neo-liberal economic policies.[33] Similarly, in the United States,

---

[27]   He does not, for example, read the parable in a way that encourages an ethics for others beyond the individual self; the primacy of the individual is the first ethical component of the parable for Howard.

[28]   Howard, 'Prime Minister John Howard's Speech', pp. 6–7.

[29]   Harvey, *A Brief History*, p. 2.

[30]   Howard, 'House of Representatives', p. 118.

[31]   Harvey, *A Brief History*, p. 69.

[32]   Ibid., p. 83.

[33]   Ibid., p. 79.

neoconservatives have suggested that neo-liberal policies ought to be accompanied by 'an overweening morality' that would serve as 'the necessary social glue to keep the body politic secure in the face of external and internal dangers'.[34] The Howard government drew on both neoconservative ideals of morality and Thatcher's populist nationalism in their framing of neo-liberal policies as good for Australian society.

Framing a national and moral order through neo-liberal economic discourse has the effect of naturalizing these political ideologies as common sense or normal. For example, Howard described liberalism as relevant 'to the concerns and aspirations of the Australian mainstream, rather than the narrower agendas of elites and special interests'.[35] As in the culture wars, there is a contrast in governance here between designing 'special' policy for a minority of constituents and a traditional liberalism that simply requires governments to foster and promote the inherent capacities and freedoms of individuals. The suggestion is that liberalism and individualism are not biased towards any specific group of constituents even though these ideas have a specific cultural and racialized history.[36]

Moreover, as Foucault argues, the individual autonomy implied by liberalism should not be understood as securing an individual's freedom from social or political constraints. Constituting national subjects as individuals is a means through which certain kinds of governance are made possible.[37] This is a central point of his theory of governmentality, an 'art of government or state rationality' that emerged in seventeenth-century Europe.[38] Governmentality comprises the strategies and tactics employed by the state to reconcile the interests of 'each individual who goes to make up the population' as well as 'the interest of the population regardless of what the particular interests and aspirations may be of the individuals who compose it'.[39] The state fosters individual freedom to the degree that individuals govern and discipline themselves according to the requirements of the state.

The Howard government's promotion of a Christian nationalism acting as a 'force for goodness' is a religious variation of this type of governmentality. Howard's Christian morality is represented as both consistent with individual freedoms yet containing those freedoms within an overarching moral and national order. The values that make up this national and moral order are then positioned as self-generating and autonomous rather than produced and reproduced according to specific political and historical agendas. This is how the privileging of citizens

---

[34]   Ibid., p. 82.

[35]   As cited in Mary Kalantzis, 'Australia Fair: Realties and Banalities of Nation in the Howard Era', *Overland*, 178 (2005): p. 12.

[36]   See for example David Theo Goldberg, *Racist Culture: Philosophy and the Politics of Meaning* (Cambridge, MA: Blackwell, 1993).

[37]   Michel Foucault, 'Two Lectures', in Colin Gordon (ed.), *Power/Knowledge* (New York: Pantheon Books, 1980), p. 98.

[38]   Foucault, 'Pastoral Power', p. 151.

[39]   Foucault, 'Governmentality', p. 100.

according to certain racialized and religious identities (of Anglo-Celtic and Judaeo-Christian values) becomes represented as simply a universal or transhistorical phenomenon. Despite a potentially radical undoing of nationalism implied in neo-liberalism's economic imperatives for freedom of choice, neo-liberalism nevertheless requires citizens to submit to a set of shared national and religious values so that coherent, nationalized governance is still possible.

For this reason, neo-liberalism's claims to foster a society of individuals, where structural disadvantage based on class or race does not effect market competition, becomes unsustainable and problematic. Before he was elected the new prime minister under Labor, Kevin Rudd was critical of the Howard government's neo-liberal economic reforms of industrial relations and welfare. He saw these reforms in tension with community and family values. 'Rampart individualism, unconstrained by any responsibility for interests beyond the individual, is inherently destructive' when aligned with neo-liberal capitalism because it 'is capable of destroying any social institution that inhibits maximisation of individual self-interest'.[40] For Rudd, neo-liberal ideas are dangerous because they privilege the individual above all else. It is misleading though, to view neo-liberalism as unconnected from social and cultural ideas about community and the state. Because neo-liberalism removes government intervention from society as a policy norm, it could be argued that national governments become more invested in the promotion of collective and community organizations to take up the slack left over from diminishing governmental responsibility for the social welfare of citizens. But only certain kinds of community organizations and collective socializing are seen to allow neo-liberal economic principles to succeed. Unions, collective bargaining or a national unity where each citizen receives an equal share of health insurance and employment protection, for example, would compromise a non-regulated and free market advocated by neo-liberalism.[41] This is why religion, and specifically Christianity in the context of Howard's Australia, is particularly suited to neo-liberal reforms because it is constructed as something that exists outside of the political. It is religion's ability to supposedly thrive without government interference that makes it compatible with neo-liberal policies.

Neo-liberal Welfare Reform

In this final section, I shall look at how the Howard government's privatization of welfare enabled church charities and agencies to be integrated into the state's delivery of social security provisions. The discursive representations of a common morality and national unity safeguarding individual freedom laid the groundwork for reorienting the welfare of citizens from a state to a private and religious

---

[40]   Kevin Rudd, 'Faith in Politics', *The Monthly*, 17, October 2006, at http://www. themonthly.com.au/tm/?q=node/300, accessed 24 September 2010.

[41]   Harvey, *A Brief History*, p. 75.

concern. The privatization of social security according to neo-liberal economic ideas attempts to give citizens more autonomy by transforming welfare into a market-based service for 'customers'.[42] In 1998 the Job Network scheme replaced the Commonwealth Employment Service by outsourcing job search provisions to private contractors, including church charities and agencies.[43] The basis for this privatization was the idea that recipients of social security could then choose an unemployment service that suited their needs. The Howard government's welfare reforms followed a model of economic rationalism whereby 'economic resources are better allocated through market forces than by government intervention'.[44] According to this theory, market competition between welfare agencies has the advantage of making social security provisions more efficient and cheaper for the government to run.

Privatized social security operates through a contractual-based system where welfare recipients are framed as customers actively negotiating with the government. A consequence of framing welfare recipients in this way is that recipients are required to take responsibility for breaches of contractual rules. This can involve penalizing tactics such as the removal of benefits to foster self-disciplinary behaviour. The disciplinary component of privatized welfare allows a behavioural emphasis to be imputed to economic disadvantage because success or failure is put down to an individual's personal choice in education, training or job network agency.[45] Former treasurer and deputy prime minister Peter Costello argued that 'income support provides insulation against poverty [but] it does not treat the cause of poverty'. Church agencies, in delivering welfare services, are 'willing to share their values in support of treating underlying causes of poverty'.[46] The behavioural aspect to poverty implied here suggests that a values approach, in conjunction with financial support, can better address and deal with economic disadvantage more so than financial support alone. Unlike the bureaucratic and depersonalized nature of state-run social security, church agencies can address a welfare recipient's personal failings at an individual level.

This fusing of bureaucratic and spiritual discipline is indicative of what Foucault called 'pastoral power'. Emerging in the medieval period of Europe, 'pastoral power' involved a Christian theology centred on the care of the individual subject and a concern with improving the life of the people within a territory rather than conquering them.[47] The individualization of subjects was a crucial element in the

---

[42]   Harvey, *A Brief History*, p. 76; see also Newman, *Modernising Governance*, pp. 148–51; Ryan, 'Reconstructing Citizens', pp. 104–9.

[43]   See Warhurst, 'Religion and Politics', p. 26.

[44]   Hogg, 'Myths and Markets', p. 239.

[45]   Harvey, *A Brief History*, p. 65.

[46]   Peter Costello, 'Address to the Anglicare Lunch, "Is Faith a Lost Cause?", Watersedge, Pier One, Walsh Bay, Sydney', 27 June 2003, at http://www.treasurer.gov.au/ tsr/content/speeches/2003/007.asp, accessed 24 September 2010.

[47]   Foucault, 'Pastoral Power', p. 123.

formation of state power in the seventeenth century and the management of an economy tied to the productivity of individual citizens.[48] Foucault argues that the welfare state epitomizes 'pastoral government' in the sense that it individualizes and cares for subjects while integrating them within the larger economic structures of the state.[49] The privatization of welfare under the Howard government constitutes a neo-liberal version of pastoral power. The spiritual guidance provided by church employment agencies ensures that the governance of welfare subjects through otherwise bureaucratic and impersonal penalties can individually and more efficiently target underperforming welfare recipients.

Even as church agencies provide this more individualized approach to welfare, the Howard government viewed the religious character of church organizations as fostering a trustworthy environment for welfare recipients, one that is free from political bias. When addressing the Salvation Army's Red Shield Appeal Launch in 2006 Howard commented on the Army's involvement, along with other church agencies such as the Wesley Mission and Society of St Vincent de Paul, in government welfare programmes such as the Joblink Plus scheme. He stated that, although the Salvation Army 'is at core and at heart a traditional orthodox Christian organisation', it also 'helps people in a non-judgemental fashion … to establish a linkage with a person … to assist them in a non-judgemental way'.[50] The framing of church agencies as both non-judgemental and strongly religious reinforces the idea that these agencies offer a more personal approach to welfare services. Their Christian ethics nevertheless maintain objectivity and ensure a non-judgemental attitude. Similar to the idea that the free market is more efficient because it is objective and caters to individual needs in a way that public services cannot,[51] Christianity's pastoral care transcends political (as well as social and personal) bias and makes church agencies uniquely suited to the delivery of welfare in the private realm.

The discursive construction of Christianity's role in welfare reform as inherently pastoral and moral removes from view the political and economic benefits for the government in outsourcing welfare delivery to church agencies. The tendering of public services to private contractors such as church agencies was based on a competitive pricing system that took into account the services being offered and their cost. Beginning in 1998 when the Job Network scheme replaced the Commonwealth Employment Service, Christian church charities comprised a significant amount of the Job Network contracts tendered by the then Department

[48]   See Foucault, 'Governmentality'; also '17 March 1976', trans. David Macey, in Mauro Bertani and Alessandra Fontana (eds), *'Society Must Be Defended': Lectures at the Collège de France, 1975–1976* (London: The Penguin Press, 2003), pp. 239–64.

[49]   Foucault, 'Pastoral Power', p. 141.

[50]   John Howard, 'Address to the Red Shield Appeal Launch, Newcastle', 31 March 2006, at http://www.pm.gov.au/media/Speech/2006/speech1853.cfm, accessed 24 September 2010.

[51]   Ryan, 'Reconstructing Citizens', p. 105.

of Employment and Workplace Relations. For example, in 2005 newspapers reported that Catholic Welfare Australia, Uniting Care, Anglicare and the Salvation Army were awarded 20 per cent of the contracts.[52] Marion Maddox points out that 'one likely reason for the tenders by church agencies being so successful is that, as not-for-profit organizations, they could provide cheaper services than private enterprise'.[53] This is because, unlike the non-charitable and non-religious private contractors, church agencies are not run according to economic profit and are more likely to be staffed by voluntary or part-time workers.[54] Consequently, the likening of Christianity's pastoral care to a force for goodness that has somehow always existed within the Australian state frames the subsequent (neo-liberal) economic benefits of welfare reform as moral rather than political.

The differentiation of Christianity's moral character from the state's political character allowed Christianity to be depoliticized by the Howard government. In tendering unemployment services to Christian charities, the government also sought to implement measures obliging religious welfare agencies to adhere to 'non-judgemental' policy advocacy. These measures included contracts for welfare and unemployment services containing '"no criticism" clauses'[55] or 'non-advocacy clauses'.[56] These measures were consistent with a broader critique made by the government against some Christian organizations for commenting publicly on secular political issues. The former deputy prime minister, Peter Costello, had this to say at an Anglicare lunch in 2003:

> The church leaders had a lot to say about Australia's involvement in Iraq. When the Government was reforming the tax system [by introducing a goods and services tax] I was amazed how many church leaders were, in fact, tax experts who had sized up the moral dimensions of a value added tax.[57]

The argument that it is detrimental for the political sphere when church bodies advocate on policy issues is not necessarily contradictory with the above praise for church welfare agencies working to implement certain policies. Christian welfare agencies were praised because of their capability, in Costello's words, to step 'outside their role as taxpayers and income beneficiaries'.[58] Christianity's

---

[52]   See Karvelas, 'Church Lobby', p. 2.

[53]   Maddox, *God under Howard*, p. 247.

[54]   Ibid., p. 250.

[55]   Ibid., p. 251.

[56]   Stephen Judd and Anne Robinson, 'National Forum on Australia's Christian Heritage: Its Importance in our Past and its Relevance to our Future Social services, Parliament House, Canberra – Paper presented at the National Forum on Australia's Christian Heritage', 2006, p. 12, at http://www.australiaschristianheritageforum.org.au/Resources/RobinsonandJuddspaper.pdf, accessed 31 March 2007.

[57]   As cited in Maddox, *God under Howard*, p. 239.

[58]   As cited in ibid., p. 236.

pastoral care is idealized as a kind of transcendental moral force, supported by understandings of religion as something external to or outside politics. Contextual approaches to social issues by various Christian churches threaten this transcendental pastoral care by reinserting religion back into the politics of the state. The neo-liberal inflection to Christianity's pastoral care of welfare subjects then allowed the Howard government to maintain a strategic separation of religion and politics during their reform of welfare services. Because the privatization of social security attempts to consign welfare problems to the private sphere, the representation of Christianity as external to politics positions religious bodies as ideally suited to carrying out neo-liberal reforms.

Conclusion

The Howard government's integration of church agencies into the delivery of welfare services constitutes a form of neo-liberal governmentality with a Christian twist. The privatization of social security is often accompanied by promises of individual freedom and choice. Individual autonomy is ostensibly provided by these policies but only to the extent that neo-liberal governance of subjects is still possible from a distance through the sanctions and penalties deployed by private employment agencies. The pastoral care of Christian agencies is then discursively constructed by the Howard government as ensuring this economic disciplining of welfare subjects is morally sound. Such a discursive construction functions to legitimize the role and importance of Christianity to the Australian state.

The pastoral care attributed to church agencies in the context of welfare reform reinforced the broader political aims of the Howard government in using a Christian national unity, represented as a permanent and transhistorical feature of Australian society, to nullify and contain the potentially alienating effects of neo-liberal economic policy. A neo-liberal understanding of social relations as organized through market choice can seem unsettling when social security is retracted and economically vulnerable citizens are left to fend for themselves. The Howard government saw Christianity's role as providing pastoral care for citizens left vulnerable by neo-liberal policies, as well as providing a set of values and morals to unite individuals within a neo-liberal society. When religion is invoked in this way to balance neo-liberalism's absolute individualism with a collective sense of belonging,[59] religion is often conceived of as an overarching and, ostensibly, non-political force for goodness. The potential to see and address structural disadvantage is rendered difficult with neo-liberalism's insistence on limited government intervention into social relations and the conception of religion as simply an antidote for the poor market choices made by individuals.

---

[59] Harvey, *A Brief History*, p. 69.

The current Rudd government has advanced an alternative view of Christianity 'informed by a social gospel or Christian socialist tradition'[60] and has rolled back many of the contractual-based forms of welfare implemented under the former Howard government. However, the Rudd government's differentiation of its own policies as socially based, in contrast to the non-interventionist and individualist policies under Howard, takes at face value neo-liberalism's claim to limited governance and indifference to social relations. There can be no real engagement with the political effects of neo-liberal policies if neo-liberalism is understood in this way. Even as the Rudd government was critical of neo-liberalism under the Howard government, it has nevertheless continued the policies of its predecessor in relation to Indigenous affairs by offering welfare, education and housing services to disadvantaged communities in contractual-based exchanges for leases and title to land.[61] Both governments, in different ways, use neo-liberalism to place the burden of addressing institutional or social disadvantage onto individuals themselves. Although associated with discourses of freedom and individual difference through choice, neo-liberalism must be located within a system of governmentality that constructs citizens as individuals so that they will organize themselves into larger systems of power. Neo-liberalism relies on hegemonic identity-based forms of power, such as nationalism, to make coherent governance possible while relocating structural disadvantage based on gender, class or race to the private sphere of 'individual problems'. The relationship between Christian nationalism and neo-liberal policy under the Howard government analysed in this chapter reveals how a religious conception of national identity can be promoted and then depoliticized through privatized neo-liberal governance.

---

[60]   Rudd, 'Faith in Politics'.

[61]   See Larissa Behrendt, 'The Emergency We Had to Have', in Jon Altman and Melinda Hinkson (eds), *Coercive Reconciliation: Stabilise, Normalise, Exit Aboriginal Australia* (North Carlton: Arena Publications Association, 2007), pp. 15–20; Chris Graham, 'Editorial: A Racist Policy for Racist Times', *National Indigenous Times*, 178 (28 May 2009): n.p.; Irene Watson, 'The Aboriginal State of Emergency Arrived with Cook and the First Fleet', *Australian Feminist Law Journal*, 26 (2007): pp. 3–8.

Chapter 16

Mediated Spaces of Religious Community in Manila, Philippines

Katharine L. Wiegele

Introduction

El Shaddai is a popular Catholic charismatic movement founded and based in Manila, Philippines.[1] It began in 1984 as a non-denominational Christian radio programme, and within a few years described itself as a Catholic lay group, in keeping with the affiliation of its founder and the majority of its followers. Within 15 years, the group had become a substantial movement with a followership in the millions.[2] The group has chapters in nearly every province in the Philippines and in over 35 countries, with overseas participation comprising around 30 per cent of the total followership. The group is best known for its massive outdoor Saturday-night rallies in Manila, which attract half a million to a million followers each week. These 'prayer and healing rallies', which feature emotional preaching by 'Brother Mike' Velarde, the group's charismatic founder and 'Servant-Leader', are broadcast on television and radio throughout the country, while tapes of Velarde's sermons circulate widely among Filipino overseas workers. Velarde is a businessman-turned-preacher, without any formal religious training. His evocative and entertaining preaching style, his populist persona and message, and the belief that he can channel miracles to the faithful, however, allow him to attract crowds and monetary collections that are the envy of clergymen.[3] Followers in Manila, elsewhere in the Philippines, and in Filipino communities overseas, have formed

---

[1]   El Shaddai DWXI Prayer Partners Foundation International, Inc.

[2]   El Shaddai estimates of its own 'followership' have been based on crowd estimates at mass rallies and other events, prayer requests and tithes, prayer group attendance, chapter membership, radio listenership surveys and official membership. 'Followership' numbers around 5 million (or even 9–10 million at one point in time), according to El Shaddai officials, were also confirmed through presidential election results. Given the nature of El Shaddai participation, and the fact that official registration of members is not stressed by the group, many participants/followers are not 'official' members. Therefore official membership numbers are much smaller: 252,463 as of 19 September 2005 (personal interview at El Shaddai headquarters, Makati City, September 2005).

[3]   For a full discussion, see Katharine L. Wiegele, *Investing in Miracles: El Shaddai and the Transformation of Popular Catholicism in the Philippines* (Honolulu, HA: University of Hawaii Press, 2005).

local El Shaddai chapters in which they gather for smaller prayer meetings. The El Shaddai congregation, and Velarde himself, have been influential in national politics during successive presidencies beginning with the term of Fidel Ramos (1992–98). While members do not vote as a block, Brother Mike's endorsement is highly sought after, and he often voices his opinions publicly on matters of national importance. He even seriously explored running for President of the country in 2010, but eventually decided against it.

El Shaddai is officially recognized by the Philippine Roman Catholic Church as a Catholic lay movement, but it appeals to many of the same desires as popular Protestant groups in Manila. As in other charismatic and Pentecostal movements worldwide, El Shaddai religiosity emphasizes the workings of the Holy Spirit (for example faith healing, miracles and emotional worship experiences) over doctrine.[4] El Shaddai can be classified as belonging to a specific wing of charismatics called the 'prosperity movement', also called 'neo-Pentecostal' owing to its origins in Pentecostalism, its acceptance of material prosperity, and its appeal across social classes and religious denominations.[5] Like other prosperity groups, El Shaddai's theology not only accepts material prosperity, but also emphasizes healing, the personal elicitation of miracles through 'seed faith', and what others have called 'positive confession' or 'name it and claim it'.[6] Seed faith has at its heart the principle that giving tithes with faith will result in miracles or even a '100-fold return'. Members practise positive confession in part through 'prayer requests' (written requests for miracles), in the belief that specific statements can claim God's generosity in the present. In this context, life events are continuously interpreted as miracles, and those who have received miracles are encouraged to testify publicly at El Shaddai rallies and prayer meetings.

Velarde's prosperity gospel affirms people's desire for upward mobility and teaches that paradise is to be achieved now, not postponed until after death. Furthermore, suffering and poverty are not in themselves virtuous, in contrast to mainstream Filipino Catholic norms that emphasize 'taking up the cross' – the idea that there is spiritual value in suffering and hardship. Like the American preacher Pat Robertson, creator of the television show *700 Club*, Velarde teaches that suffering can be alleviated by faithfully following God's principles, one of which is tithing. According to my own non-random survey of 259 people at several El Shaddai rallies in 1996, approximately 80 per cent of El Shaddai members were below the national poverty level, a statistic similar to national poverty levels at the time. Elsewhere I have described how the aspirations expressed in Velarde's prosperity theology seemed to fit with attempts in national government to focus energies on development and material well-being, especially during the decade or

---

[4]   Karla Poewe (ed.), *Charismatic Christianity as Global Culture* (Columbia, SC: University of South Carolina Press, 1994) p. 2.

[5]   Simon Coleman, *The Globalisation of Charismatic Christianity: Spreading the Gospel of Prosperity* (Cambridge: Cambridge University Press, 2000).

[6]   Ibid.

so immediately following the 1986 EDSA People Power Revolution.[7] In addition, the vacuum of power created by the end of the Marcos dictatorship, the ultimate disappointment with the subsequent leadership's effectiveness in dealing with poverty, corruption, land reform and human rights abuses, and the weakening of the communist insurgency in the 1990s and 2000s provided the socio-political context for the emergence of 'Brother Mike', whose populist message emphasized not only prosperity, but self-reliance and hope. El Shaddai reframes deterministic class-based cultural models implied in development, liberation theologist, leftist and other progressive discourses – discourses that define the average El Shaddai member as one of the oppressed. Using Brother Mike's story as a model (one of transformation from illness and destitution to health and wealth through active faith and the resultant miracles), members emphasize individual faith and action, and reject structural or historical understandings of inequality, as well as those that accept suffering as a natural aspect of spirituality. In so doing, they redefine themselves.[8]

El Shaddai's Catholic affiliation confers some legitimacy within this predominantly Catholic country. Although El Shaddai operates as if it were an independent church, local chapters are linked with local Catholic parishes, and the movement has a clergy member as a spiritual adviser. A portion of its collections go to the Catholic Church, and Mass is said at El Shaddai rallies. However, in local neighbourhoods, El Shaddai healers merge ritual elements of Roman Catholicism, prosperity theology, charismatic Christianity and local shamanic traditions to produce a revitalized spiritual arena in which so-called 'authentic healing power' has shifted to El Shaddai contexts. These ritual innovations and experiential elements, as well as Velarde's personal charisma, offer power and credence to the prosperity theology.[9]

Becoming 'Live'

As mentioned, the El Shaddai movement began as a radio programme whose listening audience soon evolved into a rally audience as people gathered outside

---

[7]   Anonymous,. 'The Prophet of Profit: El Shaddai's Mike Velarde Brings Religion Down to Earth', *Asiaweek*, 20 September 1996.

[8]   For a fuller discussion, see Wiegele, *Investing in Miracles*. Indeed, resisting class identification is itself part of a class-based discourse, as the dominant discourse is deployed in its very resistance.

[9]   The prosperity gospel's emphasis on worldly over eternal concerns has been a major point of contention with mainstream Filipino Roman Catholics and clergy. Velarde has also been criticized for preying on the needs and desires of a class of Filipinos for whom survival itself is often a struggle. In response, Velarde has begun a variety of social services for members. Furthermore, far from just giving members a way to elicit miracles, Brother Mike's prosperity message and seed-faith principle offer members an opportunity for transformations of the self.

the radio station in thanksgiving for blessings and miracles received. This gathering then became a weekly occurrence, and eventually developed into mass rallies. Radio (and later television) programmes expanded greatly to become hallmarks of the movement.

Many El Shaddai followers' first exposure to the group is through radio or television. DWXI, El Shaddai's radio station, is one of the more popular AM band radio stations in Metro Manila. The group also buys air time from other radio stations throughout the Philippines, as well as in other countries, and air time on television stations throughout the Philippines. El Shaddai produces and distributes *Bagong Liwanag* magazine (and an English version, *The Miracle Newsletter*) for free throughout the Philippines and internationally. The predominance of radio and television in El Shaddai religiosity differentiates it from mainstream Catholic experience and helps to create a new form of religious space, new understandings of religious community and a more personalized relationship with God. From its inception until now, the community is, to a large extent, a mass-mediated community. Despite the fact that El Shaddai outdoor rallies and other events are now also experienced 'live', mass media actually produce this 'live-ness'. The boundaries between these two 'communities' (radio and live rally) are blurred, both conceptually and spatially.

Going to an El Shaddai mass rally on a Saturday in Manila involves merging the world of the mass-media community with the anonymous but physically manifest congregation of El Shaddai devotees in the field of the Philippine International Cultural Center (PICC), the huge open field El Shaddai ministries have rented for their rallies. The description below, adapted from my field notes, provides an experiential account of this process.

> I am the last person to arrive at Eddie's dwelling – a two-room section of a house in a cramped semi-squatter area in the heart of Manila. Eddie's wife, Celia, and their two children, are still preparing for the El Shaddai rally, as their neighbor Josie and two other young women wait on the couch. The TV in front of them is on, competing for attention amidst the bustle of the rally preparations.

> The TV is tuned to the live broadcast coming from the stage at the rally site. The rally has not actually begun yet, but on TV we can see the activity on the stage. A series of individuals give short, impassioned testimonies of miracles they have received, a choir from a provincial chapter sings religious songs, and an emcee mediates each transition with introductions, announcements, short prayers, and pep talks about the exciting rally, or 'Family Appointment with Yahweh El Shaddai' that will begin in several hours. As the cameras pan the crowds, we see the commotion of hundreds of thousands of followers getting settled in the open-air field for the evening. Peddlers sell plastic mats, food, and other necessary supplies. Ushers keep people from sitting in the roped-off aisles, and hand out envelopes for 'prayer requests' and tithes. On the fringes, people wait in line to use portable toilets. As the emcee on stage pauses to lead

a short prayer, Josie and the others present in the living room fall silent and listen, concluding the prayer with an 'amen' spoken out loud, in unison with the emcee. Josie joins in, momentarily, as the choir sings the popular song, 'We will serve the Lord.' Josie's friend, Nhelin, sits beside her on the couch and writes her 'prayer request'.

When Eddie's family is ready to go, he lowers the volume of the TV, and we join hands in a circle for a 'binding' prayer with each other. Then Eddie turns off the TV. Although the house is less than two kilometers away from PICC field, it will take us over an hour to navigate our way via public transportation to our final destination: a spot on the rocky lawn, close enough to see the stage area, but far away enough to be able to sit comfortably, with enough fresh air.

Celia flips on the radio as we begin the journey, tuned to DWXI, where the rally is being broadcast live. We leave the house, and then the 'interior' of Sinag by walking through the many *iskinita*, or narrow corridors between houses and buildings – the dark urban footpaths that wind around and between the two- and three-story buildings. Neighbors greet us as we pass through the densely populated neighborhood where, according to the local priest, at least 85% of the residents live below the national poverty level. One neighbor greets us with 'See you there, sister!' even though she knows she'll never find us in the crowds at the rally. A young man, half-mockingly, hums the first line of the El Shaddai theme song.

After fifteen minutes waiting by a major thoroughfare, a jeepney (public jeep) finally stops for us, and the eight of us get on. As we sit in the cramped jeepney, we listen to a woman's humorous testimony coming from the radio. She is talking about her husband, exaggerating his former bad qualities, and then testifying to his transformation. My companions laugh and say 'Amen! Praise God!' as we imagine those in the crowd at the rally are doing the same.

Forty-five minutes and two jeepney transfers later, we arrive outside the Harrison Plaza shopping mall. By now, all of the passengers are hot, grimy, and a little light-headed from the humidity, heat and air pollution. Here we pile out and walk three blocks on the side of the street to a designated spot outside Rizal Baseball Stadium, where enterprising jeepney drivers have formed a new jeepney route. These jeeps go from here, to the PICC grounds, and back to Harrison Plaza, all day long, every Saturday. This particular route has expanded in recent years to accommodate the hundreds of thousands of travelers going this way to the El Shaddai rally.

As we wait in line, along with at least a hundred other people, for space on the next available public jeep, radios of various volumes and levels of clarity can be heard throughout the crowd, all tuned to the live broadcast from PICC. There is a feeling of camaraderie amongst the people waiting in line. People greet each other as El Shaddai followers – with the titles 'Brother' and 'Sister.'

Everyone inside the jeepney is going to the rally and a more powerful 'boom box' blasts the live transmission. Within ten minutes we are inside the PICC grounds, slowing to avoid hordes of pedestrians. We are dropped off near one of the parking areas and walk the rest of the way.

Outside the PICC grounds, El Shaddai activity extends as far as the highway – a good 20 minute walk from the stage. On Saturdays (the day of the rally), the area of the city surrounding PICC becomes, in effect, El Shaddai space. Not only are decorated and bannered jeeps, taxis, cars, tricycles, bicycles, buses, and mobile vending stalls blocking movement and traffic, but pedestrians and vendors adorned with markers of El Shaddai membership – El Shaddai handkerchiefs, portable chairs, T-shirts, candles, hats, and blasting radios – seem to flow from every corner en masse toward the PICC grounds. Those passersby stalled in traffic on the highway can sometimes gaze at vending stalls with El Shaddai religious items, which include wall calendars, banners, El Shaddai cassette tapes, and ritual items for the day's rally, such as eggs or flowers. El Shaddai participants get a small kick out of inconveniencing the unconverted through these huge weekend traffic jams. To them, it is a form of evangelism.

As the crowds get thicker and the back of the grandstand area is in sight, we no longer need our radio – we can hear the live transmissions from countless radios around us, of people who have decided to sit down here on the fringes. Some people can't even see the grandstand at all because their view is blocked by another building in the PICC compound. Nonetheless, when Brother Mike begins speaking in several hours, these people will listen to the live radio and face the grandstand while going through all the same motions as everyone else, actively participating in the rally.

As we head toward the grandstand, the sounds of portable radios are gradually replaced by the sounds coming from the loudspeakers near the stage. Soon we can actually see the emcee on the stage as we squint in the brightly lit area. We are now part of the 'live' rally. Huge stands with camera and audio equipment block the view of the stage as we get closer. The area directly in front of the stage is blocked off and reserved for the 'very sick' – those with terminal illnesses or deformities – so that they can receive the strongest healing power coming from Brother Mike on stage. There is a feeling of excitement, of being part of history, as a video camera's gaze passes over us and simultaneously transmits our image to people across the country. Josie told me once that she loves going to the rally at PICC, as opposed to the smaller rally in her local chapter, 'because it's live!' Were it not for the cameras, the simultaneous broadcast, and the instant playback (after the event is over), this 'live' feeling would not exist. In the floodlights and in the camera's gaze, we have come out of the 'interior' into the spotlight. For a few hours this evening we are, it seems, significant, and in a sense de-marginalized.

As the crowds of people leave the area and journey home after the rally around midnight, many radios will be tuned to the playback, a repeat broadcast of the event that just occurred.

Radio and television broadcasts of rallies are often a person's first contact with El Shaddai. DWXI announces the upcoming rally all week long, orienting followers to the stage where Brother Mike gives his 'healing message'. The journey that followers undertake each week, from areas of Manila, or from far-flung provinces, is oriented towards Brother Mike, who becomes, in effect, a locus of miracles. Yet the ritual sphere of the rally extends beyond its immediate locale because radio and television are played constantly, before and after the event. Since the broadcast is live, one begins experiencing the event even while still at home. Listeners at times 'tune in' electronically at the rally as audience-members far from the stage listen to radios and watch oversized film screens on the perimeters of the massive rally lawn. Many watch or listen to rallies without even attending them, but go through the motions, the songs and the prayers as if experiencing them 'live'. Within the PICC grounds, radios serve as links with Brother Mike at the centre. The mass-mediated community is gradually transformed into the more immediate, physical community of the rally. While leaving the rally, the opposite occurs. The rally community is transformed once again into the media audience.

Within the rally context itself, mass media help to create a 'live' feeling. The rally becomes 'live' when participants enter a zone they understand to be mediated to others who are watching or listening via television or radio. This brightly lit, colourful sphere presents a larger-than-life, amplified reality that doesn't stop with the self, but flows outwards. This feeling is enhanced by Velarde on stage, who is aware of this outward flow as he directly addresses people listening from home. 'There is a woman in Naga City listening right now who is in need of a miracle. She has been suffering from cataracts for several years. Woman, you will be healed, and you will see your son graduating from high school next year!' (Inevitably a person fitting this description will surface later to publicly tell a miraculous story of healing.) Many followers I interviewed testified to having been healed through radio or television, from blessings Velarde gave either during a live rally broadcast, or during another one of his radio programmes. Some hold up objects to the radio or television to be blessed, as is done at rallies, or use the radio or the television to keep evil spirits away from the house, for example spirits that bring drugs into the neighbourhood or cause discord within families.

Ritual Space, Community and the Holy Spirit

By expanding the boundaries of ritual space through the airwaves, El Shaddai creates a direct individual experience of sacredness, ritual blessing and the Holy Spirit in the home, within a very personal sphere. El Shaddai prayer and counselling sessions on the radio, and the implication that blessing can travel through the airwaves, allow for a personal relationship with God that is not mediated through traditional Catholic channels such as priests, saints, the Virgin Mary, the Eucharist, statues, crucifixes or the Catholic Mass. Velarde told me that the calling of his ministry was to 'free people from the bondage of religion'. He said religion builds walls that block one's relationship with the Holy Spirit. By 'religion' he meant 'tradition', or more specifically, conventional Catholic traditions (such as the mediators mentioned above) that divert people's attention away from meaningful relationships with the Holy Spirit. At the same time, he still supports the sacraments and the practice of attending Mass on Sunday and regards the El Shaddai movement as a Catholic movement.

Furthermore, by locating the channels of sacredness and blessings in radio and television airwaves and in open-air rallies, Velarde has avoided constructing a physical structure – a church. Mass media have allowed the group an independent existence as a mass-mediated congregation that transcends specific geographical, social and institutional boundaries and contexts[10] without requiring a denominational separation. El Shaddai's coexistence with the Catholic Church, then, has been unproblematic (on this level) because, from its inception, it has occupied a wholly different sort of religious space.

By claiming privilege in the realm of spiritual mediation, El Shaddai in effect relegates the Church to the position of a repository of tradition. Velarde acknowledges the need for certain 'traditions' such as the sacraments, but says the Church and its clergy are bogged down with intellectualism and ritual. Velarde himself is fond of pointing out that he is 'just a businessman' and never formally studied religion. While Catholic priests' connections with God are 'man-made' (the result of studying), Velarde's connection is 'spiritual' (the result of a more authentic connection with God). When God healed him of heart disease, he wrote, he became 'a channel of God's grace and power to heal', and 'a channel of countless miracles by appointment and prayer request'.[11] 'This is no longer the work of man,' Velarde told me personally. 'We are just willing vessels. Like me. I have a covenant with God that no man can ever understand.' Furthermore, Velarde speaks in Tagalog[12] with a provincial accent, giving the impression that he has a

---

[10]   Lawrence A. Babb, 'Introduction', in Lawrence A. Babb and Susan S. Wadley (eds), *Media and the Transformation of Religion in South Asia* (Philadelphia, PA: University of Pennsylvania Press, 1995), p. 17.

[11]   Mariano 'Mike' Z. Velarde, *El Shaddai the Almighty God, Volume I* (Makati, Philippines, 1992), p. 3.

[12]   Tagalog is the basis of Filipino, the national language of the Philippines.

'common-man' or even lower-class background. In contrast, Catholic priests, who may speak English and schooled Tagalog, are often seen by my informants as connected to an intellectual and elite class.

Velarde also uses El Shaddai in-house publications to establish contact between himself, his readers, and God. In *El Shaddai The Almighty God,* one of El Shaddai's free publications, Velarde writes:

> Do you need a miracle? Would you want me to pray with you? Wherever you may be, this Newsletter can serve as a contact point of our faith for God's miracle power to operate – if you only believe and accept Jesus Christ as Lord and Savior![13]

> I'm excited! I know something good is going to happen to you. Are you ready? Okay, let's do it. Put your hands on this page as our point of contact, as if I am with you. (Did I not tell you that wherever I go, even simply through this El Shaddai Miracle Newsletter, Jesus is with me?)[14]

Recorded-voice tapes of Brother Mike Velarde, circulated among Filipino migrants and overseas workers, function in the same way, as do his live radio programmes. *Alay Pagmamahal* ('Love Offering'), for example, is a live radio programme that airs several times a week on DWXI in which Velarde leads prayers, interprets the Bible, and takes calls from listeners asking to be counselled, 'prayed over' and blessed. Here he is addressing the general listening audience, as well as the followers in and around his office building who have gathered to listen.[15] (In the following extract, the programme is translated from Tagalog, with the exception of the words in quotation marks, which were spoken by Velarde originally in English.) Before this excerpt, he has already asked the listeners to stand up, raise their hands, and bow their heads.

> Put those hands on top of the head of the one beside you … 'wherever you may be'. The hands you lifted earlier were blessed by the Lord. Don't worry, the hands of Brother Mike and your hands have no difference. 'If only I had a million hands, I'd put them on your heads, but there is no way.' Your hands have been blessed by the Lord, so offer them to Him. Put your hand on top of the head of the one beside you. Bow and I will pray for your requests. 'It's just impossible for me to touch your foreheads.' … Ask now while those hands are laid on you whatever you wish to receive from the Lord. And I believe the hands laid on your heads are the Lord's hands more than the hands of Brother Mike. All those healed are because of the Lord's miraculous and wondrous hands …

---

[13]   Velarde, *El Shaddai the Almighty God, Volume I*, p. 5.

[14]   Velarde, *El Shaddai The Almighty God, Volume II* (Makati, Philippines, 1992), p. 4.

[15]   This programme was broadcast on 13 February 1996.

Place yourself in the presence of the Lord. 'Just continue to meditate right now. It's healing time.' If you have brought oil or if you have [bottles of] oil in your houses, get them out … Lift them up and we will pray over them … rub the oil on the forehead of the one beside you in the name of Jesus our Savior. And on their palms. We're together and one now. The Lord is rubbing your foreheads. Lift the oil and we'll pray. This seldom happens in our programme – the Lord's spirit is moving now. He knows all your needs. If you have no doubts, I believe everyone here right now is receiving an extraordinary strength and miracle in their lives.

This extract powerfully creates a moment of simultaneous, shared ritual experience, and an explicit awareness of a real-time gathering that is yet imagined and geographically dispersed (and that goes well beyond the passive 'imagined community' of nation or ethnicity described by Benedict Anderson).[16] 'We're together and one now,' he reminds them. 'If only I had *a million* hands, I'd put them on your heads.'

In addition, sacredness and the ability to heal move from conventional ritual space to Velarde's hands, which become God's hands, and which then become each and every individual's hands. 'I believe the hands laid on your heads are the Lord's hands more than the hands of Brother Mike,' he says. As with the newsletter, the blessing and the Holy Spirit also seems to move from him, through the radio, into each person's home, into each person's own hands, and in this case into the healing oil. One's body and one's home become sacred, and ordinary individuals are empowered to bless and heal. Through the radio, he is able to bring 'the Lord's hands' to people, and yet his own hands are still there to mediate this process.

Velarde's mobilization of this common ritual form (laying-on of hands) in radio and print media releases it from its more typical religio-social contexts. The classless, populist nature of El Shaddai religiosity is a point lost neither on 'Brother Mike' nor his followers, who repeatedly mentioned the absence of social distinctions as a significant difference between El Shaddai events (where, followers told me, 'an engineer stands next to a maid') and 'ordinary Catholic' rites in church. One of Velarde's favourite stories is of an illiterate man who became an El Shaddai preacher. The invisibility of social difference (between each other, and with Brother Mike) creates a feeling of *communitas* that participants have told me is transforming and empowering.

Furthermore, the mediated space of the airwaves and the open air of the rally are seen by followers as conducive to the free movement of the Holy Spirit. The Holy Spirit is at the rally, they say, in part because of the open space. Informants consistently associated the rally with God as spiritually manifested, and the Church with 'just tradition', devoid of the efficacious presence of the Holy Spirit. As one El Shaddai member said, 'At church, God is near. At the rally, He is actually there.' They say they can 'feel' God at the rally, in the open space – as energy, as heat

---

[16]   Benedict Anderson, *Imagined Communities* (London: Verso, 1983).

running through their veins, as rain water on their skin (when it's not raining), or as wind (when there's no wind blowing). Moreover, they say the feeling of God's presence follows them into their everyday lives, whereas going to 'church' (i.e. a Catholic church) is seen as limited in space and time: 'you go in, you go out,' or 'after one hour, it's over'.

It is understandable that El Shaddai followers enjoy the rallies in the open space at PICC on the coast, and that they 'feel God' there. One emerges from cramped, tunnel-like streets and neighbourhoods to a rare, wide open space with a view of the sunset, and, on the horizon, a partial view of the Makati skyline. The fresh air, sea breeze, open space and stars signify a different, liberating sort of existential state to many of those who come to spread blankets on the PICC grounds.

In this space, El Shaddai members get a perspective not only of the city, but of themselves and their own critical mass. They are able to express the force of this mass to outsiders by disrupting the city and its imposed 'order' and by occupying, even reclaiming, public spaces. They create massive traffic jams at unusual times, and take over the clean, posh segments of the city. In the interior *barrios*, El Shaddai's mass is dispersed and unseen, but a rally crowd is a totality that can be seen and felt. As part of this collectivity that is simultaneously broadcast on national television, El Shaddai members are in a sense demarginalized.[17] Seeing El Shaddai's impressive assembly, especially from atop the steps of the Film Center building (part of the PICC compound) or through the television cameras above the stage, gives participants a sense of significance, even empowerment. This view of 'the numbers' is, in part, what makes El Shaddai seem awesome to outsiders as well.

In 'coming out' from the *barrios*, El Shaddai members also enter a space where mediation with the elites and the power brokers of Philippine society seems possible. People in the rally audience are courted by politicians and candidates who 'perform' for them on stage, address them directly, and banter with Brother Mike. In El Shaddai/PICC space, formerly invisible people now exist, at least on some limited level, for the nation – they are on the national political map and in the national consciousness. Not only do politicians, candidates for political office, high officials of the Church, prominent businessmen, and so on regularly visit them, giving them a sense of importance, but these visits reach a national audience through mass media. It is thus not surprising, either, that El Shaddai followers from other provinces in the country make long trips to be part of these national rallies. Even for those who see hypocrisy in the words and actions of their visitors, the visits are important to them because, as some participants have put it, these politicians 'need our prayers'. In other words, 'they need *us*'. Furthermore, just by being at the rally, these politicians will receive the Word of God and be blessed. This, they say, can only be for the good.

---

[17]   El Shaddai is considered within the Philippines to be a movement of and for the *masa* or the masses (the common people), a group that is often marginalized from politics and from economic growth and opportunities, in a country with widespread poverty and large income disparity.

Conclusion

Early Methodism's sense of freedom of the supernatural from established religious hierarchies, and the notion that the supernatural is accessible to ordinary individuals in everyday life, is echoed in today's Pentecostalisms.[18] The emphasis on religious autonomy, individual freedom and personal choice is part of the modern message of Pentecostalism. This autonomous religious self is chosen rather than inherited, in a marketplace of religious options.[19] The El Shaddai option, like other Pentecostal options in the Philippines and elsewhere, displays these distinctly modern social forms of autonomy, achievement, entrepreneurship and personal spiritual empowerment.[20] El Shaddai followers, like their Pentecostal counterparts, redefine who they are through their deliberate religious choices, which in turn may help them find their footing in the modern world.

Congregation, sacredness and community have been transformed and expanded in El Shaddai contexts to create forms of religious experience that are very different from those of the mainstream Church. Most notable are the ways El Shaddai followers see their relationships with God and with others in the religious community, their experience of ritual, their emphasis on the spiritual manifestations of God, and their orientation toward Velarde as a conduit to God. By using mass media and open-air rallies, Velarde also puts El Shaddai ministries in a strategically favourable position with the church institution, allowing El Shaddai to remain both independent from the Church and under the wing of the Church at the same time. This gives El Shaddai a perceived distance from Catholic orthodoxy, while allowing it to capitalize on the sense of legitimacy that comes from its Catholic identity. Likewise, the fact that El Shaddai religious practice occurs mainly outside Catholic structures makes it easier for church officials to overlook or downplay unorthodox practices. El Shaddai members' use of religious programming, combined with their participation in mass rallies, extend the sacred and ritual sphere beyond the immediate locale into the home and the body, blurring the boundaries between mass-mediated religious experience and more temporal forms of religious practice.

Postscript

The evolving relationship between El Shaddai and the Philippine Roman Catholic Church (PRCC) has not been without controversy, as mentioned. Brother Mike has been summoned several times by the Catholic Bishops Conference of the

---

[18]   David Martin, *Pentecostalism: The World their Parish* (Oxford: Blackwell, 2002).

[19]   Ibid.; see also David Martin, *Tongues of Fire: The Explosion of Protestantism in Latin America* (Oxford: Blackwell, 1990).

[20]   See Katharine Wiegele, 'Catholics Rich in Spirit: El Shaddai's Modern Engagements', *Philippine Studies*, 54/4 (2006): pp. 495–520.

Philippines (CBCP), and has been involved with the CBCP in an ongoing dialogue about specific El Shaddai practices, Catholic orthodoxy, and the PRCC's role within El Shaddai, ritually, theologically and administratively, which continues to unfold today.[21] Despite their differences, my research indicates that the PRCC as well as El Shaddai have walked a mutually beneficial fine line. El Shaddai has defined itself in opposition to Catholic tradition, as well as with legitimacy from its Catholic affiliation. The Church has been able to retain a revitalized segment of its congregation that it might otherwise have been lost to Pentecostal denominations, and it has gained a renewed spiritual relevance in Philippine society.

On 20 August 2009, Velarde opened the 'El Shadddai International House of Prayer', a US$20 billion worship structure with a floor area of one hectare in the Velarde-owned Amvel City San Dionisio, Paranaque City (within metropolitan Manila). The structure is said to have a seating capacity of 15,000, with a standing-room capacity of 25,000, and an overflow capacity of 200,000. It claims to be the biggest place of worship in Asia. Philippine President Gloria Macapagal-Arroyo, among other VIPs, attended the inauguration. Joro Archbishop Angel Lagdameo, the outgoing president of the CBCP, was the main celebrant of the concelebrated Mass for the inauguration. He said, 'This is my first time to address a people equivalent to six cathedrals.'[22] A news article on the Catholic Bishops Conference of the Philippines official news website, the *CBCP News*, stated: 'after 25 years, the charismatic group [whose] membership has tremendously grown to 7 million, found its own home in Amvel City'.[23] And the Church was there to help it celebrate.

[21]   See Wiegele, *Investing in Miracles*.

[22]   Christian V. Esguerra, 'Velarde opens El Shaddai church' *Philippine Daily Inquirer*, 21 August 2009, at http://newsinfo.inquirer.net/inquirerheadlines/nation/view/20090821-221325/Velarde-opens-El-Shaddai-church, accessed 6 October 2010.

[23]   'El Shaddai P1-B church opens today,' CBCP News, 20 August 2009, at http://www.cbcpnews.com/?q=node/10155, accessed 6 October 2010.

Index